The Somali Conflict

Prospects for Peace

Mark Bradbury

An Oxfam Working Paper

First published by Oxfam UK and Ireland in 1994, reprinted in 1999.
This edition transferred to print-on-demand in 2007

© Oxfam UK and Ireland 1994

ISBN 0 85598 271 3

A catalogue record for this publication is available from the British Library.

Available from:
Bournemouth English Book Centre, PO Box 1496, Parkstone, Dorset, BH12 3YD, UK
tel: +44 (0)1202 712933; fax: +44 (0)1202 712930; email: oxfam@bebc.co.uk

USA: Stylus Publishing LLC, PO Box 605, Herndon, VA 20172-0605, USA
tel: +1 (0)703 661 1581; fax: +1 (0)703 661 1547; email: styluspub@aol.com

For details of local agents and representatives in other countries, consult our website: www.oxfam.org.uk/publications
or contact Oxfam Publishing, Oxfam House, John Smith Drive, Cowley, Oxford, OX4 2JY, UK
tel +44 (0) 1865 472255; fax (0) 1865 472393; email: publish@oxfam.org.uk

Our website contains a fully searchable database of all our titles, and facilities for secure on-line ordering.

Published by Oxfam GB, Oxfam House, John Smith Drive, Cowley, Oxford, OX4 2JY, UK

Oxfam GB is a registered charity, no.202918, and is a member of Oxfam International.

CONTENTS

LIST OF DIAGRAMS

ACRONYMS USED IN THIS REPORT

CMOC	Civilian and Military Operations Centre
DHA	Department of Humanitarian Affairs
DHRR	Division for Humanitarian Relief and Development
ELCAS	Ecumenical Liaison Committee for Assistance to Somalia
ICRC	International Committee of the Red Cross
IMC	International Medical Corps
MSF	Médecins sans Frontières
NGO–C	International NGO Consortium
ORH	Operation Restore Hope
SAMO	Somali African Mukti Organisation
SCF	Save the Children Fund
SDA	Somali Democratic Alliance
SDM	Somali Democratic Movement
SDRA	Somali Development and Relief Association
SNDU	Somali National Democratic Union
SNF	Somali National Front
SNM	Somali National Movement
SNA	Somali National Alliance
SNU	Somali National Union
SPM	Somali People's Movement
SRSG	Special Representative of the Secretary General
SSDF	Somali Salvation Democratic Front
SSNM	Southern Somali National Movement
TNC	Transitional National Council
UNITAF	United Nations International Task Force
UNOSOM	United Nations Operation in Somalia
USC	United Somali Congress
USF	United Somali Front
USP	United Somali Party
WFP	World Food Programme

PREFACE

This paper was commissioned from Mark Bradbury by Oxfam (UK and Ireland), with the main aim of identifying practical ways in which the international group of Oxfams might contribute to the peace-making process in Somalia and Somaliland. When the paper was subsequently edited for publication, the recommendations which were originally specific to Oxfam, were generalised to make them relevant to all non-governmental organisations concerned with the situation in Somalia and Somaliland.

Some of the information presented in Part II and Part V is reproduced from a study written by Mark Bradbury in April 1993 for Responding to Conflict and the British NGO ActionAid. This study will be published in 1994 by Responding to Conflict, Woodbrooke College, Selly Oak, Birmingham, under the title *Development in Conflict: Experiences of ActionAid in Somalia.*

Roger Naumann
Regional Manager, Horn of Africa
Oxfam (UK and Ireland)
February 1994

ABOUT THE AUTHOR

Mark Bradbury worked in Sudan, Somalia, and Somaliland from 1983 to 1993 on a variety of relief and development projects. In 1991/92 he was employed as the Coordinator of the Inter-NGO Committee for Somalia.

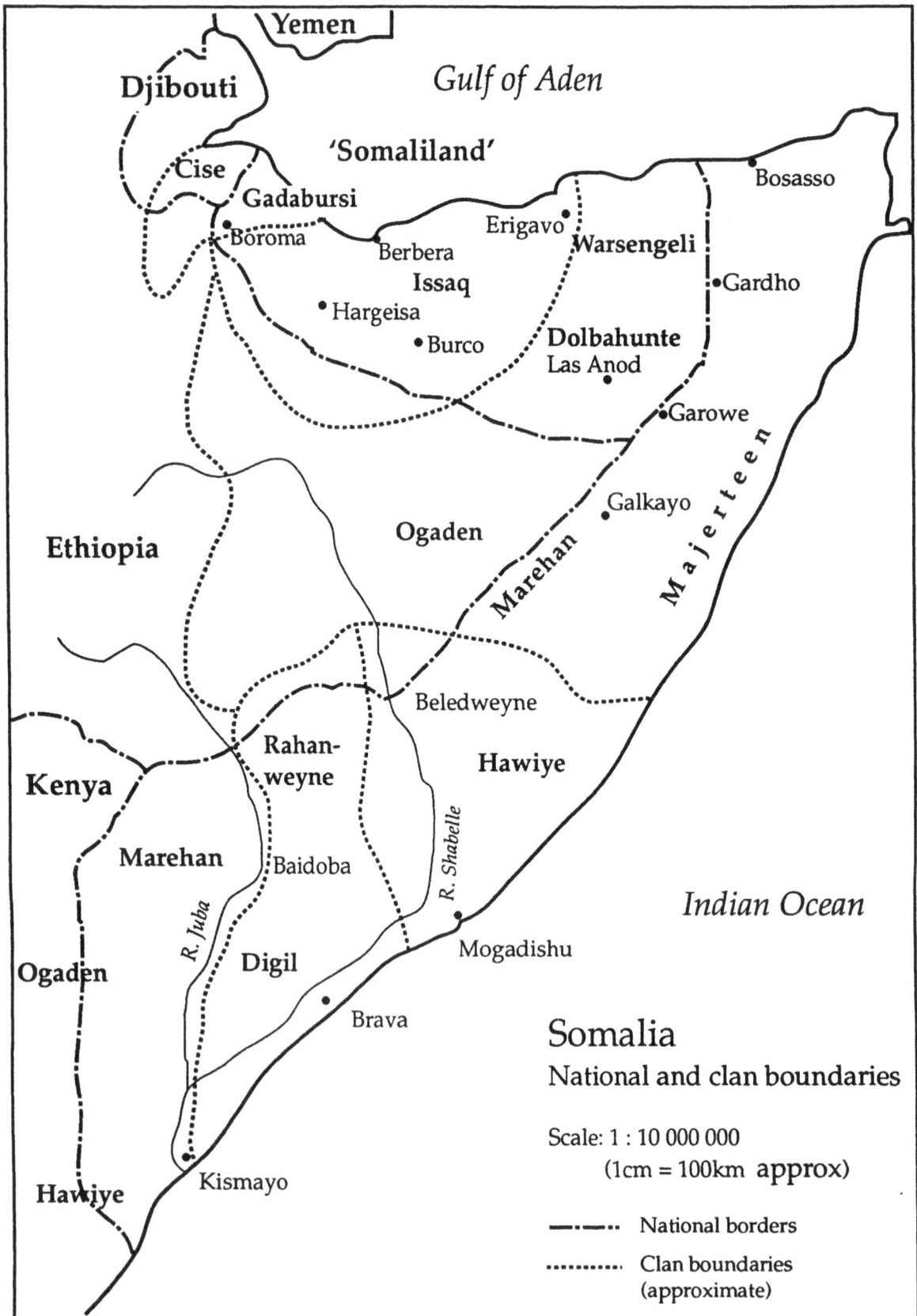

Yemen

Gulf of Aden

Djibouti

'Somaliland'

•Bosasso

Cise

Gadabursi

•Boroma

Erigavo•

Warsengeli

Berbera

Issaq

•Gardho

• Hargeisa

•Burco

Dolbahunte
Las Anod
•

Garowe
•

M a j e r t e e n

M a r e h a n

Ogaden

•Galkayo

Ethiopia

Beledweyne

Hawiye

**Rahan-
weyne**

Kenya

Marehan

•Baidoba

R. Shabelle

R. Juba

Digil

Indian Ocean

Ogaden

Mogadishu
•

•
Brava

Somalia
National and clan boundaries

Scale: 1 : 10 000 000
(1cm = 100km approx)

Hawiye

Kismayo

—··—··— National borders

············· Clan boundaries
(approximate)

PART I: INTRODUCTION

1 BACKGROUND TO REPORT

The killing of 24 Pakistani peace-keeping troops of the United Nations Operation in Somalia (UNOSOM II) in Mogadishu on 5 June 1993, and the outbreak of conflict between UNOSOM and General Mohamed Farah Aideed, started a new cycle of violence in the long-running conflict in Somalia. It brought to a halt any progress achieved in the reconciliation process in Somalia initiated by the intervention of US-led UNITAF forces in December 1992, and the Addis Ababa Agreement on National Reconciliation of March 1993.

On 17 June 1993 Community Aid Abroad (CAA) proposed to Oxfam (UK and Ireland) that the time might be right for an NGO-sponsored Peace Conference for Somalia, using the Boroma Reconciliation Conference in Somaliland as a possible model. CAA had provided support for the Boroma conference, through the Somali NGO SORRA.

A high level of interest was expressed in Oxfam (UK/I) for the idea, and in Oxfam internationally — Oxfam Hong Kong, Oxfam New Zealand, Oxfam America, and Oxfam Canada — and it was proposed that they might mount a joint peace initiative in Somalia. Preliminary research suggested that a low-key approach, supporting local, regional, or district peace initiatives, rather than a high-profile peace conference, might be a more appropriate intervention for Oxfam.

In July 1993, I was commissioned by Oxfam (UK/I) to undertake some research on the possibilities for supporting peace-making in Somalia and Somaliland. Specifically, I was commissioned to:

1.'Strengthen Oxfam's institutional knowledge and analysis of the situation in Somalia and Somaliland, to place the agency in a relatively informed position to facilitate local initiatives for peace and to assist the emerging dynamic of different levels of peace-making.'

2.'Identify options for the Oxfam family to consider with regard to how best Oxfam can assist the peace-making process.'

1.1 The Research

This report is the culmination of three months of research from July to October 1993, involving discussions with a range of people and organisations:

•International and Somali NGOs working in Somalia/Somaliland, based in the UK, the USA, and Somalia, to elicit whether there were common perceptions and approaches to peace-making in Somalia and Somaliland.

• Peace institutions involved in Somalia/Somaliland, to gain an understanding of what is already being done in this field, and what resources are available for non-governmental organisations (NGOs) to draw upon.

1

• Individuals working for the UN in Somalia/Somaliland, to gain an understanding of the dynamics of the operation.

• Somalis, men and women, both outside and inside the country, intellectuals, politicians, elders, and NGO workers, with a range of personal and professional perspectives on the causes of the conflict and solutions to it.

In order that my understanding was based, as much as possible, on the opinions and perceptions of people in Somalia/Somaliland and Oxfam, workshops on the theme of conflict and peace were held in Hargeisa, Somaliland, and in Oxfam House (Oxford, UK). Unfortunately, it was not possible to do this in Mogadishu. The minutes of the Hargeisa workshop are attached as an additional report.

On the assumption that readers will pick and choose information which interests them most, I have tried to incorporate in this report as much of the information gained as possible, in the hope that some of it will be of interest to people with concerns wider than Somalia and Somaliland.

A note of caution here. The situation in Somalia is 'complex'. Such a description is often used as an excuse by people who do not want to understand. Unfortunately, it is a feature of the current situation in Somalia that there are many foreigners with influence who do not want to improve their understanding of Somalia. I am conscious that the more I learn about the Somali people, the more there is to understand, and the more there is a need to understand. It is also true that, like Somali kinship genealogies, historical events are open to interpretation. Amnesia is an important part of remembering. Although the information presented in this report is drawn from other people, it suffers from my own interpretation.

2 EXECUTIVE SUMMARY

Armed conflict is back on the agenda of humanitarian agencies as a major contributor to world poverty. Armed conflict is nothing new to Oxfam (UK/I), which was itself formed in 1942 in response to a particular conflict (Agerbak, 1991). In this post-Cold War, 'new world order' of things, Oxfam and other humanitarian agencies are spending large sums of money in dealing with the impact of these conflicts.

The conflict in Somalia occurred at a time when the new world order was bloodying itself in the Gulf in only the second multi-lateral war, after Vietnam, since World War II. As such, Somalia has become a theatre in which many ideas pertinent to a possible future world order are being tested out. It has become a testing ground for the UN and the USA. It has also been a testing ground for many humanitarian organisations and their future roles in responding to situations of conflict. It therefore presents some fundamental policy issues for NGOs.

If armed conflict is part of the present and probable future experience of many of the countries where relief and development agencies work, there is a need perhaps to develop a greater understanding of 'conflict'. In its widest sense, conflict is a 'universal part of the way that humans organise and mediate individual and group relations, and is therefore part of our everyday experience' (Bradbury, 1993). It is something that, through its normal development and relief programmes, Oxfam deals with all the time.

2

In Somalia we are concerned with a particularly destructive form of violent armed conflict. The question is how an agency such as Oxfam responds to it. Are our normal relief and development programmes sufficient and appropriate? Are they able to provide an answer, or solution? This report, as requested, is an attempt to explore some of the options open to Oxfam, and to similar NGOs, in response to some of these questions.

2.1 Peace-making is a Long-Term Process

The present conflict in Somalia and Somaliland has been going on for five years. The conflict is protracted and has gone through numerous cycles of violence. What started as a 'localised conflict' in May 1988, when the Somali National Movement attacked government garrisons in the northern cities of Burco and Hargeisa, has become an international conflict, with the UN, under US leadership, in conflict with local factions (notably General Aideed), and with Somali refugees dispersed throughout the world, particularly the Horn of Africa. The situation in Somalia has thus become one of an increasing number of situations in the world described as a **'complex emergency'**.

A central feature of these types of emergencies is that they are protracted over a long term. The Somali conflict arises from a variety of political, economic, social, and ecological circumstances. **Part II** of this report provides a brief historical narrative on the Somali war and provides one interpretation of the causes of the conflict.

The failure of the UN to bring about reconciliation in southern Somalia attests to the failure of any 'quick fix' solutions. The Boroma National Reconciliation Conference in Somaliland, in 1993, lasted four months and was productive only because other flash points were dealt with along the way. To transform the situation into a peaceful one will take a long time.

RECOMMENDATIONS:

i If agencies are to become involved in peace-making in Somalia or Somaliland, they will need to make a long-term commitment of people and resources. Agencies need to think in terms of a ten-year perspective and probably not expect to see substantial results from their efforts in anything less than two years.

ii An understanding of both the causes and impact of the Somali conflict, the responses and possible solutions to it, is a pre-requisite for any involvement in peace-making. Agencies should consider sponsoring research on a number of different areas that will provide a dynamic analysis of the current situation in Somalia and Somaliland. The emphasis should be on commissioning Somali researchers.

2.2 Peace Cannot be Enforced

A feature of 'complex emergencies' is that they are fundamentally political in nature. In this situation, the response of NGOs, whose mandates are restricted to 'peaceful' 'humanitarian' measures, is insufficient to provide a solution, and the UN is called upon to intervene. Political problems require political solutions. Perhaps NGOs should recognise the need to become involved at a political level.

Where peaceful means fail to restore peace and security, the UN has within its mandate, under Chapter VII of the UN Charter, the authority to enforce peace. In response to the killings of the Pakistani peace-keepers, the UN operation in Somalia invoked that right to use coercive measures to restore security. Somalia is the first place where the UN has made use of this mandate. UNOSOM's policies are dominated by political concerns that have more to do with political agendas within the UN and USA than with the concerns of the Somali people. Somalia has become a testing ground for other international political concerns. By invoking Chapter VII, the UN changed its goals in Somalia, and in the process came into conflict with those of local protagonists.

Two theories dominate debate about how reconciliation can be promoted in Somalia. One proposes that a political settlement has to involve the warlords who are the *de facto* political leaders in the south, and one must find a way of working with them. The UN/USA initially did much to legitimise the warlords through the internationally-brokered peace conferences.

The alternative theory suggests that reconciliation can be built only from a base of localised, indigenous, and democratic peace-making processes. In this way the warlords will be marginalised. As implemented by the UN through the District Council programme, this approach is also failing. UNOSOM is a bureaucratic, centralist body. Constituted by governments, its mandate is to establish centralised governmental structures, albeit with some emphasis on decentralised regional structures. Centralised government is the very thing that many Somalis have been fighting against. As implemented by the UN, both approaches to peace-making in Somalia reveal the dangers of trying to impose an outside solution to the Somali conflict.

Reconciliation and resolution can work only when conflicting parties want it to happen. The Boroma conference in Somaliland succeeded to the extent that it did because the participants presumably had common goals. The UN intervention to date has failed because it was an 'intervention' and not a Somali initiative. The report therefore concludes that in Somalia 'peace-enforcement' will not work.

Part III of this report examines the origins of the conflict between the UN and General Aideed in Mogadishu. It explores the politics of the UN in Somalia, the conflicting agendas at play there, and the likely success of the peace-enforcement policy to resolve the Somali conflict. This section also comments on the UN attempts at promoting 'bottom-up' reconciliation through the District Council programme, and on the relationship between the NGOs and UNOSOM.

RECOMMENDATIONS:

i Agencies should use their international standing to advocate a return to diplomacy, and the principles of pro-active peace-making, rather than 'peace-enforcement' by the UN in Somalia.

ii Agencies should call for a commission of enquiry into alleged human rights abuses by the UN and the warlords, and consider promoting a human rights monitoring office in Somalia.

iii Agencies should consider sponsoring a series of consultations between various

4

groups in Somalia, with the aim of promoting greater involvement in political reconciliation and of creating a 'peace constituency'.

iv Agencies should consider commissioning an independent review of the District Council programme, with a view to providing recommendations on how the programme may be improved.

v Agencies should consider increasing their support to the Inter-NGO Consortium on Somalia (INCS), to strengthen its role of lobbying and advocacy throughout Somalia.

2.3 Peace-making must be Holistic and Integrative

In August 1993 a peace agreement was signed in Kismayo by parties inhabiting the southern regions of 'Jubaland', thus bringing an end to fierce armed conflict in a region that had been fought over since 1989. It is a region where Oxfam (UK/I) has a substantial agricultural programme.

The Jubaland Peace Agreement was heralded by UNOSOM as a breakthrough in the reconciliation process in Somalia, and an example of how the UNOSOM peace-keeping operation was working. To some extent the efforts of UNOSOM in Kismayo have been successful. However, the situation remains very fragile. Many of the underlying causes of the conflict have not been addressed. In particular, there is a question of land issues.

'Peace' cannot be said to exist in an environment where there is conflict. Any peace initiative will require an understanding of the factors that create conflict, and efforts should be directed towards the creation of an environment without tensions, in which peace and a return to civil society can emerge. Peace-making needs to work at a number of different levels at the same time.

Part IV of the report describes the conflict in Kismayo and the Lower Juba region. It examines the complex range of forces, including political, economic, and ecological, that lie behind the conflict, and that constrain efforts at peace-making there. It concludes that, despite some blunders, UNOSOM has been partially successful in promoting reconciliation there. The peace remains fragile and there is an urgent need to strengthen it. NGOs need to identify levels at which they can contribute.

RECOMMENDATIONS:

i Agencies in this region should consider ways of assisting with the resettlement and integration of refugees, whose return will place pressure on damaged infrastructure.

ii Agencies should consider commissioning research into the issue of land ownership and use, which is one of the main causes of conflict.

iii Agencies in the Juba Valley and Kismayo should consider training their teams in the principles of conflict-resolution and mediation, as they may be called upon to mediate, or support local mediation or peace meetings.

2.4 Peace-making and Development are Similar Processes

From an anthropological understanding, Somali society works on a system of balanced oppositions between groups, orchestrated through, and institutionalised in, a segmentary kinship system and traditional laws and procedures laid down in a 'social contract' (*xeer*). This system is inherently unstable and therefore potentially dangerous. If peace is thought to exist where there is an equitable balance, anything which upsets the balance will continue the conflict. The danger inherent in any 'intervention', be it in the form of foreign military force or humanitarian aid, or externally initiated peace conferences, is that they can upset that balance.

The spectrum of peace-making is wide, and can range from physical to social rehabilitation. Relief work, if it helps to promote a return to a stable environment, can be considered part of a peace-making process. If relief becomes a source of conflict, then it is not contributing to peace-making. It is unlikely that 'peace', in the sense of a total absence of conflict, can exist in Somalia or Somaliland, or for that matter other societies. How then does one define 'peace' and 'peace-making'? If society is always prone to conflict, perhaps all peace-making can aim to do is to turn embittered, destructive relationships into more peaceful, constructive relationships.

While Somali society may be said to be prone to conflicts, mechanisms exist within Somali society to mitigate and resolve them. Dialogue, the mediation of elders, religious sanctions, compensation, and indeed military strength are all traditional means for resolving conflicts.

The people who understand those mechanisms best are Somalis. Indeed, Somalis are as experienced at peace-making and conflict-resolution as they are at making war. Foreign intervention in peace-making should, therefore, perhaps be perceived as a process that restores or empowers the indigenous forms of peace-making and conflict-resolution to restore that balance in society.

Reconciliation will be achieved only through a process which is 'bottom-up': that is, one initiated and controlled by the participants. The aim of NGOs should therefore be to support or promote local initiatives. The term 'peace-making' itself could be construed as interventionist, and a preferable term might be 'peace-building'.

Part V of this report describes the current situation in Somaliland, and examines some of the reasons why it has been possible to make and rebuild peace in that part of the region. It suggests ways in which agencies might assist in strengthening peace in Somaliland through support for demobilisation. It examines the current debates on the relationship between central and local government. It also examines local peace-making initiatives.

It draws together some general conclusions about the role of NGOs in supporting peace-making and provides some recommendations for future consideration and action.

It concludes that conflict-resolution and peace-making should be approached in the same way that development is best undertaken: in a 'bottom-up', 'participatory' style, over a long period of time, with participants controlling the process. In this sense,

6

agencies could usefully evaluate all their work in Somalia and Somaliland in terms of the extent to which they are helping to promote a peaceful environment.

RECOMMENDATIONS:

i Agencies should make a substantial commitment to supporting the demobilisation process in Somaliland.

ii The political, economic and military situation in Somaliland is different from that in Somalia. Somalia and Somaliland should be treated separately, and agencies should consider new work or strengthening existing programmes in Somaliland.

iii One advantage of UN peace-making efforts over indigenous ones is that they receive international support. Agencies should work towards international acceptance of the legitimacy of indigenous peace processes.

iv Agencies should consider supporting further 'peace workshops' in Somaliland, specifically for Somali staff of international NGOs and Somali NGOs as a means of strengthening the capacity of these NGOs and promoting dialogue and an exchange of ideas throughout Somaliland.

v Agencies should consider supporting a workshop for Somali women, from Somalia and Somaliland. This might best done as a workshop for Women of the Horn of Africa, and might aim to identify broad issues affecting women throughout the Horn. Widening its scope to 'Women of the Horn' might help it to deflect some internal conflict. It might form part of the consultation process suggested for Somalia.

vi Agencies should consider holding a Peace Workshop on Somalia, at which current research and experiences could be presented, with the aim of helping to develop a framework and rationale for NGO peace work in Somalia and Somaliland, and to promote a more positive image of Somalia. As much work has been done by Somalis, both practical and academic, the workshop should concentrate on their work. One could usefully consider bringing people from other conflict situations.

v Agencies should consider supporting and promoting Somali cultural activities, in particular peace poetry, songs and music. This should be done both within Somalia and Somaliland and outside, as a high-profile media initiative, through the radio and television.

PART II BACKGROUND TO THE SOMALI WAR

1 INTRODUCTION TO SOMALIA

1.1 The Somali People

Somalia[1] covers almost 640,000 square kilometres in the north-eastern tip of the Horn of Africa. In the main this is a semi-desert region, with a vegetation cover and water resources that dictate a pastoral nomadic existence for the majority of the population. The exception is the area between the two southern rivers, the Shabelle and Juba, and in valleys of the northern escarpments, where higher rainfall and richer soils provide land suitable for agriculture.

The Somali-speaking people form one of the largest ethnic groups in Africa, living dispersed throughout the Horn, from the Awash Valley, through the Ethiopian Ogaden, and into northern Kenya as far as the Tana river. A Cushitic-speaking family or 'nation' of people, Somalis belong to the Hamitic group of peoples, which includes the Afar, Oromo, Saho and Beja peoples of the Horn. The Somali are distinguished by a shared common ancestry, a single language, an Islamic (*sunni*) heritage and a way of life that is overwhelmingly pastoral.

The Somali are divided into six 'clan families' — **Dir, Issaq, Darod, Hawiye, Digil, and Rahanweyne** — which are further divided, according to agnatic descent, into subsidiary clans or lineage groups (see diagram 1) (Lewis, 1961). The Somali kinship system and the flexible and shifting alliances of clan kinship groups are fundamentally entrenched in the social, political, and economic culture of the Somali people.

Until the colonial period the Somali 'nation' did not form a single political unit; any concept of political identity was based on clan affiliation. It was only when the Ethiopian empire and the colonial powers of Britain, Italy, and France divided the Horn and the lands of the Somali peoples into five states — British Somaliland, Italian Somalia, French Somaliland (Djibouti), the Ethiopian Ogaden, and northern Kenya — and the Somali Republic was subsequently created that the concept of a Somali nation state began to grow. The international colonial borders that separate Somalia, Djibouti, Ethiopia, and northern Kenya make little reference to established territories of the Somali pastoral clans. Of particular importance are the **Haud** grazing reserves ceded to Ethiopia by Britain in 1954. Since independence, irredentist policies to reunite the 'lost' Somali territories have been one of the driving forces of Somali national politics.

1.2 The Barre Regime

Created from the union of Italian Somalia and the British Somaliland Protectorate, the Somali Republic attained independence in July 1960. For its first nine years Somalia enjoyed a succession of democratically elected governments. In October 1969, amid accusations of corruption and electoral malpractice, the military seized power. Under the leadership of **General Mohamed Siad Barre**, 'Scientific Socialism' was adopted as the guiding ideology for the country's development.

Under the banner of Scientific Socialism, Barre embarked on a radical programme to fundamentally restructure Somali society. This programme initially received support from a class of urban intelligentsia and technocrats, grappling with the move from a pastoral society to a modern nation state, and disillusioned with the debilitating effects of 'clanism'. With a centrally planned programme, national development was promoted through an end to 'tribalism' and a commitment to 'popular participation', under the guidance of the single Somali Revolutionary Socialist Party. The masses were mobilised for crash development programmes, such as the 1973/4 literacy campaign; effigies of 'tribalism' were ceremonially burnt; marriages were celebrated at orientation centres and stripped of clan significance; clan elders were renamed 'peace-seekers' (nabad-doons) and made part of the state bureaucracy. This assault on the fabric of Somali society was coupled with state control of the economy. The intention was to turn this 'nation of nomads' into a modern state, in which people were required to look to the state for security and welfare, instead of the clan. Embodying the nation was the President and 'father of the nation', Siad Barre.

In 1974, Somalia suffered one of the worst droughts (dabadheer) in its history. In September of that year the regime of Haile Selassie in Ethiopia was overthrown. In 1977, taking advantage of the weakened Ethiopian state, Barre launched a war to reclaim the **Ogaden** for Somalia. The war, which met with almost universal support among the Somali people, was a high point of Somali nationalism and Barre's popularity. Defeat a year later by the Soviet-supported Ethiopian army of the new Ethiopian Marxist government caused fissures in Somalia, previously hidden by the war, to open.

In 1978 military officers of the **Majeerteen** (Darod) clan made an abortive attempt to overthrow the regime. Some officers who escaped arrest went on to form the **Somali Salvation Democratic Front (SSDF)**, which launched a guerrilla campaign against the Barre regime in the central regions of Somalia. In 1981, disaffected **Issaq** of the northern regions formed the **Somali National Movement (SNM)** and took up arms against the regime. The end of the Ogaden war destroyed any sense of national unity. The fact that both the SSDF and the SNM sought sanctuary in Ethiopia was an indication of the disintegration within the Somali state.

Diagram 1: **Somali Clans and Modern Politico-Military Movements**

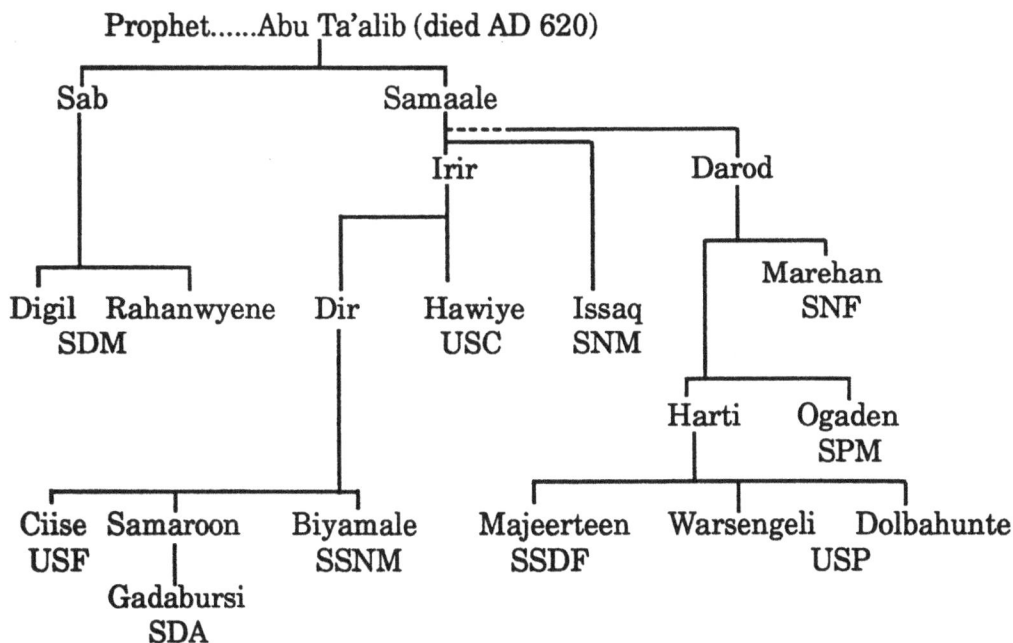

9

From that period power became more entrenched in the immediate family and clan of the President. Despite the elaborate structures of state that Barre introduced, and despite his anti-tribal rhetoric, Somalis regarded the regime as essentially clan-based, supported by those clans of his extended family commonly known as the 'MOD alliance': **M**arehan (father), **O**gaden (mother), and **D**olbahunte (son-in-law). By the late 1980s, even the MOD alliance began to break down, as the Marehan consolidated their positions in the face of growing insecurity.

Many Somalis point to the Ogaden war as the real starting point for the present Somali conflict. The 1988 peace accord between Somalia and Ethiopia brought an end to ten years of hostility between these countries. However, the accord also signalled a further demise in pan-Somali solidarity, as Ethiopian control over the Haud was finally recognised by Somalia. The accord precipitated an assault by the SNM on the northern cities of Burco and Hargeisa in May 1988, which provided the overt starting point of the present war.

1.3 The Militarisation of Somalia

As Cold War politics in the region demanded, the Barre regime was initially supported by the Soviet Union and later, when the Soviets switched support to Ethiopia, by the USA. Siad Barre was particularly adept at using the tensions of the Cold War and super-power interests to solicit a vast array of armaments for his government. Between 1969 and 1977, with the support of the Soviets, Barre was able to build Africa's largest army. After 1977, when Barre turned for support to the USA, he was able to secure $100 million a year in development and military aid, in return for US access to military facilities at Berbera port for its Rapid Deployment Force. In late 1987, at a time when Somalia was on the verge of signing a peace accord with Ethiopia, some 16 per cent of Somalia's imports were in the form of arms (*Third World Guide* 1991/2). In June 1988, a few weeks after the outbreak of war in northern Somalia, the USA delivered $1.4 million in military aid to the Barre government.

The USA and the Soviet Union were not the only suppliers of military equipment to Somalia. At different times Italy, Romania, East Germany, Iraq, Iran, Libya, South Africa, Saudi Arabia, and China have all contributed. The vast arsenals of weapons that the warlords have had at their disposal to fight the civil war have been the Cold War's main legacy to Somalia.

2 THE SOMALI CIVIL WAR

Since the late 1970s Somalia, and those areas of the Horn inhabited by the Somali people, have been in a virtually continual state of conflict. The historical origins of the present civil war lie in the defeat of Somali army in the Ogaden war of 1977 and, with it, the end of pan-Somali unity. As the Somali war has become more protracted, that sense of unity has dissipated further and Somalia has become more fractured probably than at any other time in its history.

2.1 War with the Majeerteen

The Majeerteen clan inhabit the north-eastern corner of the Somali peninsular, in Mudug, Nugaal, and Bari regions. Since the nineteenth century, they have also formed a prominent business community in Kismayo, where they are known as **Harti** (the generic term for the Majeerteen, Dolbahunte, and Warsengeli).

Since the arrival of the European powers, the Majeerteen have always played a significant role in Somalia's politics. After independence Somalia's first two Prime Ministers were Majeerteen, as was the second president, Abdirashid Ali Shermarke, who was assassinated in 1969.

In April 1978, following the defeat of Somalia in the Ogaden, Majeerteen colonels attempted to remove Barre in a coup. The coup failed, but those officers who escaped went on to form the SSDF, led by **Colonel Abdillahi Yusuf**. The SSDF launched military campaigns against the regime in the early 1980s in Mudug region, home of Abdillahi Yusuf's sub-clan. The response of the regime to the SSDF guerrilla campaigns was savage. In the months of May and June 1979, over 2,000 Majerteen were said to have died in Mudug region at the hands of Barre's crack troops, the Red Berets (Samatar, 1991). The brutality of the campaign against the Majeerteen was a forerunner for an even more vicious campaign against the Issaq people.

The SSDF collapsed in 1986, when its leader Abdillahi Yusuf was arrested by the Ethiopians, who at the time were seeking rapprochement with Barre. It was reconstituted as a political party in 1989 in Rome. In 1989, as the civil war spread into the central regions, the north-east became cut off from the south. In 1990, several prominent Majeerteen joined the **'Manifesto Group'** of politicians, businessmen, and elders who sought the peaceful removal of Barre from power. However, the SSDF played little part in the military over-throw of Barre. Since the overthrow of Barre, the north-east has remained largely free from fighting, except for a short-lived conflict with the Al Itihad Islamia (Islamic militants) in June 1992. In contrast, the southern Harti have been involved in a fierce war, under the banner of the **SPM/SNF**, against the **USC/SNA**, for control of Kismayo.

Since 1991, the Chairman of the SSDF has been **General Mohamed Abshir**, former Chief of Police in the 1960s, with Colonel Abdillahi Yusuf resuming military command of the SSDF after he was released from Ethiopian jail with the fall of Mengistu.

2.2 War with the Issaq

The Issaq, all located in the north-west of Somalia, made up the major section of the population of the former British Somaliland Protectorate.

Somaliland gained independence from Britain on 26 June 1960. Six days later it joined with Italian Somalia to form the Somali Republic. Although the Issaq lost their majority position in the new Republic, they continued to have influence in the government. Between 1967 and 1969 Somalia had an Issaq Prime Minister, **Mohamed Haji Ibrahim Egal**.

Part of the traditional grazing land of the Issaq lies in the Haud in Ethiopia. The decision to unite with the south was partly based on a belief that through unity there was a chance of reestablishing control over the Haud. The Issaq were therefore supportive of the war against Ethiopia to reclaim the Ogaden. The loss of that war resulted in a mass influx of **Ogadeni** (Darod) refugees into the north. The threat which this

11

posed to their own lands in the north, coupled with the dictatorial policies of Barre, led the alienated Issaqs to form the Somali National Movement (SNM), in London in 1981.

The SNM did not achieve widespread support until 1988. In May 1988, fearful of losing their bases in Ethiopia because of the peace accord, the SNM attacked government garrisons and briefly captured the northern cities of Burco and Hargeisa. In response to the SNM offensive, the Somali Armed Forces then proceeded to carry out a systematic assault on the Issaq population, forcing thousands of civilians, mainly women and children, to flee to Ethiopia. Some 50,000 people were estimated to have been killed between May 1988 and March 1989 (Africa Watch, 1990), and up to 600,000 fled to Ethiopia. These brutal attacks succeeded in uniting the Issaq behind the SNM.

The three years of warfare in the north were largely confined to the Issaq territories in the western regions of **Waqoyi Galbeed**, **Togdheer** and **Sanaag**. Areas inhabited by the **Gadabursi (Awdal)**, **Dolbahunte (Sool)** and **Warsengeli (Badhan)** remained largely free from fighting, and today the towns of Boroma, Las Anod and Badhan remain relatively undamaged.

When Barre fled from Mogadishu, in January 1991, the SNM took over the territory of the former British Somaliland and assumed authority. In May 1991, having reached an accommodation with the non-Issaq clans in the north, the SNM declared the secession of the north-west region and reasserted their sovereignty as the independent **Republic of Somaliland**.

2.3 War with the Ogaden

The Ogaden, a sub-lineage of the Darod, are the largest Somali clan confederacy, inhabiting the Ogaden region of Ethiopia, Somalia south of the Juba river, and north-east Kenya.

The Ogadenis did not play a prominent role in the independent civilian governments. The majority live in the Ethiopian Ogaden, and it is their location there, and the force of Somali irredentism, which has given them a particular role in Somalia's politics. The refugees who entered Somalia after the Ogaden war, by and large, provided Barre with a new, supportive constituency, which he later armed to fight the SNM.

In April 1989 Barre dismissed the powerful Ogadeni Minister of Defence, **Aden 'Gabiyo'**, thus sparking a mutiny among Ogadeni soldiers in the southern port of Kismayo. This led to the formation of a second armed opposition movement, the **Somali Patriotic Movement** (SPM), led by the brother-in-law of Gabiyo, **General Bashir 'Beliliqo'**. The sacking of Gabiyo arose out of Marehan fears of Ogadeni dominance in the army. However, the mutiny in Kismayo had its roots in a protracted conflict between the Marehan and Ogadeni pastoralists over the resources of the **Juba** region.

The creation of the Ogadeni opposition movement signalled the break-up of the Darod alliance of clans that had dominated the ruling group in Somalia for twenty years. A second Ogadeni front was formed in June 1989, when **Colonel Omar Jess** defected

12

with soldiers from the Somali army in Hargeisa. Since the overthrow of Barre, the SPM have divided into two factions, one led by Aden Gabiyo, and the second by Omar Jess.

2.4 War with the Hawiye

The final downfall of Barre was precipitated by the emergence, in 1989, of a **Hawiye**-based military force, the **United Somali Congress** (USC), in the central rangelands. As the largest clan in southern Somalia, stretching into Kenya and Ethiopia, their size, geographical spread, and economic strength within Mogadishu have made the Hawiye significant players in the country's politics. The first president of Somalia was Hawiye, and throughout the civilian 1960s they retained 20 per cent of cabinet posts. During Barre's regime, while their political power was limited, they were economically strong and benefited from the concentration of development programmes in the south. They were therefore not marginalised in the same way as the Issaq.

In October 1989 a section of Hawiye soldiers mutinied in Galkaiyo. Afterwards some 200 Hawiye civilians were reported killed. From that point fighting spread throughout the central regions of **Mudug**, **Galgaduud**, **Hiraan** and the towns of Dusamereb and Beletweyne. The USC was supported in its campaign by the SNM. Again the Somali army retaliated, with bombings of villages and massacres of civilians on a scale that matched those against the Issaq and Majeerteen.

The USC, founded in December 1989, was formed from the **Habr Gedir** sub-clan of the Hawiye, a number of whom were members of the SNM Central Committee. The first leader of the USC, Mohamed Wardhigly, who sought a peaceful solution to the conflict, died in June 1990 and was replaced by **General Mohamed Farah Aideed (Habr Gedir Saad)**, who favoured a military solution. By October 1990, having agreed a joint campaign with the SNM and SPM, the USC had reached the outskirts of Mogadishu.

2.5 The Digil and Rahanweyne

The Digil and Rahanweyne, located between the Juba and Shabelle rivers, belong to the **Sab** branch of the Somali people. Although they share the language and religion of other Somalis, they are predominantly agriculturalists and, as such, are looked down on by the Somali pastoral clans.

Their inferior status and smaller numbers have prevented them from playing a major part in Somali national politics. In 1989, a Rahanweyne opposition movement was formed, the **Somali Democratic Movement** (SDM), calling for the removal of Siad Barre. Their small size meant that they played only a limited role in the over-throw of Barre. After Barre fled, they were unable to withstand the rampaging bands of both Barre's and the USC fighters, and became the principal victims of the war and famine.

2.6 The Manifesto Group

For a year after the outbreak of war, the capital, Mogadishu, distanced from the fighting in the north and south, remained relatively calm. However, disaffection with the economic situation, the rising tide of displaced people in the capital, and the government's handling of the conflict burst into violent opposition to the regime in July 1989. Following the assassination of the Bishop of Mogadishu, and the subsequent arrest of several prominent religious leaders, some 450 people were killed during a day of riots, followed by mass arrests and executions of civilians.

The events of July signalled a turning point in the conflict. The ruthless way in which the government suppressed the riots shattered any loyalty to the regime. In May 1990, over 100 prominent Somali citizens, including the first civilian president of Somalia (**Aden Abdulle Osman**), a former police commander (General Mohamed Abshir), cabinet ministers, ambassadors, civil servants, religious leaders, elders and businessmen (including **Ali Mahadi Mohamed**), signed an open letter ('**Manifesto No 1**') condemning the policies of the regime, and calling on the government to accept a process of discussion with opposition groups to bring about a lasting solution to the political turmoil. Forty-five of the signatories were arrested and put on trial for treason, but later released after a mass demonstration in Mogadishu.

2.7 The Fall of Siad Barre

In December 1990 Italy and Egypt belatedly offered to sponsor a Peace Conference in Cairo. This was rejected by the SNM, SPM, and the USC, as the USC forces, under the command of General Mohamed Farah Aideed, were poised to infiltrate Mogadishu.

On 3 December fighting erupted in Mogadishu as armed Hawiye attacked the army garrison at Villa Baidoba and the President's residence at Villa Somalia. The battle for Mogadishu lasted almost two months, during which time attempts by the Italians, Egyptians and the Manifesto Group to broker a peaceful solution failed. On 4 and 5 January 1991, the UN and remaining foreign nationals were evacuated by helicopter from the city to the US aircraft-carrier *Guam*, which had been diverted from its duties in the Gulf War.

Barre fled from the city on 26 January, together with his son-in-law **General Said Hersi Morgan**, to his home area in Gedo region in the south-west of the country. In Gedo he reconstituted his army under the banner of the **Somali National Front** (SNF), twice attempting to recapture Mogadishu. In April 1992 Siad Barre fled from Somalia to Kenya and eventually Nigeria.

2.8 War and Famine

The fall of the Barre regime left a huge vacuum. Any control that the USC and SPM leaders exerted over the situation was quickly lost in the battle against Barre in Mogadishu. The hurried appointment of Ali Mahadi Mohamed as interim President and **Omar Arteh Ghalib** as Prime Minister by the Manifesto Group after Barre fled immediately precipitated a split among the loose alliance of opposition movements that had fought to overthrow Barre. Early attempts by the Italian government to reconcile the various factions showed some signs of promise at two conferences held in Djibouti in May and June 1991. However, without the agreement of General Aideed, Omar Jess, and the SNM, the recommendations of that conference proved impossible to implement.

14

After months of friction a second and more intensive battle between General Aideed and Ali Mahadi in Mogadishu began in November 1991. The fighting, which lasted four months, cost the lives of as many as 25,000 civilians. A cease-fire brokered by the United Nations, on 3 March 1992, coincided with a second attempt by Siad Barre to recapture Mogadishu. His forces, which came within 70 km of the capital, were repulsed by the USC, and the former President was forced to flee into permanent exile.

For some 16 months, from December 1991 to March 1992, the south suffered almost continual warfare. The coastal towns of Merca, Brava and Kismayo and the inland towns of Baidoba and Bardheere suffered waves of invasions by the undisciplined fighters of the USC, SPM, SNF, and others. Rape of women, particularly among the coastal Hamr and Bravani populations, mass executions, destruction of agricultural land, looting of grain stores and livestock, destruction of water supplies and homes led to the massive displacement of people into Kenya, Ethiopia, and Yemen, and mass starvation.

2.9 International Intervention

Throughout this period a handful of aid agencies witnessing the vicious violence and impending starvation, notably ICRC, SCF, MSF and the International Medical Corps (IMC), called on the UN and international community for a large-scale infusion of food to subdue the fighting (Africa Watch, 1992).

In April 1992, after 18 months of inaction, the UN appointed a Special Envoy to Somalia, **Ambassador Mohamed Sahnoun**, and mobilised a six-month Plan of Action to provide $23 million in aid and the deployment of 550 military personnel as peace-keepers. The operation, known as **UNOSOM**, was enlarged to 3,500 peace-keepers in August, after the UN Secretary General Boutros-Ghali accused the West of being more concerned with the 'rich man's war' in former Yugoslavia than with Somalia. In October 1992 another 100-Day Plan for Somalia, worth $82.7 million in aid, was set back when public criticism of the UN operations in Somalia by Ambassador Sahnoun caused a dispute with the Secretary General, and Sahnoun was forced to resign.

By this time inter-clan warfare had declined and was replaced by the armed looting of food aid, thus exacerbating the deadly famine that, at its height, was killing 1,000 people every day in the south. The cost of armed protection for relief supplies was equivalent to the cost of the food delivered. The inability of the UN troops to control the ports and secure the aid supplies finally led the UN Security Council to endorse resolution 794 (1992), which authorised an offer by the outgoing US President Bush to deploy 30,000 US troops in Somalia. Code-named **Operation Restore Hope**, the limited objective of the US-led **United Nations International Task Force (UNITAF)** was to 'create a secure environment for the delivery of humanitarian relief', throughout the country.

The intervention of the UNITAF was followed by two hastily arranged reconciliation conferences between the military factions, as a precursor to handing over to a UN multi-lateral military peace-enforcement administration. On 8 January 1993 in Addis Ababa, leaders of the politico-military movements, the **'warlords'**, agreed a cease-fire and signed an agreement on modalities for disarmament. This was followed on 27 March 1993 by an agreement for National Reconciliation in Somalia. By this agreement the factions reaffirmed their commitment to the cease-fire and a process of disarmament, and agreed to the formation of national transitional political and administrative institutions that would lead to the formation of a new government within two years.

On 4 May 1993, UNITAF handed over to a UN international military and civilian operation known as **UNOSOM II**, authorised under UN Security Council resolution 814 (1993). A month later 24 Pakistani UN peace-keepers were killed in Mogadishu during a weapons search of the Aideed-controlled Radio Mogadishu. The deaths of UN peace-keepers ushered in a new cycle of violent conflict in Somalia in which, by mid-September 1993, over 56 UN soldiers and several hundred Somalis had been killed.

2.10 Impact of the War

In 1992, at the height of the conflict and famine, the situation in Somalia was described as the worst humanitarian crisis faced by any people in the world. Certainly, four years of civil war and famine have been catastrophic. At the end of 1992, it was estimated that over 400,000 people had died and 1.5 million had fled from the country, seeking refuge abroad.

In the aftermath of Barre, Somalia has become divided into semi-autonomous regions, represented by clan-based military organisations and administrations. On 18 May 1991, the SNM declared the secession of the northern regions to form the independent 'Republic of Somaliland'. In the North East Region the SSDF established an administration for the regions of Mudug, Nugaal and Bari. In Mogadishu and the traditional Hawiye territories directly north and south of the capital, there were said to be some 30 military groups at the end of 1992 claiming control of different areas, as the USC had fractured along clan lines. Various areas of the densely populated and resource-rich Lower Shabelle and Juba regions have, at different times, come under the control of the USC, SPM, SNF, SDM and SSNM (**Southern Somali National Movement**).

The war has affected all parts of Somalia and Somaliland. Only the north-eastern regions of Mudug, Nugaal and Bari and Sool and Awdal regions of Somaliland have escaped the worst of the violence. However, these areas, like others, have been affected by the pressures of destitute and traumatised people displaced by the war. Whole communities have been uprooted. The majority of the non-ethnic Somali population has left the country. The war has resulted in the wholesale destruction of housing, urban industry, communications, social service infrastructure, and agricultural infrastructure. In Hargeisa alone 60,000 houses were destroyed. From Hargeisa and Galkaiyo to the Kenyan border all government and public buildings have been completely ransacked. The most resilient part of the economy and way of life has been the pastoral sector in the north-east and Somaliland.

At the same time the focus of international attention on the war and famine in southern Somalia has hidden more positive developments elsewhere in the region. Except for a short-lived conflict between the SSDF and Islamic fundamentalists in

June 1992, and intermittent skirmishes along its southern border with the USC, the North East Region has, by and large, remained peaceful. In the self-declared Republic of Somaliland, the euphoria of independence was shattered by an outbreak of fighting in Berbera and Burco in early 1992. However, after some eight months of insecurity, a political settlement was brokered by the Somaliland elders. In May 1993, the Somaliland elders went on to conclude a national reconciliation conference at the town of **Boroma**, and the election, through peaceful means, of a new government for Somaliland.

3. UNDERSTANDING THE CONFLICT

Since the beginning of this century, there has hardly been a period when the Somali nation has not been in conflict with itself or with its neighbours. This was graphically expressed in the diagram below, produced at workshop on conflict and peace in Hargeisa in September 1993 (see Appendix D).

Diagram 2: **Periods of Conflict and Peace in Recent Somali History**

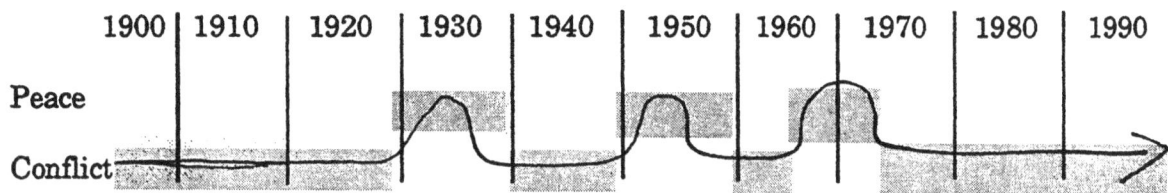

| 1900 | 1910 | 1920 | 1930 | 1940 | 1950 | 1960 | 1970 | 1980 | 1990 |

The cumulative effects of continual cycles of conflict on the development of Somalia and the lives of the Somali people must themselves be a cause of the recent conflict. While the May 1988 offensive by the SNM on government garrisons in northern Somalia stands out as the overt starting point for this conflict, the roots go much deeper.

It used to be commented that Somalia was unique in Africa, being a state founded upon a single ethnic group — the Somali — who occupy a contiguous territory and share a common ancestry, a single language, an Islamic heritage, and a way of life that is overwhelmingly pastoral. It is therefore difficult to understand why an apparently homogeneous society should be wrecked by such internal conflict. Conflict between people of different cultures seems more understandable. Until the colonial period, however, the Somali people did not form a unitary state.

One of the main legacies of European colonialism was to graft a system of centralised governance on to the highly decentralised and egalitarian political system of a pastoral people. Subsequent civilian and military governments attempted to create a unitary Somali State, by turning corporate responsibility away from sectional kinship loyalties towards the State. The development of centralised government structures reached its peak in the repressive regime of Siad Barre.

It is important to understand that the political constitution of Somali society lies not in the centralised political institutions of a Western model, but in a particular social system of a pastoral people, where the notion of a 'social contract' has more to do with regulating political and economic relationships between pastoral kinship groups than with delegating responsibility to a central polity.

17

Somali society is structured on a segmentary clan lineage system, in which membership is determined by descent through the male line. The recognisable levels of segmentation among northern pastoralists are set out below. Within this kinship system, the smallest recognisable political and 'jural' units are the *diya*-paying groups, to which all Somali belong, and whose members are pledged to support each other, to pay and receive 'blood compensation' (*diya*) (Lewis, 1961).

Diagram 3: The Somali Segmentary Lineage System

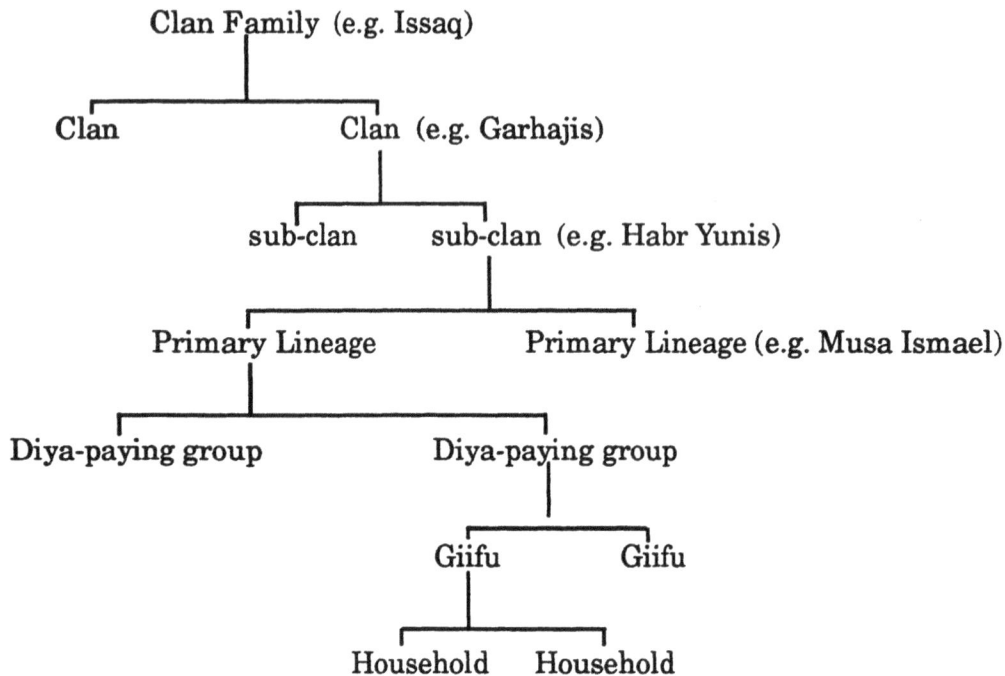

```
                    Clan Family (e.g. Issaq)
                             |
        ┌────────────────────┴──────────┐
      Clan                    Clan (e.g. Garhajis)
                                    |
                          ┌─────────┴──────────┐
                      sub-clan          sub-clan (e.g. Habr Yunis)
                                               |
                       ┌───────────────────────┴───────────┐
                Primary Lineage          Primary Lineage (e.g. Musa Ismael)
                       |
        ┌──────────────┴───────────────┐
  Diya-paying group          Diya-paying group
                                    |
                          ┌─────────┴─────────┐
                       Giifu              Giifu
                          |
                ┌─────────┴─────────┐
           Household          Household
```

The segmentary nature of this system reflects the need for pastoral groups, extracting a living from a harsh environment, to be in constant motion, expanding and contracting, in response to both internal (e.g. demographic) and external (e.g. ecological) forces of change.

It is a feature of this system that at any time one group may stand in opposition to another. The balance of opposing groups provides the 'fundamental source of order and security' (Cassanelli 1982) in Somali society. The effort to achieve this balance leads to the shifting political alliances that are a common feature of Somali politics. The system is dynamic and inherently unstable. When one group gains greater access to power or resources, or outside forces intervene, the balance breaks down and conflict emerges.

Since the creation of the Somali state and the introduction of centralised government, Somalia's politics has always been a balancing act involving the major clan families. It is true that the civil war in Somalia is the direct legacy of the concentration of power, the corruption, and the human rights violations of the Barre regime. But it has been fought along clan lines, and the 'anarchy' today must partly be understood

18

in terms of the segmentary nature of clans and their shifting alliances. The strength of Siad Barre lay in his ability to manipulate the delicately balanced clan system, supported by the means of state control. Individual access to such power goes against the grain of the Somali system of balanced groups; the imbalance needed redressing.

The civil war in Somalia has occurred at a time when the Horn in general is undergoing major social, political and economic transformations, which are directly related to global political changes, with the ending of the Cold War and the winding down of US and USSR interests in the region. The end of centralised government control, based on a single ideology, is challenging definitions of nationality, sovereignty, and the state throughout the Horn.

The most telling characteristic of the Somali conflict has been a process involving the reaffirmation of lineage identity and territoriality over national concerns. In this sense the war has been an 'ideological' struggle to overthrow a centralised government and to win greater participation, self-determination, and democracy after years of dictatorship and corrupt centralised government. The most dramatic example of this reassertion of self-determination was the declaration by the SNM, in May 1991, of the independence of the northern regions to form the 'Republic of Somaliland'.

People have also argued that an analysis of war based on clanism fails to address the external, economic, political and environmental forces that have played their part in this war. Such an analysis also, it is suggested, misrepresents the clan system as being wholly negative, and negates the more positive values of kinship.[2] Terms like 'anarchy' and 'madness' have been widely used to describe the state of disintegration that Somalia has arrived at today. They imply that there has been a complete breakdown of law and order and an absence of any sense of the 'social contract' that is required for civil order to exist. But this suggests a lack of understanding of Somali society.

Given the potential for dynamic and turbulent change inherent in the Somali kinship system, it not surprising that mechanisms should exist to mitigate tendencies to conflict. After all, mechanisms for resolving, managing, or mitigating conflict exist in all societies. In Somali society, one of the most important of these is *xeer*. This has been described as a 'contract' between lineage groups, combining both Islamic *sharia* and customary law. It defines the obligations, rights, and collective responsibilities of the group. Within the terms of this 'contract', members of a group are pledged to support each other. The *xeer* lays down the rules of corporate responsibility, and is a source of protection for both individual and group rights.

The *xeer*, however, is more than a contract. It defines the basic values, laws, and rules of behaviour. It is the closest equivalent to the notion of a 'social contract'. For those interested in peace-making and the reconstruction of Somali civil society, a fundamental question is the extent to which these values, as expressed in the *xeer*, have been lost during 21 years of military rule and four years of civil war.

Despite the assaults on the fabric of society, Barre's policies ultimately have not managed to eliminate the 'traditional' or historical value systems. In Somali society, history is extremely important. This is evident in the recitation of clan genealogies, the precedents that define customary law (*xeer*), religious knowledge and so on. Much of Somali political debate today is filled with historical references. This finds

19

expression in debates (and conflicts) over the ownership of resources in places like Kismayo, the reclamation of Somaliland sovereignty, the return to fundamental ('pure') Islam, the re-emergence of the authority of the elders, the formation of local councils such as the 'Khussusi' in Las Anod, and even the reappearance of historical figures on the political scene. There is a strong sense of people looking back to their culture, their religion and their politics, to explain why Somalia has reached the state it has today, and to find something to help them for the future. This is not regressive behaviour. It is a belief among many Somalis that future peace and stability cannot grow until people rebuild their relations of trust and cooperation from the grassroots upwards. It is to this end that people in Somaliland have looked to the reinvestiture of the traditional means of authority and leadership to rebuild society.

The Somali conflict is the result of a mixture of factors that include the legacies of European colonialism, a schismatic kinship system, the contradictions between a centralised state and a pastoral culture, east-west Cold War politics and militarisation, underdevelopment and uneven development, ecological degradation, and the lack of power-sharing, corruption, and human rights violations. Our understanding of the role that each of these have played in the war is limited and needs to be improved upon. What can be said, however, is that while climate has had its part to play, this is very much a man-made disaster, played out over four years of armed conflict. The phrase 'man-made' is used deliberately, because in this war women have been the innocent victims, if not targets, of the violence. 'Man-made' implies also that it should be resolvable.

Peace-making needs to be supported with an understanding of the causes of a conflict, and the causes of the Somali conflict are open to many different interpretations. An understanding, however, that the Somali conflict is 'created by people and can be eliminated by human action'[3] must be the starting point for any discussion of peace-making.

RECOMMENDATIONS:

Long term support: If agencies are to become involved in peace-making in Somalia or Somaliland, they will need to make a long-term commitment of people and resources. They need to think in terms of a ten-year perspective and probably not expect to see substantial results from their efforts in anything less than two years.

Research: An understanding of both the causes and impact of the Somali conflict and the responses and solutions to it is a pre-requisite for any involvement in peace-making. Agencies should consider sponsoring research in a number of different areas that will provide a dynamic analysis of the current situation in Somalia and Somaliland. The emphasis should be on commissioning Somali researchers. Agencies might consider commissioning research for a series of short briefing papers for publication. Areas for research might include:

• **History:** a historical perspective on Somalia and the creation of the Somali state, and implications of developing new models of government.

• **Anthropology/sociology:** an anthropological/sociological understanding of Somali society, its use and limitations for understanding the present conflict.

• **Politics:** an understanding of international and internal political forces in Somalia, including Cold War and post-Cold War politics, the Somali political factions and actors in Somalia, the role of African, regional politics, and UN and US policy in Somalia.

• **Economics:** an understanding of Somalia's past and present economy, resources, trade, debt, aid, and under-development.

• **Militarism:** the effect of militarism, the arms trade, NGOs and arms, mines, and demobilisation.

• **Environment:** the role which environmental factors have played in the conflict (the 'greenwar' analysis), the effect of diminishing environmental resources on modes of production, the management, control and access to land, and the impact of the war on environmental resources.

• **Social impact of the war:** at both local and national levels, the social impact of the war — population movements, refugees, inter- and intra-group relationships, trauma, social dislocation. This should incorporate a gender-based analysis.

• **Peace-making/conflict-resolution:** There is a need to identify and understand indigenous mechanisms for conflict resolution and ways in which these may be strengthened. This should also include an understanding of indigenous coping and healing practices. An understanding of the role that women are playing in the peace processes in Somalia is needed.

• **Relief and rehabilitation:** An understanding of the role that international humanitarian assistance played in resolving or sustaining the conflict would be useful to determine the future roles and policies for international NGOs in Somalia, Somaliland and elsewhere. Areas to consider might be food and health policies, NGO working practices and organisational structures, security, recruitment, and Somali NGOs.

PART III MOGADISHU: PEACE-ENFORCEMENT

1 THE INTERNATIONALISATION OF THE SOMALI CONFLICT

The killing of 24 Pakistani UN peace-keeping troops in Mogadishu on 5 June 1993 ushered in a new round of violence in Somalia. The repercussions of that incident continue to reverberate. Between then and the time of writing, over 50 UN personnel have been killed and several hundred Somalis, including many women and children. While concern has been expressed that too much attention is focused on Mogadishu, to the detriment of the rest of the country, the conflict between UNOSOM and General Aideed, and a solution to that conflict, are critically important for future progress in peace and reconciliation in Somalia. The conflict dominates the thinking of the UN; it prioritises the military rather than humanitarian role of UNOSOM; it consumes vast amounts of resources, and reinforces a negative perception of Somalia which is affecting donors. It may also have repercussions on other UN peace-keeping operations in the world. There is therefore a need to understand why the conflict has arisen. The following is an attempt to document the events which led up to the incident on 5 June, and its aftermath.

1.1 'Operation Lost Hope'

The UN Security Council Resolution (794) that authorised the intervention of the US-led, UN International Task Force (UNITAF) in Somalia in December 1992 provided 'Operation Restore Hope' (ORH) with the limited mandate to create a 'secure environment for the delivery of humanitarian relief'. Critical assessments of ORH have argued that, while delivery of food was improved, the operation failed to address wider problems in the country (African Rights, May 1993; Africa Watch, March 1993). Security declined in many areas, little progress was made on disarming the 'warlords' and gunmen, and the underlying political conflict was held in abeyance. The potential for substantial conflict remained, as was evident in the massacre of over 100 people of the Harti clans in Kismayo in February 1993, and in the re-capture of Kismayo by the SNF forces of General Morgan under the very eyes of the UN peace-keepers. The 'quick fix' solution of military intervention was itself creating long-term problems.

ORH was first and foremost a military operation with humanitarian objectives. Limited attention was given to longer-term political and humanitarian needs. The operation was initially welcomed by many Somalis. But with such a substantial force, local expectations of the intervention were more than the mere securing of routes for relief supplies. Its failure to do any more than this left many Somalis feeling bitter that their restored hopes had been betrayed.

The convening, in March 1993, of a Conference on Humanitarian Assistance, followed by a Conference on National Reconciliation, and a plan for UNITAF to hand over to a broader civilian and military operation (UNOSOM II) in May, provided an opportunity for the UN operation in Somalia to change its emphasis.

1.2 The Addis Ababa Conference on Humanitarian Assistance

In March 1993 two conferences were convened in Addis Ababa, which were intended, according to the UN, to build upon the 'dramatic changes' brought about by ORH. On 11 March, donors gathered at the Third Coordination Meeting for Humanitarian Assistance to Somalia, to discuss a request from the Department of Humanitarian Affairs (DHA) for $166.5 million, to fund a ten-month programme of relief and rehabilitation in Somalia. The UN received pledges of $142 million. Among the major donors were the EC with $43 million, the USA with $30 million, and Germany with $20 million.

1.3 The Addis Ababa Conference on National Reconciliation

The donors' meeting was followed on 15 March by a Conference on National Reconciliation. Many hopes were placed on this conference. Since January 1991, there had been three internationally sponsored reconciliation conferences, and several locally brokered meetings. If this one was to fail, people wondered whether there would be another chance.

Before it started, the Addis Ababa meeting came under criticism. The main concern was that the signatories at the conference were to be 15 political leaders, the 'warlords', who in the eyes of many Somalis were criminals, responsible for much of the suffering in Somalia. UNITAF, out of a need to protect its own forces, had sought the cooperation of the warlords, thus conferring on them a measure of legitimacy. Their participation in the Addis Ababa meeting would legitimise them further.

In response to these concerns, attempts were made to broaden representation at the conference. At least half of the 250 intellectuals, clan elders, religious leaders, women, and artists invited to the conference fell outside the narrow confines of the political factions. This broader participation was, in part, the result of efforts by some non-governmental peace institutes, such as the Life and Peace Institute (LPI), which sponsored a number of individual Somalis and NGOs to attend. Scheduling the Reconciliation Conference after the donor conference on humanitarian assistance also meant that a larger number of observers were present. In the end, however, it was the 15 factional leaders who signed the final agreement on 27 March 1993.

Somali African Mukti Organisation (SAMO) — Mohamed R. Arbow

Somali Democratic Alliance (SDA) — Mohamed F. Abdullahi

Somali Democratic Movement (SDM) — Abdi Musse Mayow

Somali Democratic Movement (SDM/SNA) — Mohamed Nur Alio

Somali National Democratic Union (SNDU) — Ali Ismail Abdi

Somali National Front (SNF) — Gen. Omar Haji Mohamed

Somali National Union (SNU) — Mohamed Rajis Mohamed

Somali People's Movement (SPM) — Gen. Aden Abdullahi Nur 'Gabiyo'

Somali People's Movement (SPM/SNA) — Ahmed Hashi Mahamoud 'Jess'

Somali Salvation Democratic Front (SSDF) -Gen. Mohamed A. Musse

Southern Somali National Movement (SSNM) — Abdi Warsame Issaq

United Somali Congress (USC/SNA)- Gen. Mohamed Farah H. Aideed

United Somali Congress (USC) — Mohamed Qanyare Afrah

United Somali Front (USF) — Abdurahman Dualeh Ali

United Somali Party (USP) Mohamed Abdi Hashi

The Addis Ababa Agreement reaffirmed the January 1993 agreement on a cease-fire and disarmament, and established agreement on the formation of 'transitional mechanisms' for the restoration of political and administrative structures. In particular it agreed upon the formation of (a) a Transitional National Council (TNC), with legislative functions; (b) Central Administrative Departments, to re-establish civil administration; (c) Regional Councils in 18 regions of the country; and (d) District Councils in all districts of the country.

The TNC is to comprise three representatives (to include one woman) from each of the 18 regions, five seats for Mogadishu, and one seat for nominees of each of the 15 factions present in Addis Ababa. This structure would be effective for two years. Four committees for Charter Drafting, the Peaceful Settlement of Disputes, Rehabilitation and Reconstruction, and Cease-fire and Disarmament were also established. A charter for the TNC was to be ready for approval at the second session of National Reconciliation on 8 June. The TNC was expected to be established by 1 July 1993.

The agreement also stated that the TNC would be the 'sole repository' of Somali sovereignty. This angered the SNM, who assumed observer status at the meeting, because it contradicted the wishes of those in Somaliland, involved at that time in their own National Reconciliation Conference at Boroma. Concern was also expressed at the legitimacy of those signatories (USP and SDA) purporting to speak for the non-Issaq clans of Somaliland, whose other representatives were also meeting in Boroma.

It has also been commented that the Addis Ababa agreement was 'so full of ambiguities' that any signatory who wished to repudiate it would have no difficulty in finding a pretext to do so (African Rights, May 1993). During the conference, fighting erupted in Kismayo between the forces of the SNF and the SPM. The fact that this could happen during the conference gave little hope that the signatories would stick to the agreements. Interestingly, one of the main complaints of Somalis (of different leanings) is that it has been UNOSOM which has repudiated the Addis Ababa agreements, by not implementing them.

While the Addis Ababa conference provided a framework for national reconciliation, insufficient time was allotted to determine clear mechanisms for implementing the agreements. In fact, the meeting was originally scheduled to finish on 23 March. Before an agreement was signed, the newly appointed Special Representative of the Secretary General (SRSG), Admiral Howe, the newly appointed US special envoy, Robert Gosende, and the Head of Political Affairs in UNOSOM, Kapungo, returned to Mogadishu. The task of overseeing the drafting of the final agreement was left to the Deputy SRSG, Ambassador Lansana Kouyate. With the assistance of the Ethiopian government and the Standing Committee on the Horn of Africa, the meeting was extended for a further five days to allow time for the signatories to reach this final agreement.

Observers of the conference have very different perceptions of its outcome. It is alleged that when Kapungo returned to Mogadishu, from his analysis of the conference he proposed to the Secretary General that the peace process should be widened, in order to marginalise the warlords. A different version purports that Aideed 'performed well' and proved to be the only person with leadership potential. It is further alleged that this version of events was vehemently rejected by others, particularly US advisers in UNOSOM, who had decided there was no future role for Aideed.

Whichever version of events is correct, the lack of clarity in the mechanisms for implementing the agreements hampered the ability of the UN to build upon any progress made at Addis Ababa. This was critical, as the Addis Ababa conference was staged to coincide with a critical juncture in the UN programme in Somalia, when UNITAF was preparing to hand over responsibility to the UN-led administration, UNOSOM II.

The conflict that erupted at the beginning of June 1993 seems to have arisen from several factors:

1 confusion during the handover from UNITAF to UNOSOM and a change in the mandate of the UN in Somalia;
2 lack of clarity in the mechanisms for implementing the Addis Ababa agreement;
3 the fact that the UN set the agenda and pace of the post-Addis Ababa reconciliation process;
4 a re-alignment among the political factions, jockeying for positions in the new TNC and jobs with UNOSOM;
5. perceived bias within the UN/US body against Aideed's faction, and attempts by the UN to marginalise Aideed;
6 perceived preferential treatment by the UN of other politico-military leaders.

1.4 UNOSOM II and a New Mandate

On 26 March 1993 the UN Security Council invoked Chapter VII of the UN Charter and unanimously adopted Resolution 814 (93) to expand the UN's role in Somalia, under a UN administration to be called UNOSOM II. By this resolution the security council approved the expansion of the multi-lateral force to 28,000 peace-keepers, with 8,000 logistic personnel, through to 31 October 1993. The budget for the military operation was $1.5 billion, making it the most expensive UN peace-keeping operation ever.

UNOSOM II has a two-year mandate, which will expire in February 1995. The objectives of the operation, as defined in Resolution 814, are to assist in the provision of relief and economic rehabilitation, promote political reconciliation and the maintenance of peace and stability, and to assist in the re-establishment of national and regional political and civil administrations in the entire country.

The formulation of UNOSOM II signalled a significant change in the UN's approach to Somalia. Under Chapter VII of the UN Charter, UNOSOM II was given powers of 'peace-enforcement', above those given to UNITAF. This enabled those in charge of UNOSOM to opt for force when 'international peace and security' were threatened, rather than normal rules of engagement which would limit UN military action to self-defence.

A further change from the UNITAF mission was the requirement that UNOSOM troops should be deployed throughout Somalia, not only in the south. While the Force Commander of UNOSOM II was required to take account of 'particular circumstances in each locality', UNOSOM II was given powers vastly in excess of those assumed for the US-led UNITAF intervention.

While Somalia was not placed under UN trusteeship, UNOSOM was given, *de facto*, international authority to make decisions for and on behalf of the Somali people. The problem is that in this process individuals and interested parties, under the UN umbrella, have been able to make decisions on behalf of the Somali people. It is partly from this change of mandate that accusations by some Somalis that the UN is 'recolonising' Somalia arise. By invoking Chapter VII, the UN fundamentally changed the nature of its operation in Somalia. In this process, the goals of the UN operation and the Somali people have come into conflict.

Authorised under UN Chapter VII, UNOSOM II is a unique UN peace-keeping operation. With military forces from 27 different countries, it is the largest multi-lateral force ever used in peace-keeping operations. It is also the first time that the USA has placed its troops under the UN flag and command. The arrival of German soldiers in Somalia on 15 May 1993 was the first time in the history of the Federal Republic that German soldiers were operating outside NATO. Unlike other UNOSOM forces, they are operating under Chapter VI.

Somalia has become a test case for a 'new world order', in which the Western-led UN will have a role to impose peace through force. In the words of one Somali: 'The UN is working under Chapter VII of the UN Charter. Is this used anywhere else in the world? There are no set formulas, principles or precedents to follow. We are witnessing trial and error. Much of it is error.'

1.5 Regional Peace Conferences and Political Re-alignments

After the Addis Ababa conference the factional leaders began to realign and strengthen their support bases in the run-up to the formation of the TNC, which was scheduled to meet in July 1993. In May two peace processes were initiated. One focused on Kismayo and the Lower and Middle Juba regions, and a second on Galkaiyo and the central regions of Mudug and Galgaduud. The Kismayo peace process, which eventually led to a peace agreement for 'Jubaland' (see Part IV below), was initiated and supported by UNOSOM. The one in the central regions appears to have been locally initiated and did not receive the support of UNOSOM.

In order to understand the significance of these conferences, it is necessary to recall that, after the overthrow of Siad Barre in 1991, two power blocs emerged in southern Somalia, centred on General Aideed and Ali Mahadi. The division between Aideed and Ali Mahadi had its roots in a dispute between the Manifesto Group of businessmen, politicians and intellectuals who sought to persuade Barre to hand over power peacefully, and the more radical military wing of General Aideed, who sought Barre's removal by force. When the UNITAF forces entered Somalia at the end of 1992, two broad alliances had been formed:[4]

(a) Ali Mahadi		(b) Aideed	
USC	(Abgal, Murosade)	USC	(Habr Gedir, Xawadle, Galjaal)
SSDF	(Majeerteen)	SPM	(Ogaden)
SPM	(Ogaden)	SDM	(Dighil, Rahanweyne)
SNF	(Marehan)	SSNM	(Dir, Biyamal)
USP	(Dolbahunte, Warsengeli)	SAMO	(Bantu)
SDA	(Gadabursi)		

26

The latter bloc (b), under Aideed, was known as the Somali National Alliance (SNA).

Militarily, Aideed and Ali Mahadi had fought each other to a stand-still in four months of brutal warfare in Mogadishu between 1991 and 1992. After a UN-brokered cease-fire in May 1992, the inter-clan fighting was mainly restricted to southern Somalia, between Aideed's SNA alliance and the SNF. In December 1992, when UNITAF intervened, Aideed was said to be losing ground, having over-extended his forces. The SNF, reconstituted under Morgan, was beginning to regain some ground. On the eve of the UNITAF intervention the SNF captured Bardheere. It is suggested that Aideed welcomed the US-led intervention as a means of shoring up his diminishing power base. In March 1993 this was further weakened when the SNF recaptured Kismayo.

On 24 and 25 March 1993, during the Addis Ababa conference, fighting broke out in Mogadishu between the Habr Gedir and Abgal. This is said to have arisen from pressure exerted on Aideed by factions that had regrouped under Ali Mahadi. During the Addis Ababa conference the SDM split into three. The loss of the SDM (Digil-Mirifle) further weakened the SNA alliance. Aideed's two-year mandate as USC Chairman was coming to an end, and was challenged by a call for a USC Central Committee meeting.[5] The initiative was unsuccessful.

Diagram 4: **Hawiye Genealogy** •

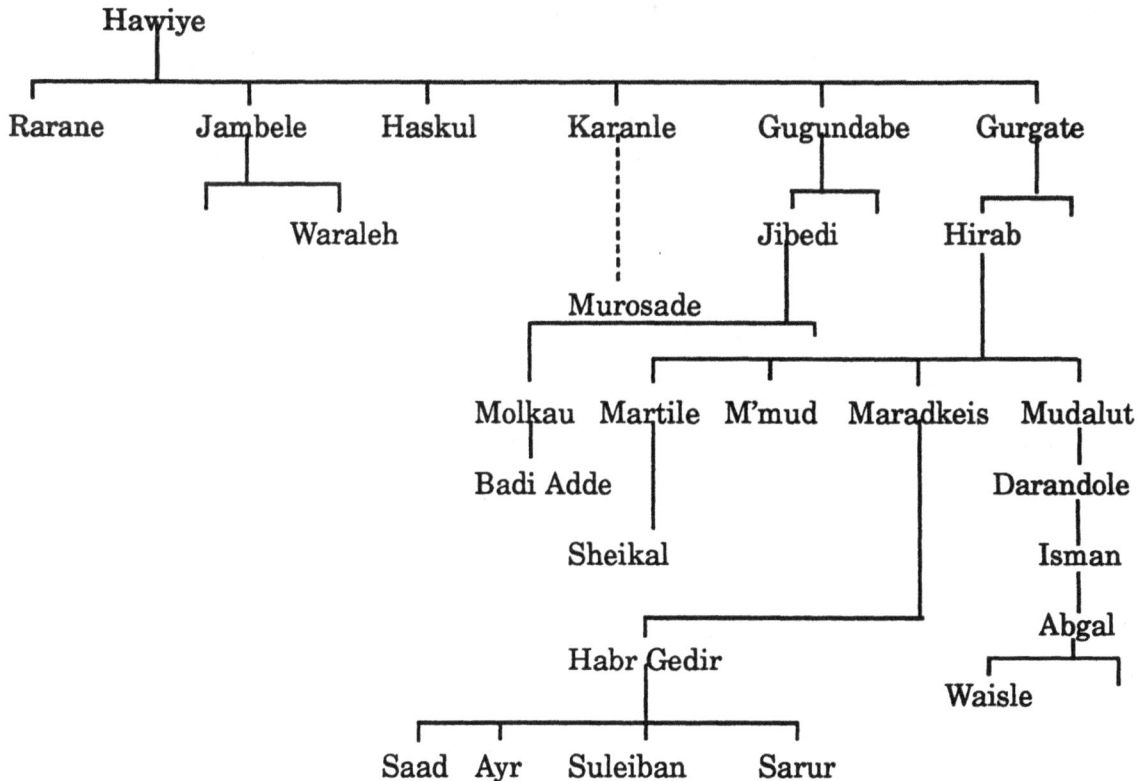

• Other clans associated with Hawiye are the **Xawadle, Degodia, Galjaal, Garre, Hober, and Aurmale.**

27

1.6 The Galkaiyo Conference and the Marginalisation of Aideed

Following the Addis agreement, elders in Mudug region, from the Habr Gedir, Majeerteen and Marehan (from Abudwak), initiated a process of reconciliation in Galkaiyo. Also involved in the process were the Lelkasse and Awrtabley (Darod). Aideed (Saad/Habr Gedir) and Abdillahi Yusuf (Rer Mahad/Omar Mahmoud/Majeerteen) of the SSDF, both of whose sub-clans come from Galkaiyo, gave their support to the meetings.

It is not clear where the initiative came from for this peace conference. One interpretation is that it was initiated by Aideed and Abdillahi Yusuf (the first leader of the SSDF, and since 1992 commander of the SSDF military), who met in Addis Ababa. Another interpretation is that it was initiated by the elders and hijacked by Aideed and Abdillahi Yusuf to strengthen their own support bases. Whatever the truth, the meeting was endorsed by both leaders. On 29 May 1993, Aideed called a meeting in Mogadishu to draft a peace agreement for the central and southern regions of the country. Under the impression that UNOSOM was supposed to provide support for such meetings, Aideed applied for financial and logistical support for the meeting.

UNOSOM, however, had not been involved in the Galkaiyo initiative and refused to recognise the conference as official, or support it. They were clearly concerned about Aideed's motives. They were suspicious that Aideed was prepared to bargain over Kismayo, in return for a settlement in Galkaiyo. They also objected to the participation of Omar Jess, who had been marginalised from the Kismayo meetings. This latter argument held little water with the supporters of Aideed, who saw UNOSOM using General Abshir (Chairman of SSDF) to broker the peace meetings on Kismayo.[6]

While the Galkaiyo and Kismayo conferences were in preparation, fighting took place in Kismayo between the SNF and the SPM. On 12 May, Admiral Howe criticised SPM/SNA for their attacks on Kismayo, stating that they were a violation of the Security Council Resolution 814 and the Addis Ababa accord. On 3 June 1993 Somali clan elders from the Kismayo area adopted a peace declaration for the Juba region.

The Galkaiyo meeting was concluded on 4 June in Mogadishu. According to Aideed, 227 people participated in the meeting, from the SSDF, SDNU (Lelkasse and Awrtabley), SNA and communities from Mudug, Nugaal and Bari regions. The meeting committed the participants to the return of property, the withdrawal of militia from Galkaiyo, and the opening of roads to traffic. (SWB 4/5/93)[7]

The meeting also resolved that UNOSOM should be asked to assist in the demobilisation of encamped militia and to store and maintain all 'technicals' (land cruisers, cut down and mounted with guns) that had been collected. The meeting was chaired by Dr Ali Ismail Abdi of the SNDU. Aideed reportedly concluded the meeting by urging delegates from Lower Juba to take seats at the negotiating table. (SWB 4/5/93)

At the same time, another conference was taking place in Karaan district of Mogadishu, involving Ali Mahadi (USC), General Abshir (SSDF), and Omar Moalim (Deputy Prime Minister to Ali Mahadi), Aden Abdille Osman (first Prime Minister of Somalia), and representatives from USC, SPM, SSDF, USF, USP, SDA, SAMO, SNF, SDM, and SNDU. (SWB 5/5/93) In contrast to the meeting called by Aideed, this meeting received the support of UNOSOM. It was concluded on 5 June.

In May, another dispute arose between Aideed and UNOSOM over attempts by the USC to set up a judiciary. They objected to UNOSOM's replacing a Habr Gedir General (Ali Kadir) with an Abgal (Jillao) as Chief of Police.

As a result of the preferential treatment shown by UNOSOM to the Ali Mahadi meeting, Aideed began to broadcast anti-UN propaganda. Aideed insisted that conferences aimed at pacifying areas in the centre and south were a Somali affair, for which the UN should provide the resources, but not the agenda. Through Mogadishu Radio, Aideed accused UNOSOM of opposing the implementation of the Addis agreement, rather than implementing it.

In the view of Aideed's people, after the Addis Ababa meeting, UNOSOM tried to set the pace and the agenda for political reconciliation in Somalia, and the form that new political structures, like the TNC, should take. This is not untrue. According to the Life and Peace Institute, UNOSOM Political Division was unhappy at the way in which the Addis Ababa meeting had further legitimised the warlords. It was their contention that a peace process should be broad-based and inclusive. At Addis Ababa it was agreed that the transitional committees should be composed of representatives of the 15 factions. The Political Division, in the interests of broadening the process, insisted that representation should be increased to 30.

From the perspective of Aideed's people, UNOSOM was therefore acting like a 'colonial power', deciding what process political negotiations should follow. This clearly threatened Aideed's own ambitions. His efforts in Galkaiyo may have been less to do with making peace than with a deliberately provocative attempt to challenge this assumption of 'colonial' authority by UNOSOM. UNOSOM were equally unsubtle. The speed at which they tried to push through negotiations and prevent Aideed from regaining a footing was at fault. Whatever crimes Aideed has committed (and in the eyes of many Somalis they are countless), there are other warlords who can equally be described as criminals. Trying to marginalise the warlords by forcing the pace of negotiations at the top, without enabling reconciliation at other levels to take place, had its inevitable consequences.

1.7 The 5 June Killings

There was much speculation that once the UN took over from UNITAF, General Aideed, who had never favoured UN military intervention, would try to test the new UN forces when UNOSOM II assumed control.

It is reported by those present in Mogadishu in May 1993 that the tension caused by these two meetings, expressed in the anti-UN rhetoric from the Aideed-controlled Radio Mogadishu, was such that conflict seemed inevitable. Perhaps mindful of the February riots in Mogadishu, stirred up by the recapture of Kismayo by the SNF, a contingent of UNOSOM troops entered Radio Mogadishu at 12 noon on 5 June, on what, according to some reports, was a staged operation and, according to UNOSOM, was a 'routine' weapons search to confiscate arms. Aideed was notified beforehand of the weapons search.

At the radio station the Pakistani peace-keepers met resistance from USC fighters. In the fight 24 Pakistani soldiers were killed, and an unknown number of Somalis. Six of the Pakistanis listed among the dead were killed away from the radio station, while overseeing food distribution at a feeding centre. Apparently unaware of what was happening at the radio station, they were pinned down by *morijan* (bandits) for five hours until their ammunition ran out. During this time, locals say that UNOSOM helicopters and vehicles passed by, but did nothing to assist them.

One of the most disturbing aspects of the killings of the soldiers, and a factor that has reinforced hardline opinion against Aideed, was the fact that many of the Pakistanis killed were badly mutilated. It is alleged that women were responsible for the mutilation.[8]

The UNOSOM action against Radio Mogadishu was seen by Aideed and his supporters as an attempt to interfere with those efforts to implement the peace resolutions reached on 4 June by leaders from Nugaal, Mudug and Galgaduud. Aideed accused UNOSOM of sabotaging the 'peace meeting'. 'Why didn't UNOSOM support the peace solution and why, instead, did they carry out this ugly act?', they asked. 'The country does not belong to UNOSOM ...'. (SWB 5/4/93)

1.8 The Significance of the Galkaiyo Conference

It is somewhat ironic, if not surprising, that the conflict between UNOSOM and Aideed arose over two such potentially important conferences. Kismayo, strategically and economically, is the second most important town after Mogadishu in the south. It has been fiercely fought over by the USC/SNA and the SSDF/SNF/SPM since 1991. Galkaiyo, which lies in the central rangelands region of Mudug on the main road connecting southern Somalia with the north, is also of critical importance. A historical political analysis of the Somali conflict suggests that, in many ways, an agreement in the central rangelands was more critical than Kismayo in the reconciliation process in Somalia.

Since independence, the clans which live in Mudug and Galgaduud region have been influential in Somali national politics. Here the Omar Mohamoud/Majeerteen, Habr Gedir/Hawiye, and Rer Koshin/Marehan share and compete over grazing lands. The coastal town of Hobbio was one of the first ports of entry for the Italians into Somalia, in 1889. Essentially a pastoral area, it is also one of the most under-developed of Somalia's regions. The Majeerteen and the Habr Gedir were some of the first to benefit from the education system introduced by the Italians, while the Marehan, smaller in number, were taken into the army.

In the first pre-independence Somali administration in 1956, the first Prime Minister, Abdillahi Issa Mohamed, was Habr Gedir Saad (related to Aideed). At independence Aden Abdulle Osman (Sheikal/Hawiye) became President, with Abdirashid Ali Sharmarke (Majeerteen) the Prime Minister. In 1964 Abdirizak Haji Hussein (Majeerteen) became Prime Minister, and Aden Abdulle Osman remained President. In 1967 Mohamed Haji Ibrahim Egal (Issaq) became Prime Minister and Abdirashid Ali Sharmarke President. The1967 elections returned the same Prime Minister and President.

In 1969, General Mohamed Siad Barre (Rer Koshin/Marehan) overthrew the civilian government, and power passed into the hands of the Marehan. In 1977, Majeerteen colonels attempted to overthrow the Barre regime. Colonel Abdillahi Yusuf (Rer Mahad/Omar Mohamoud/Majeerteen from Galkaiyo) went on to form the SSDF. Most of the military activities of the SSDF took place in the central rangelands, where they captured Galdogob, 50 km from the Marehan town of Abudwak. General Aideed (Habr Gedir) commanded some of Somali forces in the central regions during the war against the SSDF in the late 1970s.

The Habr Gedir, Majeerteen and Marehan have therefore had central roles in Somali politics since independence. It has been suggested that Aideed's opposition to Ali Mahadi, who was a member of the Manifesto Group, in which several establishment figures from the Majeerteen were prominent, stems from a fear that the Habr Gedir would lose out to the Majeerteen (Darod)-Abgal alliance. From this perspective, the war between the Abgal and Habr Gedir, who have never fought before, was fuelled by this ancient conflict.

A settlement in Galkaiyo had potential to build a broader peace and reconciliation process in Somalia. The extent to which this would have happened can only be guessed. However, a significant factor in the process would have been the traditional relationship between the clans that occupy that area.

Marriage is most common between those clans who live closest together and share resources. Their relationships are defined by common *xeer*. Political alliances are also most likely between those who share a common *xeer*. The Habr Gedir Saad share common borders with the Omar Mahmoud, and in particular the Rer Mahad (Abdillahi Yusuf's lineage of the Majeerteen) and the Rer Koshin Marehan of Abudwak. The Habr Gedir and Xawadle also border each other in the Middle Shabelle and southern Galgaduud regions. Compared with the Habr Gedir and Abgal, who traditionally inhabit different locations, do not share common borders, and do not have an established *xeer*, reconciliation is probably more feasible among the Habr Gedir and the clans in the central regions around Galkaiyo.

These clans in the central regions also share a common resource. This is the Chinese road linking Beletweyne and Mogadishu with Bosasso. After the UNITAF intervention, the Xawadle and Habr Gedir lost control of Mogadishu port and airport. One can speculate therefore that, political motives aside, it was important for those clans in the Middle Shabelle, Galgaduud and Mudug regions to open the Chinese road and enable trade to resume to the north-eastern port of Bosasso. Motivating factors such as this would have been important in the Galkaiyo agreement. Since the agreement in Galkaiyo, traffic is moving between Bakara market in southern Mogadishu and Bosasso.

After the intervention of UNITAF, much of Aideed's heavy weaponry was moved into the central regions. In April, the area north-east of Beletweyne was reported to be full of technicals and tanks.The Marehan were said to be equipped with 12 tanks, 32 technicals, several anti-tank guns and artillery pieces, and 5,000 fighters. Aideed was said to have 5,000 men with technicals and tanks. A settlement in that region, potentially, could have been important to a disarmament programme.[9]

Whether by default, design, or bad advice, the impression of Aideed and his supporters is that UNOSOM deliberately undermined the Galkaiyo meeting. The political furore this created in Mogadishu was evident from the radio transmissions emanating from the Aideed-controlled Radio Mogadishu and the UN-run Radio Manta at the end of May. It led directly to the confrontation between Aideed supporters and UNOSOM on 5 June.

UNOSOM may have made a critical mistake in under-estimating the importance of a settlement in that region. It is possible that if UNOSOM had reacted in a different way and had worked with the elders of that region, they may have achieved their apparent objective to marginalise Aideed, without bloodshed.

1.9 Resolution 837: from Peace-keeping to Peace-Enforcement

The killing of the 24 peace-keepers shocked international opinion. On 6 June 1993 the UN Security Council adopted Resolution 837, strongly condemning the attacks on UN personnel in Mogadishu. Acting under Chapter VII of the UN Charter, they authorised the Secretary General 'to take all necessary measures against all those responsible for the armed attacks, to establish the effective authority of UNOSOM II throughout Somalia [and to secure] their arrest and detention for prosecution'. The resolution called on member states to contribute military equipment to provide UNOSOM with the capability to deter armed attacks against it.

The details of the 5 June killings, the subsequent shooting of civilians by Pakistani troops, the retaliatory bombing by UNOSOM of Aideed's headquarters on 17 June and 'the house of Abdi' on 12 July (now known as 'Bloody Monday') have been documented in the press. In the bombing of Abdi's house a number of elders and businessmen, representing the Habr Gedir, Ogaden, Dir, Majeerteen, Murosade and Sheikal, were meeting to discuss dialogue with UNOSOM. The killing of these people prevented an early resolution to the conflict.

Some crucial questions have been raised over the UN's response to the 5 June incident (MSF France, 1993; African Rights, July 1993). To date, however, despite a number of critical internal documents on the affair, the UN has not provided adequate answers to these questions. Whatever opinion one holds of Aideed, one expects different standards of behaviour and accountability from the UN.

1.10 The Situation in Mogadishu as of August 1993

Since 5 June Mogadishu south has experienced a spiralling of violent conflict between UNOSOM and Aideed, with both parties accusing each other of heinous acts. The SRSG Admiral Howe (with dubious legality) offered a reward for information leading to the capture of Aideed, and Aideed in response offered a reward for the capture of 'Animal Howe'. The situation in Mogadishu has turned into an urban war of attrition between the UN and one faction in Somalia. In effect the civil war in Somalia has turned into an international conflict.

There were daily attacks by Aideed supporters on UNOSOM targets. On 8 August, four US marines were killed by a hand-operated mine in Mogadishu, and on 22 August a further six US peace-keepers were wounded by a land mine. These tactics, unacceptable by any standards, create heightened tension among UNOSOM troops who travel the roads. There was some evidence to suggest that Aideed was using children and women in the war against UNOSOM. In August an armoured personnel carrier (APC) was stopped by a crowd of children standing in front of it. They climbed on board and robbed one of the soldiers. UNOSOM troops no longer carry out any foot patrols, and travel only in convoy. The majority of UNOSOM military and civilian staff move around Mogadishu by helicopter.

The response of the UN to this situation was to strengthen their military presence. In August 1993 a further 48 APCs were imported. On 20 August, Secretary-General Boutros-Ghali called for a further 5,000 UN troops for Somalia. The USA deployed a further 400 elite Rangers and a contingent of the special Delta Force, with the aim of capturing Aideed. The aim was to create enough stability to enable the USA to withdraw its 4,000 troops 'with dignity'.

UNOSOM military operations against Aideed override all other concerns. Almost daily skirmishes between these two forces and the continual overflight of helicopters creates a repressive and frightening atmosphere for anyone living in Mogadishu. In the words of UNOSOM's humanitarian division, Mogadishu has taken on the appearance of a 'city under siege'. What signals are the United Nations sending to the Somali people?

Despite the vastly superior weaponry available to the UN and the presence of the 13,000 troops in Mogadishu, the UN do not appear to be winning the war. The failure of the US elite troops, the Rangers, and the special Delta 4 forces to capture Aideed has left the UN looking embarrassed. On 30 August, the UN was further embarrassed when the Delta Force launched a night-time raid on UNDP headquarters in Mogadishu, in the belief that it was an Aideed command and control centre. In the process they also destroyed property belonging to Oxfam (UK/I) and AICF (Aide Internationale Contre Le Faim). The conflict has also led to disputes within the UNOSOM operation itself (see section 2 below) In addition to the heavy loss of life, UNOSOM's actions have wreaked a lot of destruction. The National University, the vaccine factory, the cigarette and match factory, Radio Mogadishu, the Ministry of Livestock, and several other buildings have all been destroyed by UNOSOM in the name of security.

UNOSOM, and the United Nations, appear unmoved by criticism of their military operations in Mogadishu. After 'Bloody Monday', Ambassador David Shinn of the US State Department visited Mogadishu. Shinn left convinced that all was going well for UNOSOM. They claim to continue to have the support of the majority of the Somali population. This may have been true during the first raids on Aideed. It is clearly no longer true. The longer the military operation continues, the more they will alienate the Somali people and raise serious questions about their own accountability.

1.11 Inter-clan Conflict

The conflict between UNOSOM and Aideed has also resulted in an increase in inter-clan fighting. There are intermittent killings between Abgal and Habr Gedir, and NGO Somali staff are more cautious about travelling to different parts of the city. In early August 1993 a well-known Somali gynaecologist from southern Mogadishu was killed in north Mogadishu.

During the first two weeks of August 1993, there was an increase in inter-clan conflict around Afgoi, between the Murosade and Abgal and the Habr Gedir. The Habr Gedir are perceived to have been weakened by the actions of UNOSOM, and there were reports of Murosade attacking Habr Gedir trucks. As a result, Murosade living in the Bakara market area of Mogadishu were feeling increasingly vulnerable.

In July there was a outbreak of fighting in Brava and reports of clashes in middle Juba. In early September there was fighting in Qorioley. On 10 August there was fighting between Xawadle and Habr Gedir in south Mogadishu in which two people were killed. Later that day over 100 Somalis, many of them women and children, were killed when UNOSOM helicopters fired on crowds after Pakistani peace-keepers came under attack.

1.12 Negotiations

Following the killing of four US peace-keepers on 8 August 1993 by hand-operated mines, it was generally expected that UNOSOM would make further retaliatory strikes against Aideed. When this did not happen, there was speculation that UNOSOM might be involved in negotiations with Aideed.

It materialised that UNOSOM were attempting to start dialogue with Aideed up to the beginning of September 1993. Kouyate, the Deputy SRSG, is reported to have staked his position on being able to open a dialogue with Aideed, saying he would resign if the military would not allow him. In mid-August, through intermediaries, Kouyate was able to start a dialogue between UNOSOM and moderates in the USC/SNA.

The initial negotiating position of UNOSOM was that the USC should surrender Aideed and his new radio. In mid-August, Aideed received offers to go into exile from Ethiopia, Eritrea and Yemen. He turned these down, suspecting in them a sign of the UN's weakness. He felt his position was strong and was prepared to remain in hiding in Mogadishu, using hit and run tactics against UNOSOM, until they tired and left. He staked his own negotiating position on the call for an independent enquiry, by international jurists, to investigate events since 5 June.

On 4 September it was reported that Aideed was ready to sign a deal with UNOSOM, to include a cease-fire and the formal opening of dialogue. It is said that Kouyate asked for another 24 hours in order to convince the military. On 5 September, seven Nigerian troops were killed. Since then, it is not clear whether any further negotiations have taken place, and the violence in Mogadishu has intensified.

2 THE POLITICS OF UNOSOM II

UNOSOM II, at $1.5 billion, is the most expensive UN peace-keeping operation in the world. (The next is Bosnia, at $222 million.) Somalia is hosting the largest number of UN troops ever deployed. Under Chapter VII of the UN Charter, the UN peace-keeping role in Somalia has been transformed to one of peace-enforcement. UNOSOM Somalia is a new experiment for the UN, with very high stakes. It is not surprising, therefore, that there are internal conflicts within UNOSOM. The conflict between Aideed and UNOSOM has helped to highlight, and one suspects may arise from, divisions within the organisation. The vested interests of various parties within UNOSOM certainly impede its ability to respond adequately to the situation in Somalia. It is therefore necessary when assessing the present situation in Somalia to be aware of the dynamics at play within UNOSOM II.

2.1 New Agendas

In his Agenda for Peace (1992), Secretary-General Boutros-Ghali sets out his vision for the future peace-keeping role of the UN in the post-Cold War period. His vision gives the UN a central role in policing the 'new world order', and intervening in situations of armed conflict. This includes the ability to enforce peace, where necessary. At the same time, the USA is also looking for a new role in this post-Cold War period. The Clinton administration envisages that the USA should no longer respond unilaterally to crises, but seek to play a role of 'world policeman' through the UN. As part of his plan to restructure the UN, Boutros-Ghali believes it is necessary to establish a new UN command centre for all military and civilian peace-keeping operations.

The political dynamics that these new UN and US agendas create have a direct bearing upon the actions of UNOSOM and the situation in Somalia. The political machinations within the UN in New York over who will lead this new Peace-keeping department directly affect the UNOSOM II operation.

2.2 Structure of UNOSOM II

UNOSOM has four main divisions (see Diagram 5): Force Command, the Division for Humanitarian Relief and Rehabilitation (DHRR), the Division for Political Affairs, and the Justice Division.

These divisions are officially coordinated by, and report to, the office of the Special Representative of the Secretary General (SRSG). Since March 1993 the SRSG, and head of UNOSOM, is retired US Admiral Jonathan Howe. He replaced the former envoy Kittani. His deputy is Lansane Kouyate, Guinean Ambassador to the UN, who has been with UNOSOM since February 1993. The SRSG reports to the Secretary General in New York, as well as Kofi Annan, Under Secretary for Peace-keeping Operations and Jan Eliasson, Under Secretary for Humanitarian Affairs (DHA). A former US Admiral and National Security Advisor, he presumably also reports to the US State Department. The SRSG is advised by the Policy and Planning Group, headed by Dr Omar Halim.

1. **Force Command:** These are the military peace-keepers turned peace-enforcers, responsible for over-all security in Somalia, and charged with protecting the UN operations. The Force Commander is a Turkish General, Cevik Bir, appointed in February 1993, who reports to Kofi Annan in the Department of Peace-keeping. His second in command, Major General Montgomery, is a US military officer, who is assumed to be more influential. As commander of the US Quick Reaction Force, with their Cobra helicopter gunships and over 1,000 troops, he is responsible to General Shahin, Chief of Operations at the US Pentagon.

2. **Division for Humanitarian Relief and Rehabilitation (DHRR):**, This is responsible for the planning and coordination of all humanitarian activities. The head

of the DHRR is Hugh Cholmondeley, appointed in February 1993. He officially reports to the SRSG, but is also responsible to the Under Secretary for the DHA, Jan Eliasson.

3. **Division for Political Affairs:** This is responsible for promoting political reconciliation and building of transitional governmental and administrative structures. The head of this division since late 1992 is Kapungo. While officially reporting to the SRSG, he is also responsible to James Jonah, Under Secretary for Political Affairs.

4. **Justice Division:** This is responsible for the formation of civil police and rehabilitation of the judiciary.[10] Responsibilities also include monitoring violations of international law, and bringing to justice those guilty of human rights abuses.

The UN agencies, UNDP, UNHCR, UNICEF, WFP, and FAO fall outside this structure. Almost equivalent to NGOs, they report directly to their offices in New York. Having their own (and greater) funding sources than the DHRR, they are able to safeguard their independence.

2.3 Personal and Political Conflicts of Interest

At the highest levels of this structure there are problems, both personal and political. Plans to restructure the UN peace-keeping division have created tensions between the Peace-keeping, Humanitarian, and Political divisions. The tensions were clear in disputes over who should be in control of UNOSOM: the military, the humanitarian, or the political divisions? Relations between Boutros-Ghali and Eliasson are said to be very poor. Eliasson, an experienced mediator himself, is said to be open to more dialogue with Aideed, and has been openly critical of the military emphasis of the operation in Mogadishu.

The relationship between the SRSG and his deputy, Kouyate, is also reported to be strained. It is reported that Kouyate was Boutros-Ghali's original choice to replace Kittani as the SRSG in Somalia. His appointment was overturned when the USA insisted that an American had to be in charge, because of the large number of US troops in Somalia. Admiral Howe, a former National Security Advisor under Bush, seems to have been chosen to provide the continuity between the Bush and Clinton Administrations. Kouyate appears to have more of a political role in Somalia, involved in direct negotiations with the factions. He also has a direct line to Boutros-Ghali.

The domination of the US Administration and the Pentagon in the affairs of UNOSOM is no secret. The USA has dominated the operation since US troops led the UNITAF intervention. Somalis are aware that it is President Clinton, rather than Dr Boutros-Ghali, who speaks on behalf of the UN of the 'successful' raids against Aideed. Although UNOSOM II is a multi-lateral operation, with over 27 countries involved, the decision-makers in Somalia are primarily American. Other countries have very little representation within the overall command structure of UNOSOM. The military commanders of each contingent therefore insist on maintaining their command structures with their own governments. This has led to public disputes between the USA and UN and other countries with military forces in Somalia, in particular Italy, France, Pakistan, and Germany.

36

Diagram 5: **Structure of UNOSOM II**[11]

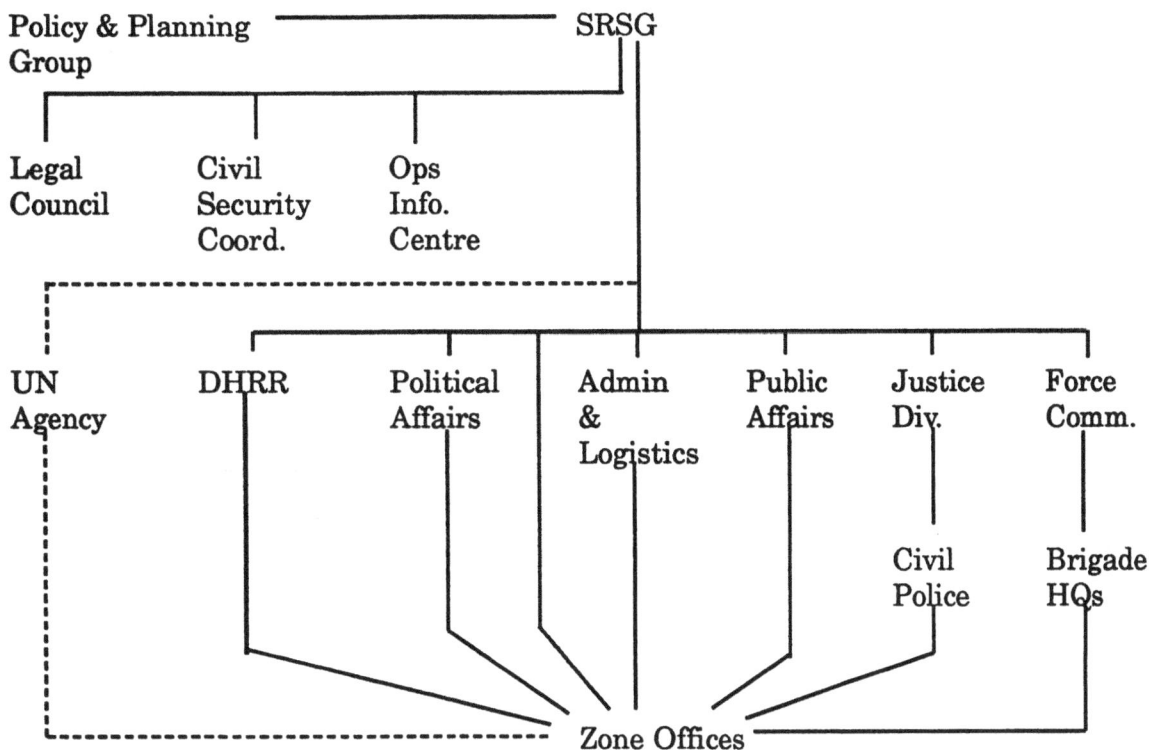

Policy & Planning Group —————— SRSG

Legal Council | Civil Security Coord. | Ops Info. Centre

UN Agency | DHRR | Political Affairs | Admin & Logistics | Public Affairs | Justice Div. | Force Comm.

Civil Police | Brigade HQs

Zone Offices

Diagram 6: **Structure of Zone Offices**

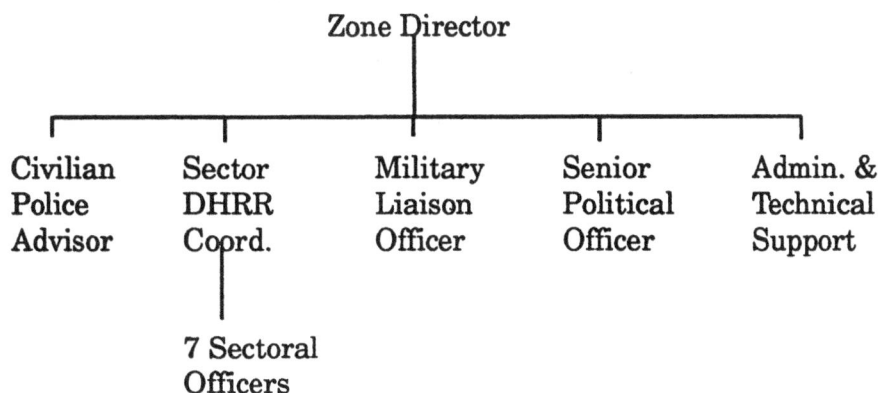

Zone Director

Civilian Police Advisor | Sector DHRR Coord. | Military Liaison Officer | Senior Political Officer | Admin. & Technical Support

7 Sectoral Officers

The UNOSOM have divided Somalia/Somaliland into five Zones:

1. Northwest — Zone Office Hargeisa
2. Northeast — Zone Office Bosasso
3. Central — Zone Office Baidoa
4. South — Zone Office Kismayo
5. Mogadishu — Zone Office N. Mogadishu

Three political factions have developed in UNOSOM. One ('the Hawks') includes Howe, US adviser Teitlebaum, the American Ambassador Gosende, Generals Bir and Montgomery and, when she was in post, Howe's senior adviser, April Glaspie (former US Ambassador to Iraq). It is this group which has dominated the policies of UNOSOM. It has been reported that Gosende and Glaspie were determined to marginalise Aideed, in preference for other more moderate leaders, such as General Mohamed Abshir.[12] Glaspie has been identified as the one who approved the arms search of Radio Mogadishu which resulted in the deaths of the Pakistani soldiers on 5 June 1993.[13] It is also reported by sources in UNOSOM that the 12 July ('Bloody Monday') bombing of Abdi's house in Mogadishu was intended to kill Aideed, and as many others as possible, an objective supported by the Hawks.[14]

A second political faction includes the Deputy SRSG (Kouyate). This is considered more moderate. It is Kouyate who has been involved in attempts to develop dialogue with Aideed. The DHRR could probably be included in this group. A third political faction is Kapungo's Division for Political Affairs. The district council programme managed by Kapungo has received a great deal of criticism from within UNOSOM.

These conflicts within UNOSOM reflect political disputes at the highest levels of the UN. The effect is that UNOSOM is dominated by political concerns that have more to do with internal political wranglings in the UN, and long-term plans for UN and US policy, than with the immediate situation in Somalia, or the Somali people.

An important division in UNOSOM is the special Policy and Planning Group attached to Admiral Howe's office. This is headed by Omar Halim, who seems to command respect among moderates within UNOSOM. The extent to which this group is actually able to influence UNOSOM policy, given the other vested interests, is unclear. To my knowledge, the Policy and Planning Group includes the only social scientist in UNOSOM whose knowledge of Somalia is based on experience.

In addition to these internal conflicts within UNOSOM and the UN, an additional factor affecting the UNOSOM operation in Somalia is an old animosity between Boutros-Ghali and Aideed. This stems from a time when Boutros-Ghali was Foreign Minister of Egypt. At the time Egypt, one of Barre's main supporters (after Italy), was involved in trying to mediate between the military factions and Barre. Aideed, who was trying to raise support for his war against Barre, was deported from Egypt. Aideed went on to become a 'warlord' and Boutros-Ghali went on to become Secretary-General of the UN. Some people (Aideed's supporters in particular) perceive a personal conflict between Aideed and Boutros-Ghali within the conflict between the UNOSOM and Aideed.

3 CONCLUSIONS

The description above is a review of the situation in one small part of Somalia. Many Somalis believe that the UNITAF military intervention was necessary, that it halted the conflict and reduced the numbers of Somalis dying. Certainly not all Somalis are opposed to the military operation against Aideed. Indeed, many support their actions. The great danger, however, is that the conflict between Aideed and UNOSOM will spiral out of control, increasing again the daily death rate and setting back recovery in Somalia.

The conflict between UNOSOM and Aideed at one level is a simple one of conflicting goals. UNOSOM has a mandate to pacify the country and support the establishment of transitional political and administrative structures in advance of elections in 1995. The mandate gives UNOSOM personnel the right to move freely throughout the country and make decisions on behalf of the Somali people.

At the same time, Aideed's aim is to gain power and influence for himself and his clan. This is to be achieved either through his presidency, or through an alliance of seats in the TNC and other national bodies such as the police and judiciary. Aideed was quick to test the authority of the UN. Power brokers within the UN, particularly the USA (and possibly Boutros-Ghali), appear to have decided that there is no role for Aideed in the future Somalia. They set about trying to marginalise him. After the Addis Ababa meeting they indicated their positions by supporting the Ali Mahadi-chaired conference rather than that of Aideed. The result is that the UN lost its neutrality, and the Somali conflict became an international conflict between the UN and Aideed.

There is a reticence among NGOs to be too critical of the UN in Somalia, in a belief that there is a need for a constructive relationship. However, while the conflict in Mogadishu between UNOSOM and Aideed continues, little progress will be achieved towards reconciliation and rehabilitation elsewhere in Somalia. Resolving this conflict is crucial. Even if there was a military solution to this conflict (and I believe the killing of Aideed is unlikely to solve anything), the means, which will involve the deaths of many Somalis, do not justify the end. There is a moral issue here that Oxfam and other agencies ought not to keep silent on.

Somalia has become an experiment for many other international political concerns. At stake in Somalia is the reputation of the UN and future peace-keeping operations, such as in Bosnia. Assuming that agencies wish to continue to have a constructive relationship with the UN, there is a need to advocate a change of approach in the UN operation in Somalia.

3.1 Recommendations

There are several areas where agencies might be able to influence the situation in Mogadishu and Somalia. They might consider pursuing the following:

Advocacy: Agencies should use their international standing to pressurise the UN into changing its approach in Somalia. The messages must be clear:

* There is no military solution to Somalia's problems in the long run, or in isolation from other factors.
* Dialogue is needed with all factions.
* The UN need to return to the humanitarian and political objectives of the mission.
* The full participation of the Somalis in the UN operation, at all levels, is essential.

In essence, peace-enforcement has failed, and agencies should advocate a return to the principles of peace-keeping and peace-making.

Lobbying should be done both individually and through the NGO Consortium. Agencies should take these messages to their home governments. Oxfam (UK/I) should take these messages to the British government and the European Union and other inter-governmental bodies. Other agencies should seek to get questions raised in their own parliaments and assemblies.

The key country in the multilateral force in Somalia is the USA. British agencies, separately or with US agencies, should be proactive in their lobbying in the USA, to advocate a thorough evaluation of the UNOSOM operation and US policy in Somalia. Integral to this message should be the need to replace the SRSG Howe with a diplomat, or someone experienced in humanitarian affairs, and probably an African.

In this vein, agencies might consider sponsoring non-official consultations between some key Somali elders, intellectuals, Somali NGOs, and businessmen from within Somalia. These consultations should not be high-profile nor be facilitated directly by the agencies, but through existing peace groups or institutes with experience, such as the Nairobi Peace Initiative, Ergada, or the Mennonites. Such consultations should happen, as much as possible, within Somalia. The objectives of such consultations would have to be clearly defined, but might include:

- to provide a forum for Somalis to meet and discuss and identify some common concerns and solutions in a relaxed environment;
- to identify individuals who might be able to influence the situation;
- to identify and empower a 'peace constituency'.

Discussions with Somaliland elders indicate that it might be possible to elicit the assistance of the Somaliland Guurti (elders' committee) to facilitate such consultations (see Part V).

It is recommended that agencies consider initiating some workshops between Somali staff of NGOs as part of the consultations process.

Human Rights: Human rights abuses by the Barre regime have been documented as one of the causes of the Somali conflict. The continuation of such abuses only prolongs the conflict. The abuse of human rights that occurred on a large scale throughout the war has not yet been documented. There is now sufficient evidence to indicate that the UN itself has, through use of excessive force, violated international humanitarian laws and is committing human rights abuses in Somalia. The warlords have shown contempt for human rights and international laws. We expect the UN to protect human rights, not to ignore them. Agencies should therefore:

1 Urge that an independent commission of enquiry is established to investigate all events since 5 June 1993, and to investigate accusations of human rights abuses by the warlords and the UN.

2 Commission a report on the legal status of the UN in Somalia. This should clarify to what extent the UN is subject to international humanitarian laws. Who is the UN accountable to? What is the legal status of the multi-national forces operating in Somalia under the UN flag? To whom are forces like the US Quick Reaction Force accountable? What mechanisms exist to investigate incidents? What training do these forces receive in international law and human rights?

3 Consider funding the establishment of a human rights monitoring office in Somalia, to document and monitor abuses by both local and international forces.

4 Consider funding the documentation of human rights abuses, especially those against women, children and minorities.

5 Consider funding local human rights organisations as they (and if they) arise, and human rights training for Somali NGOs where requested.

Media: The media played a major role in promoting an international response to the Somali crisis. There has been critical press coverage of the UN operation, but, other than CNN, litte television coverage. Agencies might consider encouraging investigative teams to cover the situation, to promote serious international debate on the situation in Somalia.

Policy: Agencies may need to review their positions on the role of military intervention in complex emergencies. Can one enforce peace? Do short-term gains outweigh long-term effects? A military solution is not an easy or necessarily quick solution. A military solution can become part of the long-term problem. Agencies should initially commission an in-depth review of the UN peace-keeping and peace-enforcement operation in Somalia.

4 DISTRICT COUNCILS

UNOSOM is mandated by Resolution 814 of March 1993, to 'assist the people of Somalia to promote and advance political reconciliation, through broad participation by all sections of Somali society, and the re-establishment of national and regional institutions'. The Addis Ababa agreement commits the Somali political factions to the formation of transitional political and administrative structures.

Since the Addis Ababa conference, UNOSOM II, in line with its mandate, has moved ahead with a programme to form District Councils. This programme is the responsibility of the Political Division. The motivation to proceed with the formation of District Councils, while the future of the TNC remains in some doubt, comes from the view that a 'bottom-up' process of political reconciliation is the best way to build peace in Somalia. It is believed that the process will eventually marginalise the warlords. Problems have arisen, however, in the implementation of this programme by UNOSOM.

The constitution for the District Councils has been drafted by the Charter Drafting Committee. By this, the councils are to have 21 members, with a 'mixture of traditional and new leaders', and one woman. Three representatives elected from the District Council will go on to participate in one of the 18 Regional Councils. Each region is assumed to have five districts. The aim was to form 39 District Councils in southern Somalia by December 1993. Somaliland will be dealt with separately. As of August 1993 UNOSOM claimed that 21 district councils had been formed.

On 22 August UNOSOM started a training programme for those Councils, using the services of the Eastern and Southern Africa Management Institute (ESAMI) from Arusha. The training programme, which covers a wide range of topics on local government management, administration and finance, lasts for six days. The Life and Peace Institute (LPI) are funding the training programme and are considering establishing a liaison post in Somalia, to coordinate and monitor the work of these Councils.

There has been much criticism over the District Council programme by Somalis, from within UNOSOM, and from NGOs. Some of the concerns raised are:

• The legitimacy of the districts (some of which were formed by Barre as late as 1988).

• The legitimacy of the council elections: as one Somali said, 'The man who slaughters ten camels will have many seats'. (In some cases Kapungo is accused of having chosen the candidates himself.)

• The representativeness of councils, given the massive internal and external displacement of people.

• In some places UNOSOM are insisting that councils should be formed, even where there is a functioning local structure of elders (e.g. north-east Somalia).

• The legitimacy of UNOSOM's insistence on equal representation of clans in the council and the inclusion of one woman on the council. It is suggested that equal representation cannot be enforced, and the one woman on a council will have no more than token authority.

• There is an opinion that DCs should not be formed until the revenue-collecting potential of an area has been assessed and added into the plan.

• There is an opinion that 'political leaders' should be involved in the process, to give the councils some legitimacy. Without the involvement of the TNC, how will they relate to each other?

• There is a lack of clarity in the functions and authority of the Councils, and there has been no dialogue about the District Councils with the Somali population as a whole.

• The Political Division and DHRR have no resources to assist the councils, once formed, and donors are unwilling to support the political process. (The exception is Sweden, which has funded the Life and Peace Institute.)

• While it has been stated that UNOSOM and the NGOs will have to work with the councils, no information has been made available to NGOs, nor consultations held with them or with UNOSOM.

The District Council programme has largely been organised by one man (Kapungo) in a division that is under-resourced and under staffed, both centrally and at a regional level. Under pressure from New York, the time allotted for the formation of these councils is seriously inadequate. This is indicated by the attempt to provide local government management training to a District Council in six days. The lack of consultation with Somalis, and mixed messages about the role of the Councils and what resources will be available to support them, have confused matters further. It is not clear whether they are to be considered permanent or temporary bodies.

UNOSOM appear to have taken no time to study how District Councils might be formed. Although they claim that elders have been 'instrumental in electing councils',[15] it is not clear how closely they do relate to indigenous councils or bodies that exist or are re-emerging. In the north-east and Somaliland, localised councils of elders have been acting with *de facto* and *de jure* authority for some time.

The speed at which UNOSOM are implementing this programme gives no time for local reconciliation to take place, which is necessary if stable and democratic councils are to emerge. The process used to form these councils suggests that UNOSOM have spent no time in trying to understand how localised political reconciliation can work in Somalia. In Somaliland, where local-level reconciliation has been going on for some time, particularly in the rural areas, the basic 'building blocks' in this process are the *diya*-paying groups.[16] Among the Hawiye, Majeerteen, Marehan, and Ogadeni this is likely to be the same. Among the Rahanweyne, the building blocks will be at the clan level.

In some cases, the District Council programme has led to armed conflict. In July 1993 fighting over District Councils led to the deaths of 100 people in Brava. In Jowhar it is reported that the Councils have created divisions among the Abgal. In the first week of September fighting broke out in Qorioley, in which some 20 people were killed and the hospital ransacked. The fighting there is said to have erupted over the formation of District Councils. While not everywhere has suffered the same problems, the District Council programme is clearly not as successful as UNOSOM would like the international community to believe.

4.1 Conclusions

Two theories have been proposed to suggest how political reconciliation can be promoted in Somalia. One proposes that there is a need to reach a political settlement between the 'warlords'. The argument goes that one cannot distinguish between the warlords and the elders, politicians and financiers, and that Aideed and the other warlords are presently the *de facto* political leaders in the south. A political settlement in Somalia is therefore not possible without them, and one must find some way of working with them. The UN initially did much to legitimise the warlords, whom many Somalis see as criminals. They have ended up with a bias towards one rather than another.

The other theory suggests that reconciliation can be built only from the base, where localised, indigenous, and more democratic institutional mechanisms of conflict resolution can be empowered to bring about reconciliation. In this process the warlords will be marginalised. As implemented by the UN, through the District Council programme, this approach is failing and leading to more conflict. The bottom-up approach threatens the interests of the warlords. As implemented by the UN, it has not been impartial or indigenous. Both approaches indicate the dangers of trying to impose an outside solution to the conflict in Somalia.

UNOSOM is a bureaucratic, centralist body in orientation. Constituted by governments, its mandate is to establish a central government structure, albeit with some emphasis on decentralised regional and district structures. Through the District Council programme UNOSOM are, in effect, supporting the formation of 'top-down', albeit localised, political structures in the hope that they will be a catalyst for a 'bottom-up', broad-based reconciliation process. This is risky. In many ways there is little difference between this system of district and regional councils and the one set up by Siad Barre during his regime. In the words of one Somali, the District Councils are 'just replicating the mess'. A centralised government structure is the very thing many Somalis have been fighting against.

4.2 Recommendations

District Councils: Agencies should commission an independent review of the District Council programme, in order that the concerns raised can be discussed openly, and provide recommendations on how the programme might be improved. This could be carried out as a joint agency initiative.

Agencies should also review the way in which their own programmes are working with and strengthening local structures — elders, councils, political parties, NGOs — however defined in the particular locality. Some useful ideas might be gained from looking at each other's experience.

Advocacy: Agencies should emphasise to donors the need to invest in political reconciliation and the development of civic institutions.

5 HUMANITARIAN ISSUES: NGOs AND UNOSOM II

The justified and vociferous criticism by NGOs of the UN's inaction in Somalia, between 1991 and 1992, was partly responsible for the eventual US-led UN military intervention. Many NGOs at that time supported military intervention as a necessary international response to Somalia's problem. Others were more cautious. This caused a serious rift in the NGO community in Somalia.

Initially, relationships between the NGOs and UNITAF were relatively good, as UNITAF was able to break the strangle-hold of banditry and extortion rackets that had held up the delivery of humanitarian relief. Since the assumption by the UN of a wider political and military role in Somalia, relationships have deteriorated. This arises from a failure by UNOSOM to create a secure environment, and the increasing prioritisation of military over humanitarian objectives. There is now deep concern among NGOs at the path the UNOSOM military operation has taken. In particular there is concern:

• that the humanitarian objectives of UNOSOM have become secondary to the military objectives, and the UNOSOM II operation risks losing direction;

• at the continuing ineffectiveness of the DHRR (70 per cent of all humanitarian assistance to Somalia is being handled by NGOs);

• that the security of NGOs' humanitarian operations is being compromised, and the lives of Somali and international staff working for humanitarian agencies put at risk (with Somali staff subject to harassment by both Somali and UNOSOM military, there is concern at continuing insecurity outside Mogadishu, particularly along roads north and south of the city);

• at the conduct of UNOSOM troops in Somalia and the lack of accountability for their actions;

• that little or no progress had been made on disarmament agreements signed by the Somali military factions;

• that few of the agreements reached at Addis Ababa in March 1993 are being implemented;

• that, since the departure of Mohamed Sahnoun, there has been no attempt at any real diplomacy and dialogue between UNOSOM and the Somali people. The level of involvement of Somalis in decisions affecting the future of their country is extremely small.

At the Second UNOSOM Informal Donor Consultation in Nairobi in July 1993, NGOs made these concerns known to the donors. They argued that, rather than military operations being a 'success', the fact that UN troops have had to be used in combat is a reflection of the 'failure' of the mission.

On 10 July, the International NGO Consortium (NGO-C) for Somalia wrote to the SRSG, expressing their concerns on the deteriorating security in Mogadishu. In July MSF France submitted an appeal to the UN for an investigation of events surrounding the 17 June UN bombings in Mogadishu. African Rights (July, 1993) and Africa Watch have made similar appeals. On 11 August, 26 international NGOs from the NGO Consortium wrote to the Secretary General, drawing his attention to their concern at the effects that military force was having on humanitarian efforts, at the moral and legal questions raised over UNOSOM's military action, and at the need to 'search actively' for alternative, durable solutions to conflict (NGO-C, August 1993).

By and large, however, there has not been the same vigorous criticism of the UN that was witnessed the previous year. This arises from the lack of unanimity among NGOs since the intervention, which some supported and others opposed. There is some reticence in criticising UN operations against Aideed, whom few would consider a legitimate representative of the Somali people. There is concern that further criticism of the UN may lead to a withdrawal of UN and donor assistance to Somalia. International commitment to Somalia is limited to short-term goals, when what is needed is a long-term commitment. The UN 1993 Relief and Rehabilitation programme was developed within the short-term framework of a relief programme, when what is needed is longer-term rehabilitation. While the USA contributed $750 million to the UNITAF operation, it has pledged only $50 million for rehabilitation.

NGOs consistently stress in their communications the need for a constructive dialogue between the NGOs and the UN. The sentiments of ELCAS[17] are not untypical, when they propose that NGOs should 'make every effort to come to a constructive and positive relationship with the UN agencies, no matter how critical we are of certain actions and policies' (ELCAS, July 1993). However, given the present domination of the military in UNOSOM, it is difficult for NGOs to build up that constructive relationship.

Although UNOSOM and most international NGOs have offices and residences in southern Mogadishu, communications between them are minimal. Contact is maintained through daily security briefings at the Civilian and Military Operations Centre (CMOC), which is part of DHRR. As most information is regarded as sensitive military information, the briefings, which are dubbed 'weather reports', are very brief and uninformative. They normally begin with a claim that the situation in Somalia is 'generally stable'.

The NGO Consortium in Mogadishu provides a useful medium of communication between the NGO community and UNOSOM. It has done much to facilitate coordination among NGOs in various sectors, a role that should have been fulfilled by UNOSOM DHRR. Relations between the NGOs and DHRR have been strained and reached a low point in February 1993, after the appointment of a new Coordinator of the DHRR, Hugh Cholmondeley. A rapprochement took place after 5 June, when DHRR and NGO international personnel were evacuated to Nairobi, and they were able to find common ground in their concerns over the military operations of UNOSOM. This was reflected in the criticism of UNOSOM by Jan Eliasson in July, that for every $10 spent on military protection, only $1 was spent on humanitarian assistance.[18]

Diagram 7 Structure of Division of Humanitarian Relief and Rehabilitation

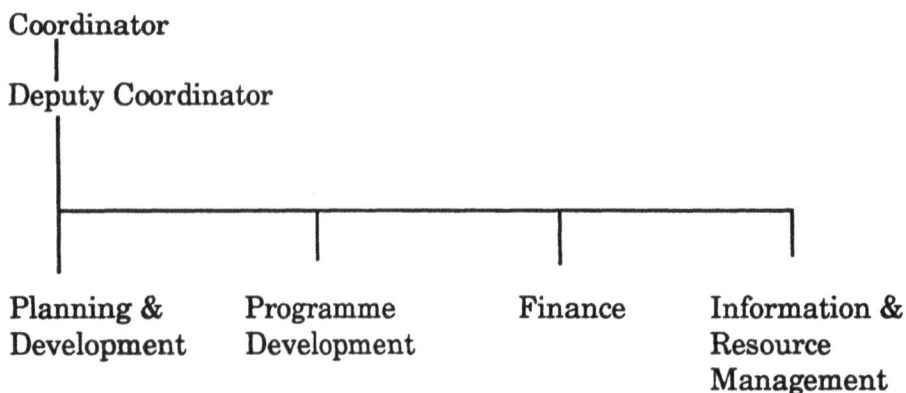

Coordinator

Deputy Coordinator

| Planning & Development | Programme Development | Finance | Information & Resource Management |

For NGOs, the DHRR should provide the best avenue to influence the military. The problem is that, while the DHRR Coordinator reports to Howe, he has limited access to him. Howe refers instead to his smaller circle of advisers. Furthermore, the DHRR is heavily underfunded; of the $166 million requested at Addis Ababa in March 1993, only $93 million was pledged and, by August 1993, only $15 million had been received. Their only capacity seems to be for staff recruitment. Some NGOs question whether the DHRR would be so open to NGOs if the DHRR had more resources of its own. The lack of funding severely undermines the effectiveness of the DHRR.

UNOSOM, more generally, has a staffing problem. At full capacity UNOSOM civilian staffing should be over 1,000. The total number of staff in the DHRR is supposed to be 59. By mid-August 1993 there were reported to be as few as 10 sectoral officers for 35 posts. Under-staffing means that UNOSOM are unable to provide full regional, political and humanitarian representation. Consequently this gives the military a greater role in these affairs. Furthermore, the majority of contracts are for a short term (six months), so there is a problem of continuity and consistency in staffing. UNOSOM salaries make Somalia an attractive option for those who want to make money in a short time. Thus the quality of those staff recruited varies enormously.

What DHRR has shamefully failed to do is respond to its own rhetoric to recruit Somalis. There remains a reluctance within UNOSOM to recruit Somali staff for any but the most junior positions. There have been demonstrations by Somalis, complaining about the small number of staff recruited by UNOSOM (NGO-C June 1993).

In August 1993 relationships between the DHRR and the NGOs deteriorated again. This arose partly through the extended absence of Hugh Cholmondeley from Somalia and the lack of clear leadership within the DHRR, but also because of the escalating conflict between UNOSOM and Aideed. For NGOs the weakness of DHRR means that there is little opportunity to influence the situation. At a time when the role of the DHA, world-wide, is under review, some aid agencies are concerned that the inability of the DHRR in Somalia to influence the military wing, and provide an alternative approach, could have serious repercussions on peace-keeping operations elsewhere in the world.

5.1 Recommendations

Advocacy: Agencies need to reinforce to donors the need to meet funding requirements for the DHA/DHRR programme. Agencies should publicly support the concerns of the Under-Secretary for the DHA in this. They should take these concerns to their own governments.

At the same time, agencies need to retain a critical perspective on the DHRR/DHA operation in Somalia. Their faults in Somalia cannot be entirely laid at the door of the military. Agencies must emphasise the need to increase Somali involvement at all levels of the DHRR.

NGO Consortium: The consortium is an important body for coordination of information on NGO activities. (One suspects that the Consortium has been important in psychological ways in providing a forum for NGO workers to meet and share common problems and concerns.) Agencies might consider increasing support to it:

1 To strengthen its political lobbying and coordination role with the UN, and its role in coordinating information on NGO operations.

2. To enable it to expand its network in Somalia. It is too narrowly focused on south Mogadishu. It needs to be aware of what is happening in other areas of the country.

3 To increase its network with bodies outside Somalia.

4 To explore whether the consortium could have a role in supporting regional Somali bodies in planning and coordination.

5 To provide the focus for inter-agency training programmes, or workshops (such as the Oxfam workshop in Hargeisa, see Appendix D), for NGO Somali staff from different regions. In this way it might have a role in peace-building.

PART IV KISMAYO: PEACE-MAKING

1 BACKGROUND TO THE KISMAYO WARS

Kismayo, the largest of the southern ports, has strategic significance, being half-way between Mogadishu and the Kenyan border. Lying at the mouth of the river Juba, it is also a commercial centre for products from the pastoral and agriculturally rich hinterland. Since January 1991, Kismayo has been relentlessly fought over by the USC, SPM, SNF, and SSDF.

The Jubaland Peace Agreement, signed on 6 August 1993, was heralded by UNOSOM as a breakthrough in the political reconciliation process in Somalia. It was presented to the international community as an example of how the UNOSOM peace-keeping operation was working in Somalia. In mid-August, Kismayo and the Juba valley as far as Jilib were, on the surface, peaceful. It was possible to drive in the valley and Kismayo without armed guards. There are, however, some concerns about the sustainability of the peace accord. There remain some groups who are hostile to it.

The Oxfam agricultural programme in the Lower Juba region is, arguably, Oxfam's most successful programme in southern Somalia to date. It is a programme that has been developed under extremely difficult security conditions. At one time the whole of the national team was forced to evacuate Kismayo, when one military faction took over from another. The success or failure of the peace accord has implications for the future of the Oxfam programme. The following endeavours to document the history of the Kismayo conflict and the UN-brokered peace process there.

1.1 Jubaland

Jubaland is the name coined by the British to describe the land between the Juba river ('the Nile of East Africa') and the Tana river in northern Kenya. In 1924 this land, as far south as Doble and Ras Camboni, was ceded by the British to the Italians.

Jubaland, according to the Addis Ababa Agreement, incorporates Gedo, and the Middle and Lower Juba regions. Up to 1975 the area consisted of two regions, Lower and Upper Juba. In 1975 these were carved into Middle and Lower Juba, Gedo, Bai and Bakool. This move was considered to be politically motivated by Siad Barre, who created Gedo as a Marehan region, including Bardheere town. Under the Addis Ababa agreement, these regions remain in place, so that 'Jubaland' refers to the whole of the area between the Juba river and the Kenyan border.

One factor lying behind the protracted nature of the conflict in Lower Juba is the complex clan composition of the area. The riverine areas of southern Somalia lack the homogeneity of the northern regions. There is a diversity of oral and material culture and a diverse complexity of social organisation not found among the more homogeneous northern pastoralists. It is an area where pastoral, agricultural, and coastal traditions meet.

In the Lower Juba region there are several large clan confederations, practising different economic activities:

Pastoralists:[19]
  Ogadeni (Awlihan, Muqaabul, Bartire, Mohamed Zubeir)
  Marehan
  Hawiye (Galjaal)
  Biyamal (Dir)

Agriculturalists:
  Hawiye (Sheikal, Xawadle)
  Bantu

Coastal:
  Banjuni
  Tuuni
  Harti (Majeerteen, Warsengeli, Dolbahunte) businessmen.

The 'Bantu' people (also known by Somalis as *tima-jereer* — 'hard hair' — or *tima-ada* — 'tough-haired' — or by the European term Gosha 'forest') are found along the course of the river Juba. They divide into two main groups:

• Mushunguli or Wa Zugua. They are thought to be descendants of ex-slaves from Tanzania, who arrived during the great drought in 1836. They retain their East African identity, and speak Swahili and *af maymay*. They are found in a fairly contiguous territory between Zunguri and Kamsuma along the Juba.

• Shanbara ('group of five'): These include the Myao, Mkuwa, Mgindu, Mlima, and Nyasa, who are also descendants of former slaves from Tanzania, Mozambique and Malawi. They are found north of the Mushunguli, north of Jilib, and have become more integrated into Somali society as bond groups to Somali clans. Most have taken on Somali names.

1.2 Historical Conflicts

Central to the conflict in lower Juba is a question of territorial ownership and control over resources. The main players are the Hawiye, Ogaden, Harti and Marehan. They all make historical claims to the control of Kismayo and its hinterland. The dispute, as it has developed, is largely between the Darod (see diagram 8), in particular between the Ogaden, Marehan and the Harti, rather than between the Darod and Hawiye.[20]

Kismayo was originally settled by the Banjuni people and only developed as an urban centre in the 1880s, when the Sultan of Zanzibar held suzerainty over Kismayo.

In 1865 the Ogaden crossed from the east to the west side of the Juba river, pushing out the Oromo, who had been weakened by a smallpox epidemic, and gained control of pastoral lands between the Juba and the Tana rivers. According to the Ogaden, the first inhabitants of Kismayo were Ogaden Muqaabul, who are now concentrated in Badade district south of Kismayo.

The first evidence of Harti settlement in Kismayo dates from the 1880s, when Harti traders from north-east Somalia established a foothold in the town. The main Harti

Diagram 8: Darod Genealogy

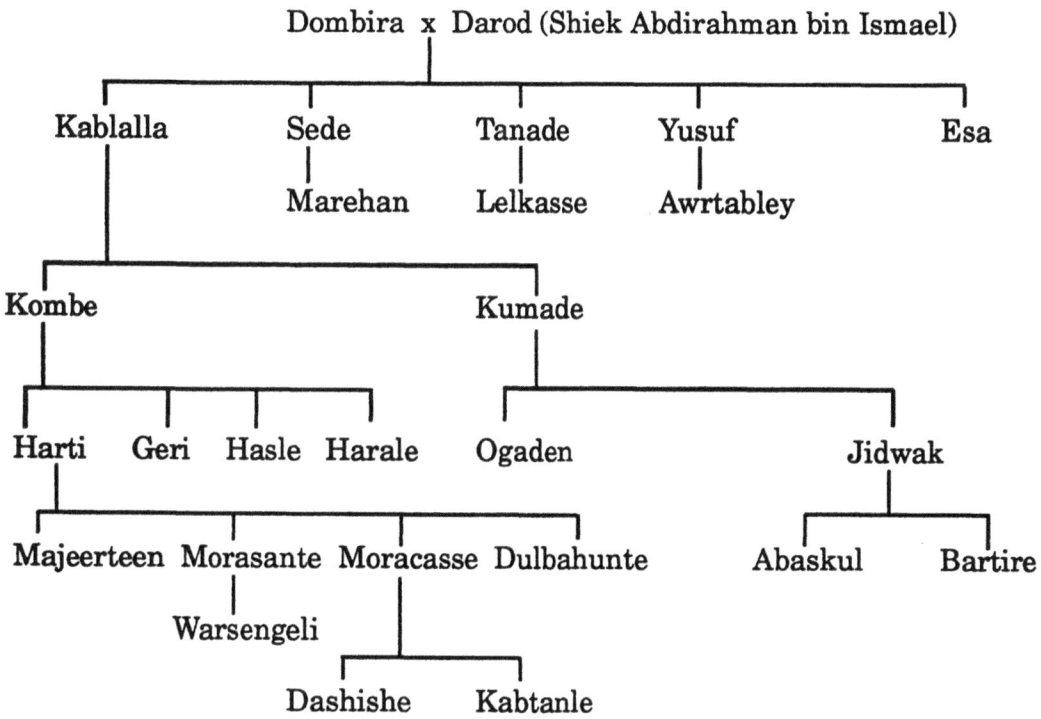

Dombira x Darod (Shiek Abdirahman bin Ismael)

- Kablalla
- Sede
  - Marehan
- Tanade
  - Lelkasse
- Yusuf
  - Awrtabley
- Esa

Kablalla:
- Kombe
- Kumade

Kombe:
- Harti
- Geri
- Hasle
- Harale

Kumade:
- Ogaden
- Jidwak

Harti:
- Majeerteen
- Morasante
  - Warsengeli
- Moracasse
  - Dashishe
  - Kabtanle
- Dulbahunte

Jidwak:
- Abaskul
- Bartire

Diagram 9: Ogaden Genealogy

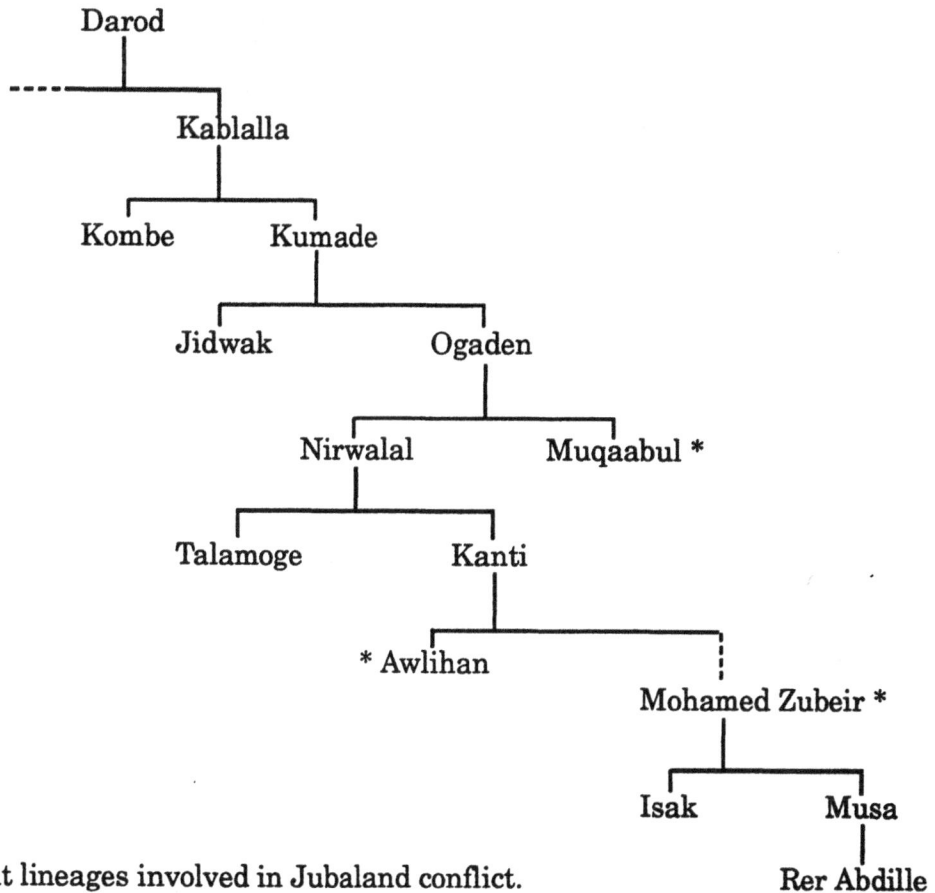

Darod
- ----- Kablalla
  - Kombe
  - Kumade
    - Jidwak
    - Ogaden
      - Nirwalal
        - Talamoge
        - Kanti
          - * Awlihan
          - Mohamed Zubeir *
            - Isak
            - Musa
              - Rer Abdille
      - Muqaabul *

*The significant lineages involved in Jubaland conflict.

51

Diagram 10: Majeerteen Genealogy

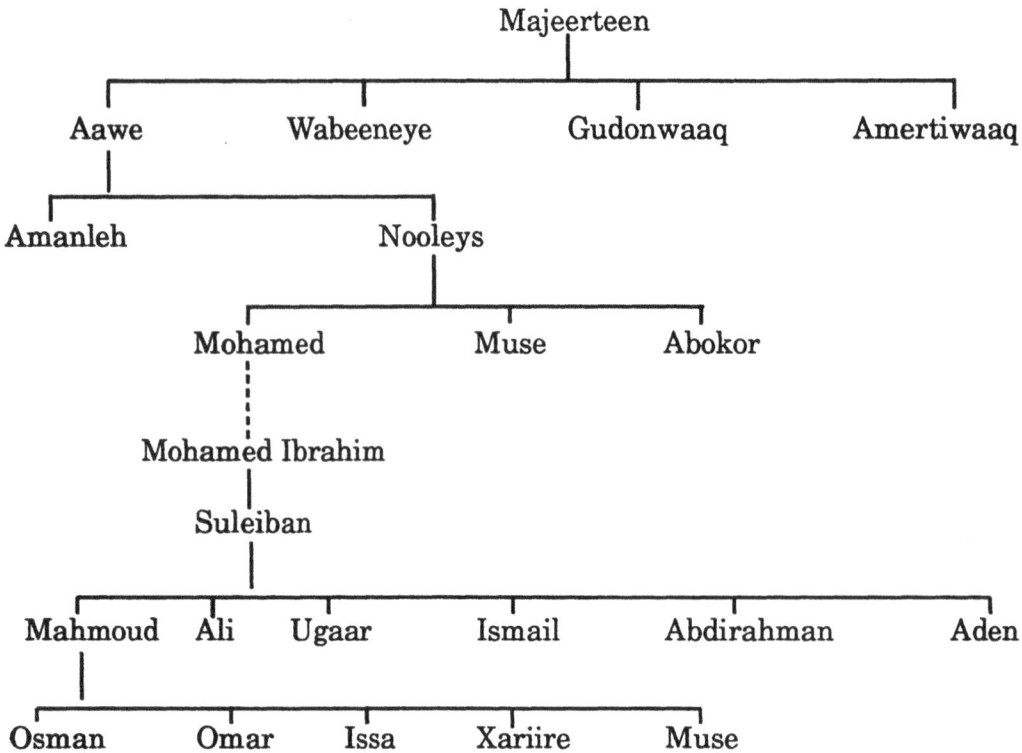

```
                               Majeerteen
        ┌──────────────┬───────────────┬──────────────┐
      Aawe         Wabeeneye       Gudonwaaq      Amertiwaaq
        │
   ┌────────────────────┐
 Amanleh             Nooleys
              ┌─────────────┬──────────────┐
          Mohamed         Muse          Abokor
              ┊
        Mohamed Ibrahim
              │
          Suleiban
              │
   ┌──────┬──────┬────────┬──────────────┬─────────────┐
Mahmoud  Ali  Ugaar    Ismail      Abdirahman        Aden
   │
┌────────┬──────┬─────────┬──────────┐
Osman   Omar   Issa    Xariire     Muse
```

group to settle in the town were Majeerteen traders from Ras Hafuun, who were known as 'Hafuuni'. Conflicts between the Osman Mahmoud and the Ali Suleiban Majeerteen, in north-east Somalia, led many of the Ali Suleiban to migrate to Kismayo (see diagram 8). Further migrations by the Issa Mahmoud and the Dolbahunte took place during the wars of the Sayid Abdulla Hassan (the 'Mad Mullah'), in the first two decades of this century.

Under the British administration the Harti became a strong mercantile class in Kismayo. They were also the first Somali employees of the British administration, thereby establishing themselves as an educated urban professional class. They maintained this position under the Italians, when Kismayo was ceded to them in 1926. The Harti therefore claim long-term settlement and trading rights in Kismayo, and cite as evidence the 1968 elections, when the four MPs from Kismayo were all Harti.

Hawiye interests in Kismayo are based on the presence of Galgaal in the area. They were displaced into the area earlier this century, having been driven southwards by the Rahanweyne. Other Hawiye clans, such as the Xawadle and Sheikal, are more recent residents in the region. Frequent land disputes between the Majeerteen and the Ogadenis took place in the early part of this century. In one famous battle some 80 Harti were killed. The Ogadenis refer to the area of the battle as 'lafara ha tiga' ('the bones of Harti'), while the Harti refer to it as 'lafara ha raga' ('the bones of men'). Jubaland was also the scene of frequent fights between the Awlihan/Ogaden and the Marehan in the first two decades of this century.

At the time when Kismayo was ceded to Italy, the British are said to have enforced an agreement between the Harti and Ogadenis. According to the Ogaden, the agreement found in favour of the Ogadenis, giving their Sultan Ahmed Magan overall authority in Jubaland. This has now passed to his grandson Sultan Abdi Ali 'Songkor'. According to the Harti, the agreements stipulated that the Ogaden (mainly Mohamed Zubeir) should stay north of what is now the Liboi-Kismayo road, while the area south of this remained under the control of the Harti. By this agreement the Mohamed Zubeir Ogaden were also given access to the port.[21]

1.3 Uneven Development

As one of the prime sites for agricultural development in Somalia, the Juba region attracted the attention of British and Italian colonial officials. Plans to develop cotton production failed, owing to labour and transport constraints. Instead, during the 1930s the Italian plantation sector was expanded through the use of forced labour.

In the 1950s and 1960s foreign assistance and development projects focused on small-scale agriculture, targeting small-holders, with small-scale cash-cropping (cotton) and the extension of social services (e.g. Jamaame Mennonite School).

In the 1970s and 1980s, foreign technical and financial assistance was invested in large-scale development projects. These included Fanoole Rice Farm, comprising 8,000 hectares, Mogambo Irrigation Project, comprising 2,700 hectares, and Juba Sugar Project, comprising 20,000 hectares. Banana plantations were expanded and a number of large state farms were created. These projects, focused on replacing staple food crops with cash crops (cotton, sugar and bananas), expropriated vast areas of land from small-holders. The effect was to marginalise the small-holders and enhance the value of the riverine lands to outside investors. Wealthy Somalis, especially civil servants from Mogadishu, used land-registration laws to expropriate village plots in the valley throughout the 1980s.

The same process occurred in the pastoral sector, where development projects which increased the number of watering points in the lower Juba attracted powerful pastoral groups from outside the region.

In addition a number of infrastructural, industrial, and service projects were undertaken in the 1970s and 1980s with foreign assistance. These included highway construction from Kismayo to Mogadishu (Italy), bridge construction (EC), a meat factory and tannery in Kismayo (USSR), port rehabilitation (USAID), primary health care (UNICEF, World Concern, CISP), Kismayo hospital (China), hydro-electric power grid to Jilib (China), Juba sugar refinery (Abu Dhabi, Saudi Arabia), and the Kismayo power plant (FINIDA). These infrastructural projects benefited Kismayo and the main urban centres, rather than the impoverished rural population (Menkhaus, 1993).

1.4 A Conflict over Resources

The overt starting point of the conflict in the Juba valley was April 1989, when Ogadeni officers mutinied in Kismayo and formed the SPM. The mutiny was in direct response to the sacking and imprisonment by Said Barre of the powerful Ogadeni

Minister of Defence, Aden Abdallahi Nur 'Gabiyo'. The sacking of Gabiyo was the catalyst for a conflict that had been smouldering over a number of years.

One analysis of the conflict in Kismayo identifies its roots in ecological pressures which caused competition over resources in the pastoral rangelands to the west of the Juba river. Gedo region is primarily a pastoral region. The predominant Marehan population there herd substantial numbers of camels. Ecological pressures in Gedo region, caused partly by the influx of Ethiopian refugees into that region in the early 1980s, resulted in a southwards encroachment of Marehan pastoralists into Ogadeni grazing lands (*degaan*). Backed by the thinly veiled Marehan regime of Siad Barre, this led to armed conflicts between the Marehan and Ogadenis around Afmedu in 1988.

A further source of dispute was the proposed construction of the Bardheere dam, which was intended to bring large areas of land under irrigation. At that time Bardheere was divided between the Awlihan on the west bank and the Rahanweyne on the east bank. (Gabiyo's sub-clan, Rer Ali/Awlihan, is from Bardheere.) The dam was never built, because of the war. The project would have reduced the available grazing lands and thus increased land values and competition between the Ogadenis and Marehan. The regional Governor at that time, Abdillahi Wagat (a Marehan recently appointed again as 'governor' in Kismayo by General Morgan), tried to mediate between the Ogaden and Marehan, but with no success. The sacking of Gabiyo, therefore, only accelerated a conflict over resources that was already spreading.

1.5 The SPM and SNF

The first leader of the SPM, General Bashir 'Beliliqo' (Awlihan/Ogaden), was a brother-in-law of Gabiyo. Through his mother's line, he also received support from the MohamedZubeir/Ogaden. The SPM was badly defeated in September 1989, in a campaign led by Siad Barre's son General Masleh, and Beliliqo was forced to flee to Kenya.

In June 1989, however, a second SPM (Ogadeni) front had been opened up in the south-west, after Colonel Omar Jess (Mohamed Zubeir/Ogaden) defected from Hargeisa. By January 1990 Jess controlled Bakool region, where he obtained the support of the Awlihan Ogaden. In August 1990, the SNM, USC and SPM agreed to coordinate operations against Barre.

In January 1991, as the USC fought Barre in Mogadishu, the SPM threatened to seal off his retreat south at Afgoi. However, after Barre fled from Mogadishu, USC leaders lost control of the situation and fighting erupted in February 1991 between the USC and the SPM in Afgoi. The defeated SPM were forced to flee south to Kismayo, where they joined up with other disparate Darod who had fled from Mogadishu. The front line between the USC and SPM/SNF passed through the Juba valley three times between February and April 1991. The USC finally captured Kismayo at the end of April 1991, and the SPM/SNF were pushed south of Doble.

When the USC overran Mogadishu, Gabiyo was released from prison. At the time Beliliqo's supporters came from the Awlihan, Mohamed Zubeir and Muqaabul in the Lower and Middle Juba, while Jess's support came from the Awlihan in Bakool, and Mohamed Zubeir in Ethiopia.

Following their defeat the various Darod factions, including the SPM (Ogadeni), SSDF (Harti) and SNF (Marehan), regrouped under the banner of the SPM. Internal Darod conflicts over land were forgotten in the face of the anti-Darod rhetoric from Aideed, who proclaimed his intention of clearing all Darod from Somalia. Gabiyo was appointed the new chairman of the SPM, and Jess the military commander. General Morgan (Majeerteen and Barre's son-in-law) was given charge of the police. The election of Gabiyo as the Chairman led to a rift between Gabiyo and Jess. It is suggested that Gabiyo was elected chairman to ensure the support of his Awlihan clan, who up until then had been supporting Jess.

In June 1991, the SPM recaptured Kismayo and Brava. A second attempt to retake Mogadishu was again defeated by the USC. In December 1991, during the re-election of the SPM chairman, Gabiyo and Morgan combined forces to remove Jess's forces from Kismayo and Brava. Jess then went on to form an alliance with Aideed's USC, which became known as the Somali Liberation Army (SLA). Their combined forces managed to push Gabiyo and Morgan out of Kismayo and in April 1992 forced Barre into exile in Kenya. Following this victory Aideed and Jess formed the Somali National Alliance (SNA), combining together with the SDM and the SSNM.

Following their defeat in Kismayo, there was an attempt by the Majeerteen to replace Morgan as army commander with General Hirani (Awrtabley). Some 40 Majeerteen elders in Kenya signed a letter replacing him, and his supply routes from Kenya were cut. Morgan responded by professing to be fighting, not just for the Majeerteen, but all the Darod. In this way Morgan managed to gather the support of the Marehan. With Marehan support, and allegedly resupplied by the Kenyan military, he was able to move up the Kenyan border to El Wak. From there he was able to recapture Gedo and went on to take Saakow, Bu'aale, and Afmedow (a Mohamed Zubeir town) and Bardheere in October 1992. He also managed to cut the Kismayo-Liboi road and capture Liboi from Jess. At this point UNITAF intervened in Somalia.

It has been suggested that when UNITAF arrived, Aideed's power was in decline, under pressure on fronts in the south and north-east. This is why Aideed is thought to have accepted the US intervention. With the arrival of the UNITAF, supporters of Omar Jess, fearful that they might lose Kismayo, were involved in the assassination of over 100 Harti people in the town between 8 and 10 December 1992.

In January 1993, Morgan attempted to recapture Kismayo but was repulsed by the US military. On 22 February, two weeks before the start of the National Reconciliation Conference in Addis Ababa, Morgan was able to infiltrate fighters into Kismayo, and after some bloody street battles routed Jess's forces and recaptured the town. Jess's forces had been deprived of their heavy weapons by the UNITAF disarmament programme.

Interpretations of the events that enabled Morgan to capture Kismayo vary. The USC/SNA alliance believe that the Belgian UNOSOM forces are not impartial, and Morgan's soldiers were allowed into Kismayo. Some Harti believe that UNOSOM allowed Morgan to re-enter Kismayo, because 'they view it as a Harti town'. This is despite the fact that, when US forces first arrived in Somalia, US Ambassador Oakley refused to meet the 'cold-blooded murderer' Morgan. The other interpretation is that UNOSOM Belgian troops were outwitted by Morgan. Whatever the truth, the

SNA/USC supporters remain extremely bitter. Their cynicism is increased by the fact that since February 1993 the US and Belgian troops have twice repulsed attacks by Jess fighters on Kismayo.

Since March, therefore, Kismayo has *nominally* been under the control of an alliance of SPM/SNF/SSDF forces (in Kismayo known as the SPM), under the overall command of Morgan. *Nominally*, because Morgan himself has not returned to Kismayo and remains in Doble, and also, because his supporters have no visible military presence on the streets of Kismayo. The rise of Morgan, as the 'champion of the Darod', seems to have sidelined Gabiyo, although he was one of the 15 signatories of the Addis Ababa agreement.

2 THE KISMAYO PEACE CONFERENCE

In April 1993, UNOSOM appointed a retired US army officer, Mark Walsh, as Zone Director to Kismayo. He arrived in a situation where Morgan's forces had recently captured Kismayo. Jess's forces had been moved north of Kamsuma, and his supporters were displaced in the Juba valley. The town and the Juba valley werepatrolled by a contingent of 850 Belgian peace-keeping forces. The political and security situation remained unstable, as Jess's supporters threatened to attack the town. In addition, there were a variety of other clan-based factions in the region.

Walsh's brief from UNOSOM was to: (1) get Jess's wounded fighters, who were in the valley, to Kismayo hospital for treatment, and (2) 'get the community back together'.[22] Two attempts to negotiate the return of the wounded to Kismayo hospital for treatment failed, and they were eventually taken to Jilib and treated by a Belgian team there.

In mid-April, Walsh made his first attempt to bring the sides together, by inviting a small group of elders from each side to meet at Madamato, 2 km north of Kismayo. The objective was to explore whether people were prepared to talk, and if it was possible to get a large number of elders together. The meeting proved a success, as it indicated that people were ready to talk.

The process was disrupted on 6 May, when Jess engineered an attack on Kismayo. The Belgians came out in force in response. On 7 May 1,500 to 2,000 people were seen moving from the valley to Kismayo, having anticipated that Jess would win. In response, a similar number of people went from Kismayo to confront them, many of them women. The Belgians placed themselves between the two sides and prevented a clash. Those from the valley set up camp at Madamato, where a 'green line' was formed, dividing Morgan's and Jess's supporters.

In mid-May, following the Addis Ababa National Reconciliation Conference, the reconciliation process was resumed, with meetings in Mogadishu. A peace initiative by elders in Galkaiyo won the support of Aideed and Abdillahi Yusuf, while Ali Mahadi was meeting in Mogadishu with General Abshir. UNOSOM were uneasy about Aideed's initiative, concerned that he was prepared to bargain over Kismayo in return for a settlement in Galkaiyo. At short notice UNOSOM asked Walsh to send 40 delegates from Kismayo to Mogadishu to reinforce UNOSOM's position. The town elders agreed, but he was initially unable to convince those elders from Jess's side in the valley.

56

By 26 May, convinced that the two meetings in Mogadishu were not going anywhere, Walsh decided to concentrate on the Kismayo problem. With the help of Omar Moalim, he was able to convince 28 elders from Jess's side to go to Mogadishu, because it was in their interests to be involved in discussions over the future of Kismayo.[23] A peace delegation, comprising Marehan, Harti and Mohamed Zubeir elders, was therefore formed. General Mohamed Abshir, of the SSDF, was asked by UNOSOM to help in mediating in peace talks.

Negotiations culminated in a conference in Mogadishu on 30 May. On 3 June 1993, a Declaration of Peace and Reconciliation was signed by elders and politicians from the Juba region. The Declaration committed them to:

1 The complete cessation of hostilities in the Lower Juba Region.
2 The reunification of the population of Jubaland in seven days.
3 The reopening of the Juba region.
4 The establishment of a working committee on the peace process.
5 The creation of an interim standing committee of elders to judicially resolve differences arising among parties in the region.

On 20 June more detailed discussions began in Kismayo, with 75 elders from each side. In these negotiations the Ogadeni (Mohamed Zubeir) were bargaining from a position of weakness, because they had broken with Jess. They were living displaced in the valley, while the other side, who had not broken with Morgan, were in town. Once the elders broke from Jess, they lost his 'patronage'. Osman Atto (a major financier of Aideed), who is said to have developed significant investments in the Juba valley during the war, had been supporting the displaced. 'Mama' Dofa (a relative of Aideed and Atto) was also feeding the displaced. Once the elders broke with Jess, this support stopped. There are also 'warlords' other than Jess, such as Ahmed Hashi, vice-Commander of SPM forces under Jess, who had significant influence on the situation. Not surprisingly the Ogadenis called for a broad representation of people at the meeting, including Hawiye.

On the other side the Harti were in little mood for compromise, They were still bitter about the Harti massacre and wanted the meeting limited to the Darod. Morgan was also uncertain whether the elders would undermine his authority.

On the first day of the meeting, the elders from the valley brought three Habr Gedir representatives. This was initially unacceptable to those in Kismayo. After three days of negotiation they were allowed to have observer status. Some groups in the area (such as the Bantu) were not invited to participate, as UNOSOM felt that, if the meeting was too inclusive, this would cause a problem.

Finally, on 23 June, 152 delegates (elders, religious leaders, intellectuals, politicians, business people, representatives of women, youth and other civic organisations) and 50 observers met at Kismayo airport to commence negotiations. Four committees were established to agree upon the following:
1 Cease-fire and disarmament
2 Reopening of roads
3 Reunification of the people and communities
4 Return of property.

This culminated in the signing of the Jubaland Peace Agreement on 6 August 1993.[24] The accord (reprinted in Appendix C) repeats the format of the Addis Ababa agreement, with conditions on the four issues listed above. In addition, there were a number of General Provisions, which call for the dissemination of the peace message, establishment of district sub-committees, reactivation of trade, restoration of essential services, reestablishment of police and the judiciary, and deployment of UNOSOM forces in each of the 14 districts mentioned in the agreement.

It is significant that UNOSOM are seen as an integral part of the agreement, in matters of security and humanitarian assistance, as the onus is now on the UN to provide the financial and material assistance to build upon the peace agreement. Despite the efforts of the Zone Director, UNOSOM provided no resources for the meeting, until the signing ceremony. It was left to the Belgians, UN agencies, NGOs, and some Somalis to provide shelter, food and blankets.

Having secured an accord, UNOSOM Mogadishu then made a major blunder, by inviting Ali Mahadi to speak at the conclusion of the peace talks. UNOSOM said that Jess and Aideed were also invited but, given the warrant on his head, Aideed was not going! Although Morgan was not invited, Howe publicly accepted a gift from him. To the USC/SNA this was seen as a symbol of rapprochement between UNOSOM and Morgan, and a further sign of UNOSOM's partiality.

3 A FRAGILE PEACE

The Jubaland Peace Agreement was signed at a time when UNOSOM was involved in a war of attrition with Aideed in Mogadishu. A success was sorely needed, to show that their policies were working. The Jubaland Agreement appeared to signal a break-through in the political reconciliation process. The agreement has brought tomany people in Lower Juba a period of relative peace for the first time in years. In August 1993 the Zone Director reported that the committees set up by the accord were still meeting, which is a positive sign. Although the green line remains, trade has increased between the town and the valley. It is possible to drive around Kismayo and in the valley without armed escorts.

The credibility of the agreement, however, was undermined by UNOSOM inviting Ali Mahadi to address the signing ceremony. Not only did it further legitimise Ali Mahadi, and indicate a bias in UNOSOM's policies, but it also had the effect of turning a local peace agreement into something national. As a result the USC/SNA supporters give little credence to the agreement. There is scepticism at the binding nature of the agreement. As one Somali commented, 'What the elders say and think are two different things.' Some of those closely involved in the peace process, including the Zone Director and Omar Moalim, also admit that the agreement is fragile. Although the shooting has stopped for the moment, a number of factors continue to make the situation delicate.

3.1 The Marehan and Morgan

The main source of instability lies within the Darod, and disputes within the Darod lost them control of Kismayo in 1991. For the Darod, Kismayo provides a place to wait for those urbanites displaced from Mogadishu. It is even possible that Kismayo could be developed as a new capital, given its port and agricultural hinterland. The stakes therefore remain high. In August 1993 Morgan's Marehan and Harti appointees controlled the town. If reunification of the city occurs, they will lose their monopoly of control. This is critical, for if economic recovery happens (and UNOSOM are developing an economic recovery plan for the region), they stand to increase their power base. For this reason they continue to block the formation of a unified police force.

Kismayo was never a home base for the Marehan. The use of the name 'Jubaland' in the agreement, which includes Gedo, gives the Marehan undue significance. They presently retain a position of power in Kismayo through Abdillahi Wagat (Marehan, and former Barre appointee) as Morgan's regional governor. The issue of Morgan himself has not yet been settled. Up to August UNOSOM were still refusing to talk to him. However, he still wields a great deal of influence and would resist plans to marginalise him. Some in UNOSOM believe there is a need to involve a broader group of businessmen and religious leaders in the peace process to off-set the influence of Morgan's appointees. WFP reported that these people have already tried to control of some of the aid resources coming into the town.

3.2 The Harti

The Harti, and in particular the Majeerteen, have been key players in the Kismayo conflict and the reconciliation process. The Chairman of the SSDF, General Mohamed Abshir, is Majeerteen (Issa Mahmoud/Majeerteen), as is Morgan. General Abshir played a central role in brokering the Jubaland agreement, investing some of his own finances in the conference. General Abshir's involvement in the Kismayo meeting angered supporters of Aideed and Jess.[25]

Since 1991, the Majeerteen-controlled north-east of Somalia has remained largely peaceful and, in places, has prospered during the war. Now that the Jubaland Peace Agreement has been signed, it is likely that division will resurface, not only within the Darod (Harti-Ogaden-Marehan) alliance, but also within the Majeerteen.

Diagram 11 : Ali and Mahmoud Suleiban Majeerteen Genealogy

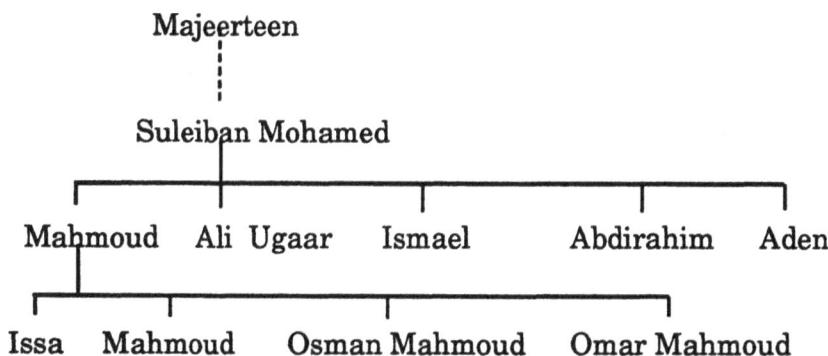

Majeerteen

Suleiban Mohamed

Mahmoud Ali Ugaar Ismael Abdirahim Aden

Issa Mahmoud Osman Mahmoud Omar Mahmoud

In May, divisions became evident between the Chairman of the SSDF, General Abshir, and the military commander, Colonel Abdillahi Yusuf, when Abdillahi Yusuf was involved in negotiations with Aideed over Galkaiyo. In Kismayo it is said that the majority of Harti support Morgan rather than Abshir, while some Harti are suspicious of Morgan's relationship with the Marehan. At one level these divisions represent differences of opinion over whether Majeerteen interests are best served, at present, by a military strongman or 'warlord', or a politician. They also represent different economic and political clan interests within the Majeerteen.

The two largest lineages in the Majeerteen are the Mahmoud Suleiban and the Ali Suleiban (see diagram 11). Many of the Majeerteen politicians and military have come from the Mahmoud Suleiban. In the 1960s the Mahmoud Suleiban dominated Somali politics, with Ali Sharmarke (President 1967), Abdirizak Haji Hussein (Prime Minister 1964), and General Mohamed Abshir (Police Commander). In the 1970s Colonel Abdillahi Yusuf (Omar Mohmoud Suleiban) formed the SSDF and led a guerrilla campaign against the Barre regime. Barre's retribution against the SSDF in the early 1980s forced many Majeerteen, particularly from Mudug, to flee to Kenya and the Gulf states, where they later established substantial business interests. These interests have been important sources of finance for the SSDF and the SNF/SPM at different times.

The Ali Suleiban, in contrast to the Mahmoud Suleiban, are known more as businessmen. Coming from Bari region in north-east Somalia, they have access to the port of Bosasso and financial trading links with the Gulf. In the 19th century many Ali Suleiban traders migrated to Kismayo and are now the largest Majeerteen group in Kismayo.

The rapprochement between Aideed and Abdillahi Yusuf in May 1993 caused a division with the Majeerteen.[26] Abdillahi Yusuf is supported by his own clan, the Omar Mahmoud (except for Rer Hersi, which has a strong lobby in east Africa). He is also said to have the support of the Ali Suleiban and the Awtabley and Lelkasse (non-Majeerteen Darod). One of the wealthiest Majeerteen in Kismayo, called Unlaye (Ali Suleiban), is said to support Abdillahi Yusuf.[27] The Ali Suleiban are said to be supportive of Abdillahi Yusuf, because they need security for their businesses. General Abshir is said to have the support of the Isa Mahmoud and Osman Mahmoud. One of his main sources of financial support, however, comes from a member of the Rer Mahad of the Omar Mahmoud, the particular sub-clan of Abdillahi Yusuf. He is the owner of a large bus transport company in East Africa (Ohan). The concern expressed to me by some Majeerteen is that conflicting political and economic interests may lead to a dispute within the Majeerteen, which could upset the peace agreement in Kismayo.

3.3 The Ogadeni

The Ogadenis, particularly the Mohamed Zubeir, have the most to lose if the Marehan and Harti retain control of the city, as they are left with nothing. There remains a great deal of bitterness among those who have been displaced from Kismayo into the valley. They feel that UNOSOM is keeping them out of their town. On the other hand, those in town accuse UNOSOM of doing nothing to clear 'gun-men' out of Madamato. The Madamato displaced are mainly from two Ogadeni groups, one originally from Ethiopia who moved in with Jess (Rer Abdille), and the other Mohamed Zubeir Ogadeni from within the region.

60

In the words of one, 'We defeated them before UNITAF put them in Kismayo, and when we try to retaliate, the Belgians stop us. We will wait until UNOSOM leave.' In response to a comment that the Harti and Ogadeni used to live together, the reply was: 'Will last night come back again?' It will take a major psychological change to bring people back together and to reshape the thinking of people, away from conflict.

3.4 The Refugees and Displaced

The issue of the displaced remains very sensitive. The Tuni, Harti and Banjuni make up a large number of the refugees in Kenya. Their inclusion in the peace agreement means that they should be able to return. With few economic opportunities, this will place pressure on the region's damaged infrastructure and resources. The Harti are also nervous that the return of refugees from Kenya may undermine their trading monopolies.

3.5 The Land Issue

The focus of the peace talks was Kismayo, because of its strategic importance. However, it is the agrarian areas along the Juba and the pastoral areas which provide the wealth of the region. Issues of land ownership were not dealt with in the conference, and therefore disputes over agrarian land rights and pastoral rights still have to be settled. The Marehan are more concerned with pastoral areas, and there are indications that the old Marehan-Ogadeni conflict is re-emerging around Afmedu.

The Bantu groups, who suffered most in the war, and for whom agricultural land is the critical issue, were not represented at the peace conference.

3.6 Impact of the Mogadishu Conflict on Kismayo

The conflict in Mogadishu between UNOSOM and General Aideed has an impact on the situation in Kismayo, and the resolution of that conflict will have repercussions on the Lower Juba. Aideed and Omar Jess were both marginalised from the Kismayo peace conference. Depending on the outcome of their conflict with UNOSOM, they will continue to oppose the Jubaland agreement and are likely try to influence the situation there.

The concentration of UNOSOM in Mogadishu necessarily diverts resources from elsewhere in the country. In Lower Juba, for example, there are only 850 soldiers covering a region 36,000 sq km, compared with 13,000 in Mogadishu. During the Kismayo peace conference, the Zone Director complained that he was not able to obtain a mere $7,000 from UNOSOM for food and shelter for the participants.

UNOSOM Kismayo are also critical that policies made in Mogadishu may not be appropriate for the regions. In August 1993 the Zone Director was still uneasy about the peace agreement and tried to forestall the Political Division from establishing the District Councils. He felt there was a need to allow more time for local reconciliation processes to work. In an area which has suffered such massive displacement, there are questions over the legitimacy of any District Council formed now. For example, at a meeting in Jamaame in mid-August, elders read out a list of 23 clans whose representatives had come to meet UNOSOM. The list did not include Bantu or

Ogadenis, who made up a large part of the pre-war population of the town. The Zone Director, however, was unable to stop the Political Division from pursuing its programme, as per schedule.[28]

A further problem for UNOSOM is that most of the UNOSOM team in Kismayo will leave in September at the end of their contracts. UNOSOM will lose the knowledge and experience which these people have developed over the past year.

4 CONCLUSIONS AND RECOMMENDATIONS

In mid-August 1993, the Somali Red Crescent expressed concerns at continuing armed theft and rape in Kismayo; banditry was still a problem north of Jilib, and there have been questions about the behaviour and activities of the Belgian peace-keeping troops (African Rights, July 1993). However, the situation in Kismayo and Lower Juba in mid-August was as peaceful as at any time since January 1991.

This peaceful appearance does conceal a number of problems, which arise from several sources: bitterness among the Ogadenis and supporters of Jess displaced from Kismayo; the impact of returned refugees from Kenya; unaddressed land-ownership issues; political and economic divisions within the Marehan-Ogadeni-Harti alliance; the continued presence of large quantities of weapons within the region; the unknown effects of the District Council formation; and unresolved conflicts suspended due to the conflict in Mogadishu. Some or all of these are to some extent being held in abeyance by the presence of Belgian troops, and could re-emerge to destabilise the region in the future.

Economic interests are intrinsic to the war in Somalia. All the warlords have their financial backers, the 'godfathers'. Osman Atto, one of Aideed's main financiers, is one example. Many other Hawiye in Somalia and abroad have undoubtedly helped finance Aideed's campaign, both to protect their own kin, but also as a future invest-ment. The same is true for all the other clan factions. The SNM, for example, were dependent on remittances from abroad to sustain their campaign against Barre. The brief description of the Harti factor in the Kismayo conflict and their financial net-works in East Africa and the Gulf only begins to hint at the complex range of factors and invested interests that can influence political reconciliation and peace-making.

Economic interests, however, can be as much a driving force for peace as they are for conflict, as will be seen in the description of the Sanaag peace meeting in Somaliland, in Part V. The challenge is to look for ways in which conflicting interests can be trans-formed into common interests.

UNOSOM should receive some credit for helping to restore a semblance of peace to the Juba region. This achievement probably has more to do with the individuals involved in the process than with UNOSOM's own policies. One can draw out the fol-lowing elements that contributed to the success of the reconciliation process to date:

• The Zone Director, Mark Walsh, was able to win the confidence and respect of the elders on both sides.

• He was able to draw on the support of Ken Menkhaus, a social scientist with a good knowledge of the Lower Juba region. He is the only foreigner in UNOSOM with specialised knowledge of Somalia.

• The presence of elder 'statesmen', Omar Moalim, Mohamed Abshir, Aden Abdille Osman, and particularly Omar Moalim, who is from the area, acting as mediators, helped the process.

• While their own behaviour has come under criticism, the Belgian UN troops have been able to stop the fighting, and therefore break the cycle of violence. Restrictions on the movement of heavy weapons (technicals) have helped to keep the peace. This improved security environment has helped to encourage the resumption of trade.

• The negotiations took place within Somalia, and more specifically within Kismayo.

• The negotiations were primarily between 'elders'. It was possible to marginalise the influence of the military warlords. That committees have continued to meet since the conference indicates that there was an interest on the part of the participants to see the process through.

• The negotiations took place over a period of two months, thus allowing time for some confidence building.

• Financial interests on the part of some members of the business community may also have been an important factor.

• The inter-marriage among clans in that region may also have helped the process. While Lower Juba is heterogeneous in its clan composition, many of those clans are linked through marriage. As seemed apparent in Galkaiyo, and can be seen more clearly in Somaliland, it may be easier for those groups linked affinally and with common xeer to reconcile their conflicts.

RECOMMENDATIONS:

Expanded programmes: Agencies should consider ways of expanding their work to cover both sides of the 'green line'. This would provide the opportunity to avoid accusations of bias and the chance to understand the context and issues from different angles.

Refugees: The return of large numbers of refugees to the region will place a lot of pressure on damaged infrastructure and resources, and could be a major source of tension. Agencies might consider ways of scaling up their programmes to assist in the resettlement and reintegration of these people. Many will be destitute and will have become dependent on HCR rations.

Staff Training: Agencies may be called upon to mediate, or support local mediation or peace meetings. They might therefore consider a pilot training programme for staff in conflict resolution/mediation. Local resources are available in Nairobi through the Nairobi Peace Initiative.

Land Ownership: Land ownership is an unresolved issue in the region. It has been suggested that the conflict such as that in Kismayo can only finally be resolved through agrarian reform. Agencies might consider commissioning research to look at the issue, to help both their own understanding of the nature of the problem, and to inform future UN strategies in the region.

Research on the Jubaland Agreement: This report has been able to provide only a brief sketch of the peace-making process behind the Jubaland Agreement. Agencies might consider commissioning a thorough piece of research in order to understand better the successes and potential obstacles of this peace process. Such a study is necessary, in order to be able to anticipate future scenarios and to be able to plan for the future. In particular it is important to know the extent to which the agreement is based on a solid foundations of inter-clan agreements. Preferably a Somali should be commissioned for this work.

Trauma: Much bitterness remains among people on both sides of the 'green line', as a result of the trauma of years of war. MSF Belgium, World Concern, Somali Red Crescent, and the WAMO Women's Organisation have all identified psychological trauma and post-traumatic distress as a problem among the population in Kismayo. This needs to be addressed. Rape has also been identified as an on-going problem. Agencies might consider ways in which they could support a trauma programme for the victims of war.

Agencies might consider commissioning such bodies as the Medical Foundation for the Victims of Torture, with experience in this field, to assess the issue professionally and provide some detailed recommendations. Particular attention should be given to indigenous healing practices.

UNHCR Kenya are presently implementing a rape-counselling and protection programme in Somali refugee camps in Kenya. Some of the victims may return to Kismayo and require further assistance. Information from the Somali Red Crescent and others suggests that it is an on-going problem in Kismayo. Agencies should consider linking up with the UNHCR on this and, in particular, with Fauzia A. Musa, who has pioneered their work.

Disability: This problem is not yet being addressed in Kismayo. Agencies might consider jointly commissioning a study to look at the extent of the problem. The Chairman of the former Association of Physically Disabled of Somalia, Abdulkadir Abdillahi Farah, is in Nairobi and would be a suitable person to do such an assessment.

PART V SOMALILAND: PEACE-BUILDING

1 SECESSION AND CESSATION

On 26 June 1960, Somaliland obtained independence from Britain. Six days later, on 1 July, under the premiership of Mohamed Ibrahim Egal, Somaliland united with the former Italian Somalia to form the sovereign Somali Republic. In May 1991, following the overthrow of Siad Barre, the Somali National Movement (SNM) declared the secession of the northern regions to form the independent 'Republic of Somaliland', the territory of which corresponds to that of the former British Somaliland Protectorate. In May 1993, Mohamed Ibrahim Egal was elected President of Somaliland.

The people of Somaliland are of the Issaq, Gadabursi and Ciise (Dir), and Dolbahunte and Warsengeli clan-families. The latter two belong to the Darod confederation of clans. The Issaq, which formed the backbone of the SNM, are the most populous clan in Somaliland.

The declaration of Somaliland secession went against the previously stated policies of the SNM, who had insisted that they sought only to change the Barre regime. The decision to declare independence at the Grand Shir ('gathering') of northern clans in Burco, in May 1991, resulted from a popular expression of opposition to further rule from Mogadishu. This was an understandable reaction to the suffering inflicted on the Issaq people by the Barre regime during three years of war, and to the manner in which Ali Mahadi's USC assumed power in Mogadishu.

Reinforcing this decision may have been a realisation that the original goal which led Somaliland into unity with the south was no longer tenable. The decision in 1960 to unite with Somalia was driven by nationalistic aspirations to join all the five Somali territories into a Greater Somalia. In that Greater Somalia, the Issaqs stood to re-establish direct control over the Haud grazing areas, which were ceded by the British to Ethiopia in 1954, and which are vital to the pastoral economy of the northern clans. The defeat suffered by the Somali army in the Ogaden war of 1977 destroyed any pretence of achieving that goal. Years of operating a guerrilla campaign from within Ethiopia and the mass movement of Issaqs into refugee camps in the Haud in 1988 may have persuaded people that the needs of the northern pastoralists for unhindered access to the Haud grazing lands can be better achieved through cooperation with Ethiopia rather than unity with the south. It may not be wholly coincidental that, prior to Burco 1991, the last Grand Shir of the northern clans occurred in 1954, in response to the British decision to cede the Haud to Ethiopia.

The restoration of Somaliland sovereignty brought an end to three years of war. Abdulrahman Ali 'Tuur', Chairman of the SNM, was elected President of an interim Somaliland government, with a two-year mandate.

The transition from war to peace was not easy. Given the traumatic experience of the Somali people and the schismatic nature of Somali political culture, it is not surprising that conflict returned to Somaliland. The initial euphoria of independence was shattered by an outbreak of fighting in Berbera in December 1991 and Burco in

January 1992. The conflict, which stemmed partly from a struggle over the control of Berbera port and its revenues and partly from old rifts within the SNM, lasted for some eight months. It was eventually concluded through a political settlement on 7 October 1992, at the town of Sheik, brokered by the Somaliland elders. In May 1993, the Somaliland national committee of elders (the Somaliland National *Guurti*) went on to conclude a Conference on National Reconciliation in Boroma, at which a new President for Somaliland, Mohamed Ibrahim Egal, was elected.

Diagram 12: Primary Issaq Clans

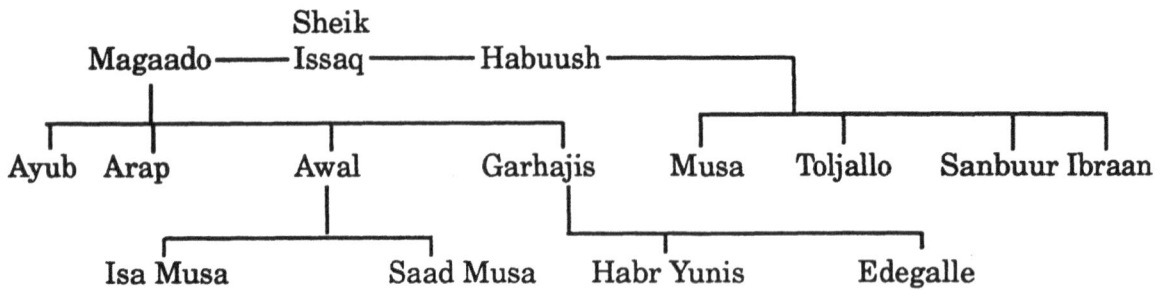

1.1 Towards A More Stable Environment

Despite the conflict and insecurity in 1992, the situation in Somaliland, compared with the south, has been very stable. The reason why Somaliland did not dissolve into the military quagmire and famine of the south is explained by a number of factors:[29]

a) Extent of the War

During the three years of war, the SNM guerrilla campaign was largely restricted to the Issaq territories in the regions of Waqoyi Galbeed, Togdheer and Sanaag. Areas inhabited by the Gadabursi (Awdal), Dolbahunte (Sool) and Warsengeli (Badhan) remained largely free from fighting, and today the towns of Boroma, Las Anod and Badhan remain relatively undamaged. While Hargeisa and Burco were extensively damaged, it meant that killing and destruction of property between the northern clans was limited. In contrast to the south, there was little retribution by the Issaq against the Hawiye, Ogaden, Oromo, Dolbahunte and Gadabursi soldiers who made up the remnants of the Somali army in the north. This helped to prevent a cycle of revenge between the clans, once Barre was defeated.

b) Common Values

For the SNM to be able to convene a conference in Burco between clans who two months previously had been at war assumes the existence of a certain amount of common understanding and trust between the different clans. In Somaliland there is not the same heterogeneity of clans and social organisations as in southern Somalia. Clan territory is more easily defined in the north. The social and cultural values and economic and political interests are closer among the northern clans than in the south.

Some Somalis suggest that the indigenous social institutions in Somaliland were less affected by British colonialism than they were in the south by the Italian administration.[30] Urbanisation was much greater in the south than the north, and new forms of habitation, integration and education had an impact on social institutions. Thus, they suggest that the north has retained its indigenous institutions, customs and value systems, which include peace-making, to a greater degree than the south.

The northern clans, Issaq, Gadabursi, Dolbahunte and Warsengeli, are inter-married and have a long history of interaction, including cooperation and competition (hostility and hospitality). As a result the clans and sub-clan have evolved common *xeer*. Elders have commented that during the war in Somaliland certain basic rules of behaviour (*xeer*) were adhered to between the northern clans.[31] These included the protection of women, children and prisoners. The retention of such values helped later in resolving conflicts.[32]

Although the SNM was primarily an Issaq organisation, it was able to attract individuals from other clans. Of particular importance is Abdulrahman Aw Ali (Gadabursi), now Vice President to Egal. He was able to mediate between the SNM and Gadabursi and prevent further fighting between the Issaq and Gadabursi in 1991.

Also important is the Dolbahunte Garaad Abdulgani. From 1989, in defiance of Siad Barre and Dolbahunte supporters of Barre, Garaad Abdulgani sought a relationship with the SNM, to prevent an escalation of conflict between the Issaq and the Dolbahunte. Thus local-level diplomacy and peace-making was happening even during the war. This helped to prevent retribution and revenge and an escalation of conflict once the SNM had defeated Barre's army.

c) Common Interests
As the Issaq have benefited from access to the Haud, so too have the other northern clans. The Dolbahunte and Warsengeli have investments in the northern towns of Berbera, Burco and Hargeisa. There is therefore an incentive for peaceful cooperation.

d) Military Sanction

Another important factor is that the SNM effectively won the war in Somaliland. The Issaq are the largest single clan and, having won the war, militarily were the most powerful clan. In Somali pastoral society, military strength, as Lewis (1961) has written, is a final sanction in any relationship. The victors were therefore able to sue for peace from a position of strength.

e) Indigenous Institutions

In marked contrast to the ideology of the former regime, under which 'tribalism' was banned, the SNM constitution recognises the significance of the clan system and, within this, the role of the elders as peace-makers and mediators. The elders have therefore played an important role in reconciliation between the clans.

f) Different Resources

Service infrastructure, industry and agriculture were more developed in the south than in the north. Between 1987 and 1989, some 41 per cent of development aid to

Somalia was concentrated in the south. Somalia's main agricultural resources were in the south. The south therefore presented a wealthy resource-base to fight over. From 1991 onwards this was supplemented by relief aid. Mogadishu itself, as the capital and therefore 'centre of power', psychologically, is a prize to fight for. Through the act of secession, the Issaqs made a psychological break with Mogadishu and the south. Mogadishu was no longer an object to fight over. After Hargeisa and Burco were destroyed in the north and much of the wealth had been plundered, there was little else left for people to fight over. Ironically, the conflict in Berbera was sparked off by the resumption of relief aid to Somaliland.

A significant proportion of the southern population depends on agriculture for its livelihood. The destruction of the agricultural infrastructure and disruption to cropping cycles by the war quickly left a large destitute population. The pastoral economy of the north, which is more mobile, was less vulnerable to the ravages of war. The refugees in Ethiopia also provided a food chain for Somaliland which helped to stave off starvation.

At the same time there was in the south a larger population of urban destitute, alienated by years of economic stagnation. They provided ready recruits for the warlords — especially the large number of destitute street kids in Mogadishu in 1990. In the south there was also a greater stockpile of weapons to fuel the fighting.

1.2 The Elders and Peace-making

One distinction which many Somalis (northerners and southerners)make between the north and south is that 'traditions' are more embedded in the northern culture than in the south. The SNM constitution recognised the importance of the clan system in Somali society and, within this, the role of the elders. The SNM constitution, therefore, sets out a bicameral legislature with an upper house of elders and a parliament of directly elected politicians. In Somaliland it is the elders who have taken a leading role in restoring peace to the region. The example of the Somaliland elders bringing a chaotic situation under control provides an alternative model for the peace and reconciliation process attempted by the UN in Somalia to date, and is thus worth commenting on.

The institution of elders (sing. *oday*; pl. *odayaal*,; as council *odayasha*) and their role in Somali society can be confusing to a non-Somali. It is often not clear who is an elder, when he (it is always 'he') is an elder, how he becomes an elder, and what authority he possesses.

Somali pastoral society has no hierarchy of political units or political and administrative offices. Investing an individual with power goes against the egalitarian nature of Somali society. It is only at the level of the clan that one finds a post approximating to a leader or chief, known as a Sultan (among the Issaq), Garaad (meaning 'wisdom', among the Darod), and Ugaas or Boqor (among the Darod).

The position of Sultan is hereditary, although it is not always the first-born son who inherits that position. Not all clans have them, nor are they indispensable; in 1992 the Habr Yunis Sultan was killed in a house of disrepute in Hargeisa. Where they exist, they are a symbol of the unity of the clan over its constituent lineages. This symbolic role is reflected in the inauguration of a new Sultan, which should always take place in the rainy season, a time of prosperity. A Sultan enjoys respect, but not reverence. His personal qualities are as important as his position in determining his authority. At the same time his structural position, above sectional lineage differences, enables him to function as an arbiter and peace-maker, mediating relations with other clans, and settling disputes within his own clan. His authority, however, is often symbolic. In a peace meeting (*shir nabadeedka*) it is the elders who undertake the negotiations, while the Sultan approves the results, in his position as head of the clan.

Unlike Sultans, elders are found at all levels of lineage segmentation. A father is, for example, the elder of a nuclear family. All adult males at every level of segmentation can be elders, with a right to speak in council (*shir*). In principle all can have an equal say. In practice some elders are more influential than others.

The position of an elder is not hereditary. Over time it may become hereditary, as people may prefer elders of one lineage to play a leading role in lineage affairs, for fear of upsetting relations. The *akil* (from the Arabic *wakil*, 'deputy'), for example, or elder of a *diya*-paying group, often passes from father to son. Sheik Ibrahim, Chairman of the Somaliland National Council of Elders (*guurti*), comes from a long line of elders, the founders of Hargeisa, guardians of the Sheik's tomb, and is respected for his religious knowledge.

Elders are sometimes described as 'chiefs'. It is misleading to call elders chiefs, for it suggests a traditional position of authority which does not exist. They achieve their positions through a variety of attributes, of which age, wealth, wisdom, religious knowledge and piety, political acumen, powers of oratory, or a combination, are important. However, in this acephalous Somali society, an elder is a representative, who receives delegated authority, rather than assuming it. In council meetings they are delegates or emissaries of and for their clans, whom they represent and by whom they are supported.

An elder's authority is the reflection of a number of different qualities or skills. Different elders will have different roles in different situations. Certain elders have greater knowledge of, for example, genealogy, *xeer*, or politics than others. These skills will be better used in some circumstances than others. For example, when two clans are to meet to discuss peace, they will send to each other lists of delegates for the meeting. Each side will know whether the other is for peace or not by the names of the delegates, because their character, kinship and political leanings will be known.

Elders operate, not secretly, but in open councils (*shir*), which all adult males, or their representatives, may attend. A *shir* can be summoned at every order of segmentation, as required. They are called to discuss relations between groups, to work out *xeer* contracts, to settle disputes, or to decide upon war or peace. Elders are professional negotiators and mediators in all clan matters and it is from this position that they have been able to assert their authority in Somaliland.

Other people in Somali society who have a role in peace-making are the *wadaad*, or Sheiks, the men of religion. They play no role in lineage politics, having only spiritual authority. Owing no allegiance to clan interests, they are ideal mediators. However, they do not settle disputes themselves, judge or make judgements. The role of the *wadaad*, or sheik, is to add sanction and the seal of religion to the proceedings.

It is also misleading to talk about 'traditional elders', for this suggests an institution. One of the powerful attributes of Somali society is its dynamism and ability to adapt to change. Since the arrival of the colonialists the system of elders has been changing. The colonial administration in Somaliland changed the role of Akils by paying them stipends to act as go-betweens, between the administration and the clans. Under Barre, the government appointed *nabadoon* (peace-makers), to replace the role of the elders and represent the interests of the government.

During the early SNM guerrilla campaigns, the prestige and influence of the elders was eroded, because the movement was spearheaded by the politicians and military. Elders initially cautioned restraint to avoid bloodshed. It was only after the outbreak of full-scale war in 1988 that elders took an active role, and a council of elders was formed in exile. The elders then became instrumental in organising recruits for the SNM *jabhad* (guerrillas).

After the fall of Barre, with no functional government or security, people looked to the elders to reassert some control. Their peace-keeping role was a difficult one to carry out, given the numerous young militia and proliferation of heavy weapons in the country. The elders themselves, to whom some of the militia owed some allegiance, were not without their own vested interests.

Elders are chosen not just for their age, but for their ability to negotiate or influence a situation in favour of their clan. That 'ability' can include a number of characteristics, as described above. However, influence can also arise from wealth (and hospitality is a characteristic looked for in elders) or the military strength of the clan. One therefore often hears elders described as 'the biggest *deydey* (bandits)'. Equally, it can be difficult to make a direct distinction between elders and politicians, as they support each other. A distinction might be that elders deal with 'clan politics', while politicians deal with politics of the state. The dividing line, however, is thin.

It is wrong therefore to regard elders as people who are above day-to-day happenings and intrigues. Indeed, the knowledge of elders is drawn from their day-to-day involvement in matters of the clan. Rather than talking about the traditional institutions of elders, it may be more appropriate to think of elders as representatives, maintaining the 'traditions' of the clan.

In 1992, as the initial unity of independence disintegrated into anarchy, elders were called upon to take some control of the situation. In January 1992, as Habr Yunis and Habr Toljallo militia fought in Burco, elders physically stepped between the parties to stop the fighting. At the same time elders in Sanaag region formed a regional *guurti* of elders to begin a process of reconciliation. In October 1992, a national *guurti* of elders stepped in to mediate in the conflict over Berbera. The Sheik conference (known as 'Tawfiq') marked a turning point in the reconciliation process in Somaliland, and led directly to the Boroma National Reconciliation Conference, January — May 1993.

As representatives of their clans, the elders have been able to achieve what they have done in Somaliland only because they were invested with the authority to do so by the people. There was thus, I suggest, a change in 'collective consciousness' in Somaliland during 1992 which enabled people to pull the country back from the brink of a dangerous civil war. In looking to the elders to restore stability, people turned back to their 'traditions' as a source of knowledge and experience for solving their problems.[33]

The point is that the peace-making role of elders cannot happen without other people, forces and factors to help them. One section of the population who appear to have played a significant role is women.

1.3 Women and Peace-making

There is little understanding of the role that women have played both during and after the war in Somaliland and Somalia. Little has been written about this to date. And yet it is clear that women have played a significant role in a number of ways.

During the famine in the south, women ran food kitchens and food distribution. As one Somali man said, 'During the war, while the youth destroyed, women saved the families'. Since the end of the famine, women have adopted many of the orphaned children.

In Somaliland, women were an invisible front for the SNM, working as nurses and medics. They were a lifeline for the family, taking relatives out of the country. As refugees in Europe they were able to bring out other members of the family and transfer money back to the country. Able to travel more freely than men, they established channels of communication and were extremely important as traders. In the Ethiopian refugee camps, Issaq women established trading networks that involved sending ghee to Djibouti and the Gulf, cloth from Djibouti to Mogadishu, and Somali shillings from Mogadishu to the refugee camps. Some of these networks still exist. Since then, women have been among the main providers of family income, as petty traders selling tea, *kat*, gold and other items.

In some instances, women have also played a pro-active role in the war.[34] Women were active in demonstrations with children in Hargeisa before and in the early days of the war. Most recently in Mogadishu, women have been prominent in the anti-UN/US demonstrations of Aideed supporters. Women poets and singers have also actively supported the different factions in the south.[35]

In Somaliland women have returned from the war with a greater economic independence and stronger role as decision makers, while men have returned chewing even more *kat* than before. Many of the most active Somali NGOs in Somaliland are headed by women, such as Al Amil, the Somaliland Women's Association, and SOMRA. In Erigavo, one of the most active NGOs is the Women's Family Life Institute. In Mogadishu Idda is a powerful women's NGO. Many women are also active in the new Islamic movements.

Some women express discomfort with this role.[36] They were brought up as unequal, but now are forced to take on greater responsibility as bread winners for the family and extended family. As a result they are unable to give as much time to the household or to take their children to the mother-and-child health clinics.

71

On 7 January 1993 five women were stoned to death in Hargeisa by followers of a Sheik. It is not clear why this happened. Some women believe it was an attempt to undermine the influence of women on the eve of the Boroma conference. Others believe it was a ploy by the government then to silence the Sheik, who had been openly critical of the government. The Sheik was subsequently jailed. While women believe it is unlikely to happen again, it demonstrated to them their vulnerability in this new situation. It is one reason why some women's NGOs would like to see the *kat* trade reduced. Women have always been involved in the *kat* trade as petty traders. It is reported that in some cases men encourage their wives to take it up, because it is lucrative. However, it is also a role that is looked down upon. Equally there is concern at the relatively high level of prostitution in Hargeisa among women forced into the trade by lack of other sources of income. One NGO has identified a particular group of teenage women who grew up during the war and became companions of the fighters. They have become ostracised from their families. There is a fear among women that the religious movements may begin to target women involved in *kat* and prostitution.[37]

It is clear that women have played a significant role in supporting peace and reconciliation in Somaliland. Some women claim that it was largely as a result of pressure exerted by women that the elders became active in the reconciliation process over Berbera. During the negotiations the Somaliland Women's Organisation organised demonstrations in Hargeisa in support of peace. They were also the only group to openly petition the government of Abdulrahman Tuur to sue for peace. At Sheik they were active in providing the logistics for that meeting, and it is said that some women gave financial support to the *guurti*.Women have also been supportive of the police in Hargeisa.

Although men are the public face at peace meetings, women claim to be able to influence things, both publicly and in domestic settings. Women will often listen in on meetings, and interject if necessary. Through marriage, women can also be an important channel of communication between conflicting parties. As such they can act to influence both sides in a conflict and may be used as emissaries. Symbolically this female role finds expression in the *diya* (blood compensation) paid for homicide, which is paid in the form of female camels.

The Somaliland *guurti* have recognised in their speeches at peace meetings the role played by women. A women poet was, unusually, given the opportunity to recite peace poems at the Boroma conference.[38] And in recognition of the role of women should play in Somaliland, in September 1993 Egal appointed a woman as a Minister of State to the Presidency.

The importance that women can have in peace-making is recognised in the following Somali proverb:

Dumarka kolbay kay raacaan baa reeya.
Those whom women cheer for surely win.

2 THE BOROMA CONFERENCE

The Boroma Grand Conference on National Reconciliation has been described as a 'make or break event' in the creation of the Somaliland nation, a process which was severely set back by the conflicts in Somaliland during 1992.

The conference was opened on 24 January 1993. It is significant that Boroma, a Gadabursi town, was chosen as the site for the conference. The Gadabursi had helped to mediate in the conflict within the Issaq in 1992. Boroma provided a relatively secure environment away from Hargeisa, Berbera, and Burco, where security was still fragile. It was also a non-Issaq town, which gave non-Issaqs a more active role in determining the future of Somaliland. Boroma also had an active police force to provide security for the conference.

The conference was attended by 150 voting delegates, comprising elders from all clans in Somaliland. They were accompanied by a further 150 observers and advisers. During the four-month conference an estimated 2,000 people participated in the meeting at different stages.

The strength of the Boroma Conference arises from the fact that it was largely financed by communities in Somaliland, with additional support from external sources, including Community Aid Abroad, the Mennonites, Life and Peace Institute, Somali communities abroad, and the French and US embassies in Djibouti. The conference was also well supported by Somali NGOs. UNOSOM provided no support.

The Boroma conference lasted nearly four months. Given the Somali penchant for oratory, and the jealously guarded right of all *not* to remain silent, and given the issues discussed, it is not surprising that it should have taken so long. One observer commented, 'It was nothing compared with your Maastricht debate'.

Peace-making is a long, painstaking process. The Boroma conference was the culmination of previous peace meetings at Hargeisa and Sheikh in 1992. The Boroma conference succeeded, to the extent that it did, because time was allowed for issues to be thoroughly debated and for flashpoints to be dealt with on the way in order that consensus could be achieved.

The conference had two agenda items: reconciliation and security; and state formation.

2.1 The National Peace Charter

The outcome of the deliberations on reconciliation and security was the formulation of a National Peace Charter (Axdiga Nabadgalyada ee Beelaha Soomaaliland). The Peace Charter, as stated, is an attempt to 'rectify past mistakes' that led to a situation of insecurity and ineffectual government and 'to promote the strengthening of security and stability [and the] peaceful co-existence among all the communities of Somaliland.'

This Charter establishes a national security framework. It details the mechanisms for the registration and storage of weapons, the demobilisation of militia, the disarming of bandits, the formation of local police forces and judicial institutions, and the securing of roads. The Charter also defines the responsibility of elders in ensuring that these security arrangements are put in place. The Peace Charter requires every community to take 'a solemn oath not to attack another community', and defines the responsibilities of elders in mediating and settling outstanding disputes and any conflicts that might occur in the future.

The Peace Charter sets out a *code of conduct* for the people of Somaliland, in 'accordance with our traditions and along the principles of Islam'.[39] In effect, the peace charter represents a national *xeer*.

2.2 National Charter

The discussions on state formation produced a decision on the structure of national government enshrined in a National Charter, which will be the constitution of the Somaliland government for a two-year period. The government is charged with drafting a full national constitution to be ratified by referendum within two years. The National Charter was signed by 150 delegates.

The National Charter reaffirms the independence and sovereignty of Somaliland, as obtained on 26 June 1990, and 're-possessed' on 18 May 1991. The Charter sets out the transitional structure of government for the following two years. This will consist of:

The Council of Elders (Upper House)
The Elected Council (Constituent Assembly)
The Executive Council (Cabinet)

The Charter also defines the functions of those councils, and the qualifications for election. Significantly, the Charter defines the role of the elders, 'to encourage and safeguard peace [and] creating new or enforcing existing Code of Conduct [*xeer*] among the clans', thus institutionalising their role as peace-makers. The authority of the elders is also confirmed in their right to appoint the members of the Constituent Assembly.

According to the Chairman of the national *guurti*, Sheik Ibrahim Sheik Yusuf Sheik Madar, the elders are confident of being able to keep the situation in Somaliland secure, because 'we have our eyes on the politicians ... we have the constitutional right to dismiss them'.

The charter also separates the judiciary, Auditor General, and Central Bank as independent agencies from the government.

2.3 Councils of Elders

The Boroma conference is an impressive example of an indigenous Somali reconciliation process in practice, in which the responsibilities of the function of elders as mediators in the internal affairs of the communities are clearly displayed. One commentator described it as 'a triumph of discourse over armed conflict' (Omar 1993).

There has been much debate on the future role of elders in Somaliland and whether they have the ability to play a constructive role in modern government. There is a concern among intellectuals and politicians that the continued presence of elders always brings things back to clans, and that a modern government needs to overcome those divisions to be effective.

The authority of the elders arose from the failure of the first SNM government and a country paralysed by the conflict in Berbera. In the absence of credible government, elder committees became active in all regions of the country in resolving disputes and establishing nascent administrations; in Boroma in July 1991 a permanent *Guurti* of 21 elders was established by the Gadabursi; in Burco a committee of elders was established in January 1992; in Erigavo a regional *guurti* of Issaq was established in January 1992; in February 1993 a regional administration (called the Khussusi[40]) was established by Dolbahunte elders in Sool region.

Interestingly, many of these councils have been formed in response to a particular crisis: the Boroma *guurti* in the face of retaliation from the SNM; in Burco as a result of the conflict in that town; in Erigavo to prevent conflict spreading from Burco; in Las Anod following several security incidents over foreign aid; in Sheikh in response to the Berbera conflict. The Somaliland National *guurti* has its origins in the 1988-1991 war, when elders were responsible for supporting the SNM militias. Sheik Ibrahim, now Chairman of the National *Guurti*, was also instrumental in organising the evacuation of Issaq from Hargeisa to Ethiopia in 1988. The origins of these committees are therefore firmly rooted in conflict-resolution. The question arises as to whether they have any further role than that.

In recognition of their contribution and the continuing need for their skills, the National *Guurti* was written into the first constitution of Somaliland. With the National Charter their role is much more clearly defined. The separation of the elders and politicians into two houses explicitly recognises the division between domestic clan politics and national and international politics. It implicitly recognises 'clanism' as a source of potential conflict, particularly in this post-war period, and the need to have an institutionalised mechanism to deal with potential conflict. The elders do not see themselves as having an administrative role in government. As Sheik Ibrahim has remarked, 'Our task is to ensure security and reconciliation. The government's responsibility is management, administration and development ...' (Omar 1993). At the same time, they explicitly recognise the realities of the stressful environment in which they live, and the need to work with that in order to form a stable government.

3 POST-BOROMA

On 5 May 1993 the Boroma Conference elected Mohamed H.Ibrahim Egal as the new President of Somaliland. Abdulrahman Aw Ali was elected Vice President. The election of Egal, first Prime Minister of Somaliland in 1960, and an experienced politician and diplomat, was met with general approval. He was welcomed into Hargeisa on 16 May by a crowd of 10,000, anticipating a new beginning for Somaliland.

Things, however, did not start well. When he announced his first cabinet in June, two out of the 13 ministers appointed — one Habr Yunis and one Warsengeli — refused their posts. The Habr Yunis, and to a lesser extent the Warsengeli, have since emerged as vocal critics of Egal. Other critics initially included the Arap and the Edegalle. The Arap appear to have settled their differences and have thrown their support behind Egal. In July the Habr Yunis held a conference in Burco (the Liiban Congress), at which they announced their decision not to take up their seats when the Constituent Assembly and Upper House met on 31 July. They went on to state that they would not be bound by the laws passed in the current session of parliament, and accused Egal of forming his government from a 'single political wing'.

The grievances of the Habr Yunis are two-fold. Firstly they believe that the system used at the Boroma Conference for the distribution of seats for the Constituent Assembly and the Upper House was unjust. The Habr Yunis are divided into four sections: Hargeisa, Burco, Berbera and Erigavo. They believe that they are the largest of the Issaq clans and that the four seats allotted to them for the Constituent Assembly and the Upper House are insufficient. They complain that this compares unfavourably with the Ayub, for example, who are smaller in number and were allotted three seats. They claim that seats were allotted on a clan basis rather than by proportional representation, and refer back to 1960 and the Burco conference of 1991, when they had a greater share of seats. They have called for another national conference to resolve the issue.

Their second complaint concerns Egal's first choice of cabinet ministers. Among those ministers Egal has appointed some of the most aggressive opponents of the government of the former president Abdulrahman Ali 'Tuur' (Habr Yunis). These include Musa Bihi (Minister of Interior),[41] Suleiman Gaal (Minister of Education), and Dayib Gure (Minister of Commerce). All these were members of a faction within the SNM known as the 'Red Flag', who had supported the opposition to Tuur in the conflict in Berbera in 1992. The Habr Yunis accuse Egal of opening old rifts within the SNM, which were supposed to have been settled at the Sheikh conference. The impression given is that those who openly fought against the Tuur administration won the war.

Egal has some room for manoeuvre. He can change his cabinet, and there are some unfilled ministerial posts with which to appease the Habr Yunis; as of September 1993 Foreign Affairs, Defence, Planning and Reconstruction, and Religious Affairs were vacant. It is unlikely, however, that the elders will accept another long conference to debate the parliamentary structure again.

Some observers feel that the dispute between the Habr Yunis and the Egal administration is not too serious. Egal's mother is Habr Yunis, as was his paternal grandmother. Both these sub-clans of the Habr Yunis are said to be supportive of him. To date the Habr Yunis have been conciliatory in their opposition. While publicly critical of Egal, they have made it clear that they are prepared for dialogue. In September their elders were in discussion with the administration.

The Warsengelis' position is less clear. They are divided in their attitude towards Somaliland, with a minority favouring a closer association with Somalia, in particular Bosasso (see below). Their lack of participation in Egal's government is probably more influenced by their relationship with the Habr Yunis of Sanaag than by any major differences with Egal.

The Gadabursi and Dolbahunte appear supportive of the Egal administration, content with their Parliamentary seats and cabinet posts. The only woman (Deeqa Cooljool) appointed to the government, as a Minister of State to the Presidency, is Dolbahunte from Erigavo. The Commissioner of the Police Abdi 'Depot' is also Dolbahunte. Since the Boroma Conference, however, several senior Dolbahunte statesmen, who were members of the Dolbahunte Khussusi, have taken up parliamentary and cabinet posts. It is said that their seats in the Khussusi have been filled by Dolbahunte with southern leanings. Some Dolbahunte and Warsengeli were represented by the USP at the Addis Ababa conference in March. The USP has been campaigning with UNOSOM against the Somaliland secession. However, their credibility, even among those Dolbahunte and Warsengeli in Somaliland who are opposed to secession, is smaller than UNOSOM have given them credit for.

Among the Gadabursi, there remains a small section who are still opposed to Somaliland secession. These come from the Rer Nur sub-clan from Dilla, a town which was destroyed by the SNM at the end of the war. This faction was represented at the Addis Ababa Conference in March by the SDA. The credibility of the SDA among the Gadabursi, like the USP, is minimal.

Despite the four months of meetings, political divisions remain to divide people in Somaliland. Such divisions are nothing new. To date the debates are public. Even the fiercest critics of Egal, such as Jama Mohamed Qalib (Edegalle), have their opinions published in the Hargeisa newspapers. As one Somali in Mogadishu pointed out, in the south he would have been shot. There is no indication of a return to the conflict and insecurity experienced in 1992. The question is the extent to which these divisions will again bedevil attempts to develop effective government. Central to this is the issue of regional government.

3.1 Decentralisation

Article 21 of the Somaliland National Charter states that 'the principle of decentralisation' will be applied to administration in the regions and districts, through the creation of regional and district councils. The Charter further states that the relationship between the regions and the central administration will be determined by a parliamentary decree. For debate is the extent to which central government will determine the form which that relationship will take.

Since 1991 regional councils have been established in Awdal and Sool, and one is in the process of formation in Sanaag region. It is clear from discussions in Erigavo that there will be some resistance from the regions to a central government making political appointments, like governors, to the regions. Some in Hargeisa, however, insist that the administration should make such appointments. It was a common practice under Barre. Abdulrahman Tuur attempted to do this and failed. After years of centralised government, people are protective of a new-found autonomy. What is being debated is more than clanism or territoriality. It is a political issue about governance, about how people want to see the country run, and how they want to manage their lives. The way in which decentralisation is handled will be critical to the success of the Egal administration.

3.2 UNOSOM

Another problem facing the Egal administration is that of Somaliland's relationship with the UN. This came to a head on 13 September 1993, when Egal asked UNOSOM personnel to cease operations in Somaliland and to leave the country.

Somaliland's relationship with the UN has never been good. The UN and the international community continue to entertain no possibility of recognising Somaliland's declaration of independence.[42] In the year since the UN opened offices in Hargeisa (in June 1992), they have failed to provide any meaningful assistance for rehabilitation and development.

The dramatic decision of Egal to expel UNOSOM arises from two sources. Firstly, his government is bitterly frustrated with the lack of support that UNOSOM have provided, despite many promises. And secondly, there is a very deep suspicion among the population in Somaliland of UNOSOM's intentions for that area.

On 27 May 1993 Admiral Howe visited Hargeisa for the first time as the new SRSG. During his meeting with Egal he made commitments to support the Hargeisa police and the demobilisation of the militia. On 3 July Dr Omar Halim (Director of UNOSOM Policy and Planning Group) visited Hargeisa and, after discussions with the administration, made a detailed proposal to UNOSOM for assistance for the police and demobilisation. While some assistance was secured for the police (500 uniforms and food provided from EC funds), no assistance was received for demobilisation. At the beginning of September, with government plans for demobilisation about to be completed, the need for that assistance became critical. The condition for this assistance, however, appears to be agreement by the Somaliland administration to allow UNOSOM to have more control over the process. In UNOSOM's eyes this would mean the deployment of some troops. Although in May Egal had indicated a willingness to accept troops to help with the demobilisation programme and infrastructural rehabilitation, events in Mogadishu had warned people against this.

The deployment of UNOSOM troops in Somaliland is a very sensitive issue. UNOSOM II is mandated to deploy its peace-keeping forces throughout Somalia and Somaliland. However, even at the height of the conflict in Berbera, this idea was rejected by Tuur's government and the opposition. There remains a very deep suspicion among the population at large of the intentions of the UN to reunify Somaliland with Somalia. UNOSOM II, they say, has 'II agendas', one of which is reunification. An announcement by Boutros-Ghali on 3 March 1993 that UNOSOM troops would be deployed throughout the region, including Somaliland, met with a sharp response from the Somaliland elders meeting in Boroma. They considered 'the arbitrary dispatch of [UN] troops into our country as an alien invasion, which we will resist with our utmost resolve'. Since the outbreak of conflict between UNOSOM and Aideed in Mogadishu, the people in Somaliland are even more adamant that they do not want the deployment of UN troops.

In an atmosphere charged with suspicion, a dispute arose between Egal and UNO-SOM over a number of diplomatic blunders by UNOSOM. In August UNOSOM personnel made two visits to Erigavo. The first was by the US envoy Gosende and the US Ambassador to Djibouti. The second was by the Deputy SRSG, Kouyate. Gosende also went to Badhan, where he reported that he met with the Warsengeli Garaad and was told that the Warsengeli did not support Somaliland. In August the Deputy SRSG Kouyate also visited Erigavo, during the peace conference, taking with him the northeast Zone Director from Bosasso. He is also reported to have held a meeting in Las Anod. The impression given was that UNOSOM was taking heed of an open letter from the USP (as representing Warsengeli and Dolbahunte) to Admiral Howe, stating their opposition to Somaliland. It was further rumoured that UNOSOM planned to open sub-offices in Erigavo and Las Anod which would report to Mogadishu. The visit was interpreted by Egal as an infringement of Somaliland's integrity and the authority of the Egal administration. In response, Kouyate is reported to have stated that under UNOSOM's mandate he was free to travel where he wished.

At the root of this conflict is the UN resolution, which does not recognise Somaliland's independence, and gives its representatives the authority to make decisions, without necessarily consulting local authorities. Through this action, the UN ignored the four months of meetings in Boroma at which people reaffirmed their belief in the sovereignty of Somaliland. This rift with UNOSOM is a gamble for Egal. It could be used as a reason by his critics for why Somaliland did not receive external support. On the other hand, one effect of this rift is that Egal has now formally submitted a request to the UN for recognition. Allegedly, this was never done by the Tuur administration.

The attitude of UNOSOM Hargeisa could not be more different from UNOSOM in the south. Their position, as stated by the Zone Director in August, was that in Somaliland there was a 'partner' with whom they could work. Their policy was that there would be no deployment of troops without an invitation. Their brief was 'listening and watching and not interfering, demobilisation and to support the police'.[43] They appear, however, to have failed to convince UNOSOM in Mogadishu of the same and to provide the resources with which to work. In September 1993 resources were desperately needed to support the demobilisation programme that was underway.

4 DEMOBILISATION

4.1 Introduction

Prior to May 1988, the SNM were estimated to have had some 3,000 trained fighters. In 1988, when the war escalated and the Barre government took fierce reprisals against the Issaq, there was a general mobilisation of the male Issaq population. Like other political factions in Somalia, the SNM was based upon a coalition of allied clans and sub-clans. The SNM military was recruited along clan lines and fought in small clan-based units (*jabhad*), supported by their clans. Since the ending of the war, many of the SNM guerrillas have laid down their arms and returned to civilian life. Many have remained together as military units with a clear command structure. The current figure used by the Somaliland government for numbers of armed militia in Somaliland is between 40,000 and 50,000. Others have turned to banditry in order survive.

In Somaliland people now make a distinction between the SNM *mujahid* and the *deydey* or *budhcad*. The *mujahid* are the proper long-term SNM fighters, some of whom had been fighting with the SNM since 1981. They are also known more generally as *mana gaaho*, taking their name from a road called *gaaho*, in Ethiopia, behind which the SNM had its rear bases. Another category of *mujahid* are the *jama rah* ('went on Friday'): those who joined the SNM on the Friday in May 1988 when the SNM first attacked Burco.

The *deydey*[44] or *budhcad* are the armed bandits. The word *deydey* means 'searching' and originates from the idea of 'the lost ones', that is those who got separated during the war and whose parents are looking for them. It has now come to have a second meaning of 'those who do the searching', meaning the looting. In a situation where there are few employment opportunities, war-hardened youths have resorted to banditry to survive. Indeed, a common explanation given in Somaliland is that *deydey* are a 'disease born of poverty'. Another common name used to describe the *deydey* is *malin dagal*, 'million a day', the idea being that they need to make a million shillings a day in order to pay for ammunition, alchohol, women, and *kat*. Another name used to describe the bandits is *hadaba marido*, 'those who start shooting now', that is those who picked up arms after the war. Many of these *deydey* know no other life.

Attitudes towards these *deydey* are ambiguous, for one clan's 'army' can be another clan's *deydey*. Like the SNM *mujahid*, a group of *deydey* will generally come from the same clan. In a conflict these gangs can be your means of protection, and are therefore your 'army' or 'militia'. At the same time, the concept of corporate responsibility means that your clan can be held accountable for the activities of your *deydey*. The *deydey* can therefore be a threat to your own security. In some places where *deydey* have become a threat to their own clan's interests, elders have taken extreme measures and killed them.

It is suggested that probably 25 per cent of the militia fall into the category of *deydey*. In principle, people say it is the *mujahid* who should be helped first. However, it is the *deydey* who continue to cause much of the insecurity. Any demobilisation programme needs to address ways of disarming these gangs and re-integrating them into society.

4.2 A Framework for Security

After the war the first government of Abdulrahman Ali Tuur made a cursory attempt to integrate the militia into a unified army. This failed, and energy was squandered on factional disputes among politicians and military officers, which led to an outbreak of fighting in Burco and Berbera.

The Peace Charter, adopted by the elders at the Boroma Conference in March 1993, sets out to rectify the mistakes of the previous government by establishing a framework for future security in Somaliland. The Charter recognises that lack of security was the single most important factor that led to the failure of the previous Somaliland administration. The Charter also recognises that the militarisation of society continues to cause destruction of assets, undermines peaceful co-existence of communities and commercial enterprise, encourages banditry, disrupts humanitarian, rehabilitation and developmental activities, and leaves the population in a state of perpetual fear and insecurity. The Charter therefore seeks to address this by setting out the principles on which security of the individual, community and nation should be based, and the responsibilities incumbent on each community to ensure such security.

The future stability and economic recovery of Somaliland will depend on the ability of the new administration to carry out a comprehensive programme of demobilisation and disarmament, coupled with the formation of a police force and a judiciary. Through the Peace Charter the elders made it incumbent upon the Egal administration to formulate a plan for demobilisation and disarmament.

4.3 Plan for Demobilisation

In contrast to the former administration, the policy of Egal's government and the military commanders is that there should not be a national army. The commanders say that they do not have the resources to build an effective army that could prevent an invasion. They are now convinced that disarmament is an important step for Somaliland towards achieving autonomy. Without disarmament, they contend that there will be no peace, and without peace Somaliland cannot maintain its independence. Their best security, they assert, is therefore in disarmament. 'Next time the clans quarrel, it must be in Parliament.[45]

By 31 July 1993 Egal had reached had reached an agreement with the militia commanders and elders on a plan for the collection of militia in cantonment sites. The government would provide rations for ten days, and the militia would leave their arms with the clan elders and move to camps to commence separate training programmes. This was to be the first step in the demobilisation programme.

The disarmament and demobilisation programme comes under the responsibility of a Ministerial Committee on Security and Demobilisation, comprising the Vice President, Ministers of Interior, Defence, Education, Finance and Information. The planning and implementation of the programme will be carried out by a 12-member Technical Committee, comprising both military and civilians in cooperation with regional Security Committees.

The programme will involve the demobilisation of 50,000 militia.[46] Estimates of militia by region are: Awdal 8,500, North West 24,450, Togdheer 7,400, Sanaag 5,400 and Sool 4,250. From these, 9,000 will be trained as police, 3,000 as border guards, 5,000 as coastal guards, and 1,000 as prison warders. It is envisaged that the remaining 42,000, who include 10,000 disabled men, will be trained in farming, fishing and vocational training programmes to last from three to six months.

In August, two Zimbabwean consultants (Paul Nyathi of the Zimbabwe Project and Jeremy Brickhill, a former ZIPRA officer and former member of Oxfam UK/I's Africa Advisory Committee) were seconded by UNDP-OPS to the Egal administration to advise the administration and UNOSOM on planning a programme for the disarmament and demobilisation of the militias. At the beginning of September, consultations produced an outline plan for demobilisation and re-integration of the militias.

The demobilisation plan envisages the training of police forces from all six regions in Mandera Camp, between Berbera and Hargeisa. The police, as envisaged, will comprise:

    regional police   1950
    special police force 1407
    striking force   260
    mobile force   850
    traffic police   107
    finance guards   190

4.4 International Response

In drawing up the plan for demobilisation, Egal had anticipated that assistance would be forthcoming from UNOSOM for its implementation. When SRSG Howe visited Hargeisa in May 1993, he had promised assistance from UNOSOM for demobilisation. In early July the UNOSOM Director of Policy and Planning, Omar Halim, visited Hargeisa and agreed that, once procedures had been finalised, UNOSOM would provide the wherewithal for the establishment and maintenance of assembly camps. Halim reported to UNOSOM in Mogadishu that the disarmament programme in Somaliland was voluntary and should be accorded the 'highest priority'. Futhermore, he stated that the assistance which the Egal administration was requesting for demobilisation, the police, and judicial system was consistent with UN resolution 814 (1993), and affordable within UNOSOM's $18 million budget for demobilisation. The attitude of UNOSOM Zone Office in Hargeisa was equally supportive of the proposed plans.

Some support had been secured from UNOSOM for the police in Hargeisa (500 uniforms, rations and equipment). UNICEF were installing water for the prisons. Under the auspices of UNOSOM, a Dutch and Canadian police adviser had been seconded to the Hargeisa police and two British police advisers were expected in September. UNOSOM had also assisted in transporting some ICRC food from Djibouti to Mandera police training camp. World Food Programme, USAID, UNOSOM and the Ministry of Planning had discussed a further $1.5 million worth of food vouchers, to provide food for some 9,000 militia for six months.

Other agencies were also involved. UNDP-OPS seconded two consultants to the demobilisation Technical Committee (see above). Rimfire were proposing to hire a further 800 militia to train for the mine-clearance programme. CARE had supported Sooyaal, the SNM veterans' association, to build a vocational training centre for ex-combatants.

Events moved more quickly than planned. In mid-August 1993 there were some 200 militia from Berbera in Mandera camp undergoing police training. By 4 September the number had increased to 800, and by the 7th to between 2,000 and 3,000. It was expected to increase to 5,000. With insufficient shelter, food, water or medical facilities for the 5,000 militia, the situation was potentially explosive. The sudden rush of militia to the camp had arisen because the clans were anxious not to miss out on the benefits of retraining and employment in the new security forces.

On 31 July, when Egal wrote to UNOSOM Zone Director in Hargeisa, informing him that his government had reached an agreement with the militia leaders and clan elders on the cantonment of militia, he requested assurance from UNOSOM that assistance would be available. By the end of August UNOSOM had given no indication that the promised assistance would be forthcoming. Angry at their failure to respond, Egal sent a letter to UNOSOM on 9 September, requesting them to cease their operations and leave Somaliland.

The immediate reason for Egal's action had been a diplomatic incident involving the Deputy SRSG Kouyate (see 3.2 above). However, Egal has largely staked his presidency and the success of the government on being able to disarm the militia. While UNOSOM Hargeisa stated that the demobilisation programme had the full support of UNOSOM Mogadishu, there was little material evidence of this. Without the promised resources, the demobilisation programme would be difficult to implement.

At the time Egal made this request for assistance, UNOSOM's attention was focused on the conflict in Mogadishu. This undoubtedly restricted its ability to respond with any speed. It is suggested, however, that UNOSOM is unwilling to provide the resources asked for unless they are able to exert some control over the process. In this respect, they have continued to insist on the need to send uniformed and protected (armed) advisers to Somaliland if they are going to support the process. The most cynical critics suspect that UNOSOM assume that without their support the demobilisation programme will fail, and this will justify a military intervention.

The extension of UNOSOM military operations to Somaliland would be disastrous. Although Howe and UNOSOM Hargeisa have publicly stated several times that they will not deploy troops unless invited, this has not quelled fears among the population. The disregard shown to the authorities in Hargeisa by Kouyate has not helped in that matter. Even if UNOSOM were to extend their military operations to Somaliland for purely humanitarian purposes, there is little confidence that they would be able to handle a demobilisation programme in a sensitive manner, especially given their recent actions in Mogadishu. Such is the concern that the military commanders in Somaliland say they would be forced to resist militarily if UNOSOM attempted to deploy troops.

4.5 Recommendations for the Support of Demobilisation

Security — stable central and regional government and the successful demobilisation of armed militias — has been identified as the key to the rehabilitation and development needs in Somaliland. As agencies' programmes change from relief to development, the emerging emphasis of the programmes will also change. There are two groups on which programmes should, for the mean time, have a strategic focus: refugee returnees and demobilised militia. The latter is a recognition that insecurity is an inhibition to economic development in Somaliland. There is a strong argument for agencies to develop a further 'sectoral' activity that focuses exclusively on demobilisation.

Demobilisation should be seen as a long-term process, requiring a substantial commitment of resources. Such a programme, if supported by agencies, should be placed firmly within the framework of a comprehensive plan initiated by the Somaliland government and implemented, as much as possible, through local non-governmental or community-based organisations. Given their previous experience in this field, Oxfam and others could make a major contribution to such a programme.

The Somaliland Peace Charter clearly identifies demobilisation and disarmament as a fundamental building block for peace and stability in Somaliland. Assistance with demobilisation therefore provides agencies with a clear opportunity to support peace-building in Somaliland. The following are some recommendations on how they might support demobilisation and disarmament in Somaliland.

Planning and Preparation: Agencies should be prepared to make an immediate provision of resources to the Technical Committee, to enable it to gather the data needed to prepare a plan for demobilisation.

Advocacy: Demobilisation has been identified as the priority issue by the Egal administration. The administration is convinced that voluntary demobilisation is preferable to assisted (or forced) demobilisation by UNOSOM, and that UNOSOM should not take control of the process. The administration needs support for this strategy. Agencies should make it an essential part of their strategies to lobby their governments to fund this process, and to put pressure on UNOSOM to refrain from acting other than as funders or monitors.

Agencies might explore, with their governments, acceptable ways of monitoring and verifying the process. This would not only be useful for advocacy purposes, but it might also help internally to have an independent body for verification. If it was acceptable to the government, agencies might consider funding an appropriate international body to visit Somaliland on a regular basis to do this. A team might be combined with elders and local NGOs.

Publicity Campaign: Public communication, civic mobilisation, confidence building, and cultural activities will be key to the success of the demobilisation process. The rehabilitation of Hargeisa Radio could be an essential contribution to this.

Peace-Building/Conflict-Resolution Training: Somaliland women have played an important role in the peace process in Somaliland as a community pressure group. Organisations of women (Somaliland Women's Organisation, Committee of Concerned Somalis, Somaliland Women's Development Organisation) have all mobilised women at peace conferences. Agencies might help to strengthen this work, where appropriate, by supporting a series of training workshops and seminars for women extensionists/mobilisers.

Agencies should consider commissioning a Somali women's NGO to look at what role women might play in assisting with demobilisation, and the possible effects on women of the process.

Agencies should look for ways to ensure that elders are fully involved and consulted in the demobilisation process. Community support for the programme will be critical to its success. Their authority, as well as their skills in mediation and trouble shooting, should be fully utilised.

Vocational Training: Some agencies have developed proposals to support the establishment of a Technical Training Institute in Hargeisa with the Ministry of Education. This might provide training opportunities for demobilised militia, and should be pursued. Agencies might also consider funding the Ministry to design and undertake education programmes for the ex-combatants while in the camps, such as basic literacy, numeracy, and Koranic education. This would also provide increased training opportunities for unemployed teachers. Agencies might also consider ways of supporting education development in the region, to assist in general rehabilitation and development to fulfil the huge need for education provision.

84

Agencies should also consider contracting local, private training institutions in Hargeisa to provide training for the militia, as required. They might consider contracting these institutions to consult with the militias and government to identify their training needs. This would have the advantage of both developing the capacity of the training institutes and providing the required training.

Trauma: The Somali psychiatrist, Dr Omar Duhod, estimates that as many as 5 per cent of the ex-combatants will be in need of psychiatric counselling. Agencies should consider ways in which they can support the reintegration of ex-combatants into society through counselling programmes. Agencies might consider consulting agencies such as the Medical Foundation for the Victims of Torture, or consultants such as Dr Derek Summerfield, Dr Twi, and Dr Duhod.

Cultural Programmes: Agencies should also consider funding cultural activities — bands, artists, poets, etc. — to provide entertainment both for the ex-combatants, as part of their psychological rehabilitation, and also more generally in Somaliland. This would probably require identifying Somali artists outside the country and sending them on tour.

Disabled War Veterans: Agencies might consider commissioning Action on Disability and Development, or others, to assess ways of strengthening the formation of an association for disabled veterans.

International Media: Agencies should use their resources to generate international media interest in the demobilisation process in Somaliland.

Disarmament 'Think Tank': Agencies should consider ways of integrating/linking this work with that of the Conrad Grebel College, Canada, and its 'think tank' on disarmament in the Horn.

Demobilisation Fund: Agencies should consider contributing to a demobilisation fund for Somaliland, for an initial two-year period. It would be used to employ on a full-time basis an individual (expatriate or Somali) to coordinate agencies' work in this field, and be used for funding any or all of the above activities. A sum of approximately 500,000 would probably be needed.

5 SHIR NABADEEDKA EE SANAAG: 'The Sanaag Grand Peace and Reconciliation Conference'

5.1 Introduction

The introduction to this report suggests that conflict is inherent in all human societies, 'a universal part of the way that humans organise and mediate individual and group relations'. If conflict is part of everyday life, then mechanisms must also exist within society to manage or resolve those conflicts. Mediation, peace conferences, peace-keeping, peace-enforcement, monitoring, military intervention, safe havens, humanitarian aid, and legal and judiciary procedures are just some of the overt and obvious mechanisms.

The response of humanitarian aid agencies to conflict tends to focus on the appalling impact of conflict and the provision of external solutions, or 'interventions'. There is, perhaps, an assumption that because a society is in conflict, local mechanisms for resolving conflicts no longer exist, or have ceased to function. Recent studies by NGOs on conflict (such as Duffield, 1990) have tended to look at the causes of conflict. While the understanding which these studies provide is essential to reorientate our thinking, perhaps there is a need to place more emphasis on looking at solutions.

By concentrating on the causes of conflict rather than the solutions to it, perhaps we fail to look for, and see, those indigenous processes or mechanisms which exist to bring about resolution or peace. Lewis (1961) has commented on Somali society that 'hostility and hospitality are important social parameters between pastoral groups'. In Somalia, to date, the emphasis of analysis has been on 'hostility', and perhaps we now need to look at closer at 'hospitality'. When we look at solutions, we should remember that, from our experience, the best development projects are those that utilise and build upon local knowledge and experience, where communities have a control over the process. It is for this reason that I present this brief case study of the 'Sanaag Grand Peace and Reconciliation Conference'. [47]

5.2 Sanaag Region

Sanaag, in the north-east of Somaliland is a semi-arid, mountainous and semi-desert region. The livelihood of people in the region is based on pastoral nomadism and small-scale sedentary agriculture, practised in the valleys of the Gollis mountains. Erigavo is the regional capital and largest town.

Historically, Sanaag is important to the Somali people as the place where many of the eponymous ancestors of the clan-families lived and are buried. Several of the tombs of the ancestors are important pilgrimage sites, in particular the tomb of Sheik Issaq in Mait. Sanaag is also the only region in Somaliland where Issaq (Habr Yunis and Habr Toljallo) and Darod (Warsengeli and Dolbahunte) live together and share (and compete over) common resources of grazing and water. The division of the region into three districts broadly reflects the demographic division of resources. The Habr Toljallo mainly inhabit Eil Afweyne district to the west, the Habr Yunis and Dolbahunte live in Erigavo district in the centre, and the Warsengeli are in Badhan district to the east. Inter-marriage between Issaq and Darod, however, is more common in Sanaag than other regions of the country.

A number of minority clans also live in the region. These include the Jibrahiil, Minsale, Magadle and Gaheyle, as well as lineages of the 'sab' (outcast) clans, the Tumale, Yibr, and Midgan. Most of these are bonded to the Issaq or Darod clans. The Gaheyle, however, claim genealogical attachment to the Majeerteen (Darod).

With pastoralists competing over diminishing grazing and water resources, Sanaag region has always experienced tensions among its population. During Barre's government, the Darod clans in Sanaag (Dolbahunte and Warsengeli) gained access to resources, such as land and property, within areas traditionally considered to be Issaq. They were able to retain control over these through the power of the state. The civil war, as experienced in Sanaag, was therefore partly fought by the Issaq, under the banner of the SNM, to regain control over those grazing and water resources.

86

Prior to the war the populations in the main towns of Erigavo and Eil Afweyne were a cosmopolitan mix of clans. However, the war led to a large displacement of people and changed the composition of many settlements. When the SNM 'liberated' Erigavo, the Darod left the town, the Warsengeli going east to Badhan and the Dolbahunte south to Las Anod. Other groups such as the Gaheyle and the 'sab' clans who had taken up arms on the side of Siad Barre were also displaced from the Issaq areas. In 1992 Erigavo's population was less than half its pre-war size.

Under the terms of a cease-fire concluded in 1991 after the war, the Issaq, Warsengeli and Dolbahunte agreed to remain within their traditional borders. Clan territories became 'safe havens' for Darod fleeing both from SNM 'liberated' areas and from the war in southern Somalia. Contact between the Issaq, Warsengeli and Dolbahunte was limited to the radio and to trading at market places along the borders. Only women were able to cross the borders.

This process of creating 'safe havens' during war, where lineages acquire a territorial reality, is described by Lewis (1961): 'Opposed groups ... withdraw from each other, leaving an area of neutral or no-man's-land, along the fringes of which guards (kojoog-ka) are posted.'

5.3 Restoring Peace

Although the SNM united the Issaq in their opposition to Siad Barre, the movement was constituted on a political alliance of clans who, in 'peaceful times', would themselves fight over resources. During the war there were conflicts in Sanaag between sub-clans of the Issaq. After Erigavo was captured by the SNM in February 1991, the town was initially occupied mainly by the Habr Yunis clan, with only a limited presence of Habr Toljallo. A Habr Yunis militia commander assumed the position of 'Acting Governor'. As the Habr Toljallo owned property in the town, this situation was clearly untenable, and a process of reconciliation was started to enable other Issaq to return to Erigavo.

The reconciliation process was led by two prominent elders from Eil Afweyne, who are closely related; their two sub-clans are known as 'Habr Labada' (the 'two Habr', or 'twins'). As a result of their efforts, a committee of 43 elders (*guurti*), representing the Issaq clans in the region, was formed in January 1992 to settle inter-clan disputes, restore stability, and appoint a regional administration.

The regional *guurti* initially reaffirmed the position of the 'Acting Governor' to head up an interim administration. However, after a series of security incidents in August 1992, the Acting Governor was asked to resign by the elders. The administration was disbanded and the elders assumed authority through a number of committees. The *guurti* also decided that there should be no regional administration until such time as all the clans in the region, both Issaq and Darod, had reconciled their differences. This assertion of authority by the elders took place at the same time that the Somaliland National *guurti* intervened to stop the conflict in Berbera.

5.4 The Peace Conference

The 'Sanaag Grand Peace and Reconciliation Conference', between the Habr Yunis and Habr Toljallo (Issaq), and Warsengeli and Dolbahunte (Darod), opened in Erigavo on 19 August 1993. The meeting was opened with the reading of the Koran by Sheik

Ahmed Edleh, one of the two Issaq elders who had helped to form the Issaq regional *guurti*.

The Sanaag Conference is an impressive example of an indigenous Somali peace and reconciliation process. Much time and thought was expended on the structure, process and organisation of the meeting. It stands in marked contrast to that initiated by the international community through the United Nations, and it is useful for the purposes of this report to draw out the main characteristics of the meeting and the process that led to it.

5.5 Peace-making from the Grass Roots

The Somali saying *nabad iyo caano* ('peace and milk') stresses the important relationship between peace and prosperity. Plentiful milk means healthy livestock and good grazing. 'Good grazing' refers not only to the quality of the pasture, but also to access to it. Access to pasture and water is assured through peaceful cooperation. Another Somali proverb, *nabad iyo rob* ('peace and rain'), complements that and stands in opposition to the proverb *ol iyo abaar* ('conflict and drought').

In the introduction to this report, I commented that there are two theories of how peace-making can work in Somalia: one a top-down process that recognises the political legitimacy of the 'warlords'/politicians, and the other a bottom-up approach where people rebuild their relations of trust and cooperation from the grassroots. The model in use in Sanaag region is the latter. The process is neatly described in the story that is now used to explain the beginning of the peace process in Sanaag.

It is said that in late 1991, the Banadde and Karaman plains around Eil Afweyne in western Sanaag received good rains, while to the south-east around Buhodle the rains failed. Pastoral families of the Dolbahunte, from the east, who needed access to the pastures used by the Issaq in the west, sent women envoys to the Issaq to ask if they could have access to their grazing areas (*degaan*). In order for this to happen, the Dolbahunte and Habr Toljallo needed to establish an agreement or 'contract' (*xeer*). The new *xeer* needed to involve the elders of each clan, and it is from this point that the peace process has been built.

5.6 A Long-Term Process

The peace and reconciliation process has been very protracted, and all sections of society have had the right to participate. Peace-making demands that people at every level of clan segmentation should reconcile their differences before they are able to meet as a larger body.[48] The process is necessarily slow, in order to be inclusive, rather than exclusive.

Between August 1992 and June 1993, seven peace meetings were concluded between sub-clans of the Issaq and Darod in Sanaag region: August 1992, between the Habr Toljallo, Warsengeli and Dolbahunte at Shimbiraale; November 1992, between the Habr Yunis and Warsengeli at Jidalle; November 1992, between the Habr Toljallo, Warsengeli and Dolbahunte at Garadag; January 1993, between the Habr Yunis and Dolbahunte at Dararweyne. Further meetings took place at Yobe and Armale, between the Habr Yunis, Warsengeli and Dolbahunte.

While the details of the meetings differed, depending on the nature of the conflict (e.g. a dispute over a water point, grazing land, or personal property), the general conclusions were the same, namely:

- 'to establish peace in the region';
- 'to establish the means through which outstanding conflicts between clans can be resolved';
- 'to enable the free trade and movement of people'.

With a view to establishing peace in the region, it was also determined that a final meeting of all clans should take place in Erigavo in 1993.

5.7 Preparatory Meetings

The regional peace meeting in Erigavo was originally scheduled to start in early 1993. However, the opening was delayed by the convening of the Boroma conference in January 1993, which ended in May, and separate meetings among the Dolbahunte at Boame in February, among the Warsengeli at Hadaftimo in July, and among the Habr Yunis in Burco in July.

Potentially the Boame, Hadaftimo and Burco meetings could have upset the peace process in Sanaag. In particular, the Warsengeli meeting in Hadaftimo (when divisions within the Warsengeli over their relationship to Somaliland came to the fore) could have resulted in the Warsengeli pulling out of the Erigavo Conference.

The Warsengeli are divided into two. One group in eastern Badhan are more closely associated with the Majeerteen, having economic links with Bosasso. The majority Rer Nooh Omar, to the west of Badhan, are inter-married with the Musa Ismael (Habr Yunis) of Erigavo and have economic links and property with the town. They are supportive of the Sanaag meeting and links with Somaliland.

The Warsengeli Garaad, Sultan Abdisalam Sultan Mohamed, is old and bedridden in Hadaftimo. His representative, his brother Ismael Sultan, who participated in some 41 meetings in Somaliland (including Burco and Boroma), issued a communiqué at Hadaftimo in support of Somali unity and of UNOSOM activities in Somalia. Although the communiqué supported the promotion of peace talks in Sanaag, he refused to attend the Erigavo meeting. As a result, the Warsengeli Garaad had no representative at Erigavo. However, the Garaad himself is said to be supportive of the meeting, because the meeting was able to proceed. [49]

There was also a last-minute hitch with the Gahayleh. The Gahayleh are a small clan, but are considered to be one of the original clans of Sanaag. They are thought to be related to the Habr Magadle, whose daughter Sheik Issaq married. Before the war they used to live among the Rer Abdi Hamud of the Musa Ismael (Habr Yunis), in Sanaag. However, they are what is known as a *sheegad* ('pretending'; claiming to belong to a lineage to which one does not belong by birth), and declare a genealogical affiliation to the Majeerteen. During the war they sided with the Darod against the Habr Yunis. When the SNM gained control, the Gahayleh fled en masse to Garowe and Bosasso. As a result they have lost their farms and frankincense trees.

Just before the Sanaag Conference was due to open, the Gahayleh requested a place in the meeting. They were refused, because they had not taken part in any previous preparatory meetings. The consensus was that they should solve their problems with the Musa Ismael before they could take part in the meeting. The Musa Ismael offered them the opportunity to meet after the peace conference at Yobe, but they have apparently refused this.

The Sanaag Conference is therefore a culmination of a series of peace meetings that had taken place over a twelve-month period. The long-term nature of this process is essential to the success and sustainability of any agreement reached at Erigavo.

5.8 Peace-making to Peace-Building

Somali society is essentially a democratic society in which individual (male) opinions and the right to participate in decision-making are jealously guarded. The authority of the elders who negotiate at the peace meetings is not inherent, but is delegated to them by their clans.

All opinions have to be canvassed, and different interest groups which cut across clan alliances have to be co-opted into the process. In Somaliland, for example, the Issaq people categorise themselves into the *mana-gaaho, mana-festo,* and *mana-seer*. The *mana-gaaho* are those who fought in the bush against the regime; the *mana-festo* (associated with the Manifesto Group[50]) are those who stayed on in Mogadishu; and the *mana-seer* ('who drink sweet drinks') are those who fled abroad. These groups represent different ideas and interests. In addition there are the 'politicians', 'intellectuals', 'army', 'religious groups' and the *'deydey'*. In a country where 'few among the population would admit to being unsuitable for Presidency' (Drysdale, 1992), everybody's opinion has to be taken into account.

The long-term nature of the reconciliation process was necessary to ensure that the different clans of the region participated and supported the process. The dismissal of the acting regional administration by the Issaq *guurti* in August 1992 was a clear recognition that a narrowly based administration could have no authority and that the reconciliation process needed to be inclusive rather than exclusive.

Given the length and intensity of the conflict, it would be impossible in a single meeting to deal with the vast range of grievances that stand between the different clans. The advantage of the series of preliminary meetings meant that many issues had been dealt with along the way. The implementation of decisions of the previous meetings, such as the return of property, helped to strengthen ties and reinforce final decisions reached in Erigavo. In essence this is 'peace-building'.

The Erigavo meeting was therefore seen by participants as the formal confirmation of a long-term peace and reconciliation process. In the words of one delegate, 'Now everyone is purely for peace ... everyone has tasted war and peace and has chosen peace.'

5.9 Common Objectives

The protracted process also meant that it was possible to define the objectives of the

Erigavo meeting clearly, and agree a common goal. There were only two items on the conference agenda:

1 Confirming Peace.
2 Establishing a regional administration.

Participants and observers in Erigavo firmly stressed that the primary objective was to establish peace between the clans that would allow for the return of the Darod to Erigavo, the settling of all disputes, and the return of all property. The fact that many Warsengeli and Dolbahunte returned to Erigavo at the start of the meeting was an indication of the confidence which people placed in a successful outcome.

5.10 Equal Representation

Each of the four clans participating in the meeting had equal representation in all the committees of the meeting, despite the fact that not all of the Warsengeli were present (see diagram 13).

5.11 Structure of Meeting

The organisation of the meeting was impressive. There were over 400 delegates, security personnel and labourers.

8 Sultans/Garaads
7 religious leaders
8 members of the Chairing Committee
200 delegates
22 on the Preparatory committee
130 police (100) and (30) prison staff
50 workers in the hotels and conference venue.

All representatives to the meeting were identified by official cards and had clearly defined roles and functions.

i) *Guurti* Suldaan\Garaad — Council of Sultans and Garaads

The Council of Sultans consisted of seven Sultans and Garaads:

Dolbahunte	- Garaad Abdelgani
	- Garaad Ismael
	- Sultan Suleiban
Habr Toljallo	- Sultan Abdillahi Ali (Garadag)
Habr Yunis	- Sultan Esa (Burco)
	- Sultan Saed (Erigavo)
Edegalle	- Sultan Mohamed (Hargeisa)
Warsengeli	- Garaad (not in attendance)

The Garaad of the Warsengeli was too old to attend the meeting. The Edegalle Sultan was present, because the Edegalle come from the same clan (Garhajis) as the Habr Yunis.

The Sultan and Garaad is the focus for the moral and ethnic solidarity of the clan. He therefore carries responsibility for the clan in a religious and political sense. The traditional function of Garaads and Sultans is as mediators. Their authority primarily derives from their expertise in mediation and problem-solving. They stand above the narrow divisions of the clan interests and 'can see beyond the fight'. The mechanism of mediation in Somali society is therefore institutionalised through the office of the Sultan or Garaad. At the beginning of the meeting the Sultans and Garaads let it be known that they were ready to sign an agreement, on completion of the conference. Thus they indicated that the meeting should conclude in peace.

ii) Sheiks

There were seven religious Sheiks attending the Sanaag Conference. Somali law combines both customary law and Islamic sharia. Religious leaders (*wadaad*) have an important role alongside elders at peace meetings, providing religious sanction to decisions. The religious leaders can influence the meetings, by reference to the Koran, by reminding participants what the Koran has to say about certain actions and behaviour.

iii) *Shir guurti* — Chairing Committee

The Chairing Committee consisted of eight members, two from each clan, one Chair, two Vice Chairs, and four secretariat:

Ali Warsame (Chair)	- HY
Saed Mohamed Nur	- HY
Mohamed Ali Shire	- DH
Mohamed Ahmed Abdulle	- DH
Mohamed Haji Ducale	- HT
Hassan Haji Ducale (Hassan Sheik)	- HY
Mohamed 'Borasab'	- WG
Mohamed ?	- WG

The Chair, Ali Warsame, was a wealthy businessman who left Mogadishu as late as 1992. It is not clear why he had been chosen to act as the Chair, but it is likely that he was able to provide some resources for the conference. He may also have had plans to invest in the region and therefore had a commitment to the success of the conference.

iv) *Shir Ergo* — Council of Delegates

The main council of elders involved 200 delegates (*ergo* — 'emissaries'), 50 from each clan. Thirty members from each clan were official voting members, with a further 20 (*murti sheraf*) in observance. The function of the Ergo was to review the agreements signed previously and to decide on the resolutions to the meeting. All the delegates were elders who had the authority to make decisions on behalf of the clans. According to informants, the elders and the members of the chairing committee are selected according to their 'ability' rather than the strength or size of their clan or sub-clan. Thus while 'politicians' were strictly excluded from the conference (although some MPs were present in Erigavo), some of the elders were businessmen.[51]

v) Conference Preparatory Committee

This had 20 members, five from each clan, with various responsibilities for finance, logistics, and reception of VIPs. The preparatory committee was also responsible for organisation of police and labourers. The Committee was chaired by Ismael Haji Nur, a Habr Yunis businessman and elder from Erigavo.

vi) Clan Preparatory Committees

Each clan had its own preparatory committee, with responsibility for preparing the clan's agenda for the meetings and logistics.

5.12 The 'Intellectuals'

Somali Development and Relief Association (SDRA) is a Warsengeli NGO, with strong links in the USA. One of its members, Mohamoud Jama, is a member of the US Ergada (Somali Peace and Consultation Committee). Another important member is Mohamed Abdi Ali 'Bayer', one of the few Warsengeli members of the SNM, and a Minister of Planning in the first Somaliland government.[52] He was also a member of the Somali Intellectuals for Peace and Democracy who, with the Ergada, the Somali Peace and Development Society, the Somali Peace Initiative, and Somalis in UNOSOM, formed an *ad hoc* peace coalition of Somalis at the Addis Ababa meeting in March.

The SDRA has had an influential role in the Sanaag peace process, particularly between the Issaq and Dolbahunte. Mohamoud Jama, as early as September 1992, wrote to the UN for assistance to fund a meeting in Sanaag, and was one of the first to record the meetings. They have been proactive in the cause of peace and have been the channel for funds from the Life and Peace Institute for the Sanaag Peace meeting.

SDRA formed one of the groups of 'intellectuals', observing and supporting the peace conference in Sanaag. Other (though less well-defined groups) existed among the other clans.

It can be seen from this that the conference involved a wide range of different interest groups.

5.13 Consensus Decision-Making

A fundamental principle of the conference is that all decisions should be achieved by consensus, rather than through voting. It is believed that voting, even if only one person is in disagreement, can leave a grievance. A consensus decision results in a 'win-win' situation and is considered more sustainable.

5.14 Problem-Solving

An important feature of the way that elders work at problem-solving is their ability to deconstruct a problem and solve first those issues which are deemed solvable. As

93

Diagram 13: Shir Nabadeedka ee Sanaag

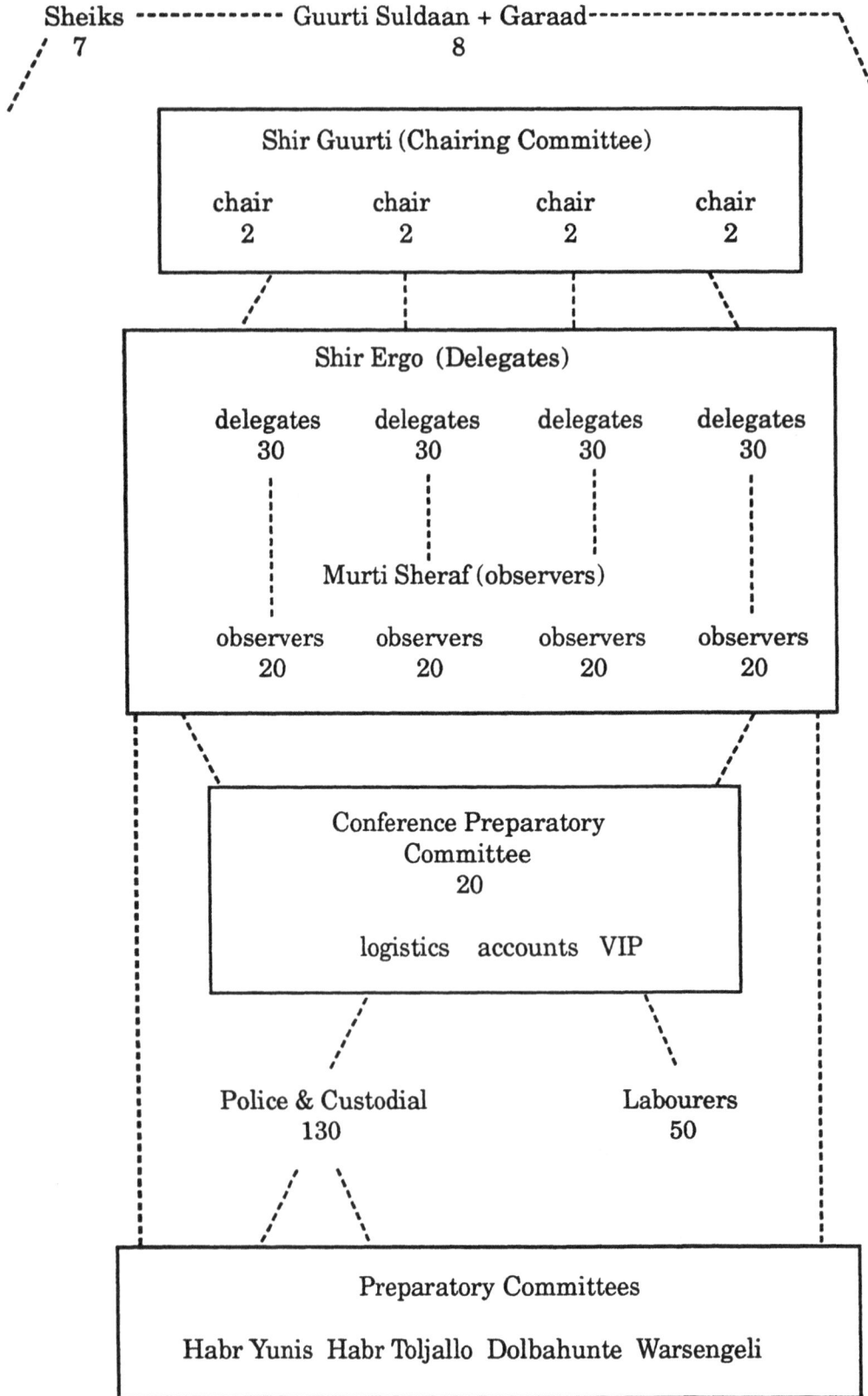

Sheiks - - - - - - - - - Guurti Suldaan + Garaad - - - - - - - - - - - - - -
7   8

Shir Guurti (Chairing Committee)

chair	chair	chair	chair
2	2	2	2

Shir Ergo (Delegates)

delegates	delegates	delegates	delegates
30	30	30	30

Murti Sheraf (observers)

observers	observers	observers	observers
20	20	20	20

Conference Preparatory
Committee
20

logistics   accounts   VIP

Police & Custodial   Labourers
130   50

Preparatory Committees

Habr Yunis Habr Toljallo Dolbahunte Warsengeli

94

described above, the whole reconciliation process itself from the beginning was constructed around that principle, so that through a series of preparatory meetings problems were dealt with along the way.

The first week of the Sanaag conference was spent reading over the agreements that had been reached by the preceding meetings, electing a chair, and agreeing on the agenda and the rules for the meeting. The second week was set aside for the individual clans to hold their meetings and to solve any outstanding issues that had not been solved during their previous meetings, or that had arisen since.

The meeting was structured in a way that recognised the different relationships and grievances between the clans and the need for these to be dealt with separately. For example, the Habr Yunis have a different relationship with the Dolbahunte and Warsengeli than with the Habr Toljallo. The Habr Yunis share common boundaries with the Dolbahunte and Warsengeli and a different set of rules (*xeer*) thus governs their relationships than those with the Habr Toljallo. The Habr Yunis have intermarried more with the Warsengeli than the Habr Toljallo have. Within the Habr Yunis there are also different relationships. The Musa Arreh, for example, who live in Mait, share no common borders with the Darod, so the rules which govern their relationship are different from those of the Musa Ismael.

As indicated above, competition over the ownership and usage of land and resources was a driving force behind the war. The various clans who share boundaries will have different land issues to resolve. For example, the Masagan valley was developed for farming by the Dolbahunte prior to the war, having previously been grazing land used by the Musa Ismael (Habr Yunis). The Musa Ismael recaptured it from the Dolbahunte during the war. Who the land now belongs to must be sorted out by the Musa Ismael and Dolbahunte themselves. Other clans would not intervene unless asked to.

The Habr Yunis and the Warsengeli similarly have specific problems to resolve. The Habr Yunis and Warsengeli own the largest numbers of houses in Erigavo. Return of property was therefore a big issue for these two clans. In contrast, the Dolbahunte and Warsengeli do not share a common border and there were fewer contentious issues to resolve.

The elders understand that different problems exist between different groups. During the war the *xeer* which governed those relationships was broken. It is much more traumatic to be in conflict with a neighbour than with a stranger. Repairing that relationship is likely to be much harder. Time was therefore set aside for the clans to discuss their problems in separate meetings, and more time was given to those clans with a greater number of more difficult problems to solve. For example, the Dolbahunte and Habr Toljallo took two days to reconfirm their previous agreements, while the Habr Yunis and Warsengeli were given four days.

Interestingly, it was said that the Issaq (Habr Yunis and Habr Toljallo) had not settled their own problems before the meeting, and it had been agreed to deal with them once the meeting was concluded. The reason for this was not clear. In 1991, they made a list of their grievances and demands (*diya* blood payments, return of looted items, etc.). It was perhaps felt that solving the larger problems between the Issaq and Darod would help them to solve their internal differences. Moreover, the issues within the Issaq were perhaps clearer and could be more easily settled within the existing rules of *xeer*.

The elders are pragmatic in dealing with problems. It is understood that there are things that can be settled, and there are others that cannot. For example, it was possible to list the grievances between the Habr Yunis and Habr Toljallo, but the grievances between the Issaq and Darod were too many. What happened between the Issaq and Darod therefore had to be dealt with in a different manner. While assets (houses, vehicles, land) can be returned, the norm has been in all such meetings in Somaliland to draw a line under the past and to declare that any homicide that took place before the cease-fire has to be forgotten. Incidents from that time on will be dealt with through joint committees. The principle is to avoid things that will create further problems: a recognition of the limits of law.

From an outsider's perspective, this insistence on forgetting and hiding grievances (institutional amnesia and amnesty) makes it difficult to understand whether trauma is in fact an issue and, if so, how it can be dealt with. It makes it difficult to address issues of war crimes and human rights abuse. History is important in Somali society and feuds can last generations, so it is difficult to see how crimes can be truly forgotten. Perhaps there is in such an agreement a recognition of common guilt.

5.15 Mediation

The primary function of the conference was to provide a forum in which the clans could solve their differences. The conference offered a forum for facilitation rather than mediation. The clans were expected to solve their own problems. At the same time the meeting did provide a structure for mediation. The clans were expected to reaffirm their agreements at the main conference. If they were unable to do this, the *ergo* were given the opportunity to mediate. If they were unable to solve the problem, it went to the Chairing Committee, and if they also were unable to solve it, it passed to the Sultans. The Sultans would if necessary be the final mediators and final decision-makers. However, they prefer to approve decisions, rather than enforce them.

Having an equal number of delegates in each committee was essential for mediation. In Somali society mediators have to be equal in number in order to represent equally the interests of the different parties.

5.16 Resources

The meeting was largely funded by the communities in Sanaag. Some support has been received from ActionAid and the Life and Peace Institute through SDRA. UNOSOM promised to transport 30 tonnes of food for the meeting, donated by the American Embassy in Djibouti, but at the time of the visit this had not been forthcoming.

The funds from the LPI has been used for food, blankets and utensils. Each delegation contributed 75 head of goats, and some fuel. The cost of keeping over 400 delegates was in the region of So.Sh 680,000 ($200) per day. By the end of the second week of meeting they were said to be 60,000,0000 ($20,000) in debt.

96

5.17 Security

By common agreement, all militia were kept away from Erigavo for the duration of the conference. 100 policemen were recruited from the Habr Yunis (50) and Habr Toljallo (50) for the meeting. They were identified by red arm bands. They were the only people allowed to carry guns during the conference. It is significant that the security police were provided by the Habr Yunis and Habr Toljallo. Erigavo is traditionally an Issaq town, primarily Habr Yunis. It is customary in Somali society that hosts are responsible for the security of their guests. In providing the security, the Habr Yunis were therefore confirming their role as hosts.

5.18 Defining the Peace

The conference in Erigavo was first and foremost a peace meeting between the clans. However, if peace is merely defined as an absence of armed conflict, then peace could be said to have been established by the cease-fire agreed between the clans in 1991. However, a cease-fire is only the first part, a precursor to peaceful cooperation. Peace has to be built upon and institutionalised. The series of peace meetings that were concluded prior to the Erigavo conference laid down the parameters for sustaining new relations and peaceful cooperation, namely the rights to:

- freedom of movement
- freedom of trade
- access to common grazing areas
- access to common water sources
- return of property.

5.19 Property Issues

It has been assumed that sorting out issues of property and land rights will be problematic in any peace process in Somalia. In Erigavo, this appears to have been less of an issue than one might assume. In principle it is an issue open to negotiation. In Erigavo it was consistently stressed that people who live (or lived) together know who owns what. People distinguish between private and common property, in the same way that pastoralists distinguish between common and private wells. For example, in Sanaag on the Guban coastal plain where water is abundant, no specific rights are exerted over wells; on the Ogo plateau small lineage groups exert some ownership rights; in the dry Haud individuals exert rights over wells.

Houses and movable property such as animals and vehicles are relatively easy to deal with. The owners are known. The issue, once the principle is agreed that property should be returned, is partly a private matter. For example, a person whose house has been captured or squatted in by another may negotiate for its return and agree to pay some money to the squatters for 'looking after' the property. Other property may have been protected by affinal relatives, in which case the return of that property is easy. By the start of the peace meeting many people had already begun to exchange property — animals and movable assets.

A more problematic issue is land. As described above, some of the valleys of Sanaag had been expropriated by others prior to the war for farming land, and the war had

97

been partly fought over this issue. In Sanaag a major issue will be the farms and grazing areas which the Habr Yunis have declared as rightfully theirs and which used to be farmed by the Darod. The significance of the land issue was made clear by the fact that fencing of enclosures was going on in Erigavo town even during the conference. Equally significant will be the lands of (23) former cooperatives and reserve areas which were declared open at the Dararweyne meeting. Closures and exclosures will ultimately damage the interests of the pastoralists, and affect their coping strategies, by restricting their movement.

Somali pastoralism is a highly developed system of range management that utilises resources which other modes of production may not be able to utilise so effectively. The conflict in Sanaag has had an effect on the relationship between different interest groups and how they perceive the management of resources in the future. The changing population and market forces will bring new investment strategies and changes in the use of rangeland resources. One is likely to see greater 'opportunistic' development or exploitation of resources by wealthy people wanting to invest in the region, now they can no longer invest in the south. The extent to which the meeting in Erigavo, and any peace meeting, is able to address these long-term issues will be crucial for future peace in the region.

5.20 Commonality of Interests

Why, after all the years of repression, death and mistrust, should people in Sanaag want to restore peace? What are the common interests among people that motivate the desire for peace?

Because the war has been fought along clan lines, analysis of the conflict to date has tended to emphasise the agnatic relationships and conflict-prone nature of the segmentary clan system. We tend to look at the clan system vertically. However, clans segment through marriage and demographic growth. Too much emphasis on the agnatic links means that we forget the affinal links. Some Somalis have joked that 'Habr' ('mother', e.g. Habr Toljallo, Habr Yunis, Habr Awal) is the problem. While this recognises the problem of the segmentation of clans, it is perhaps also a comment on the fact that it is difficult to be hostile to someone to whom one is related. What was consistently stressed at the Erigavo conference was the affinal links and the high level of inter-marriage between the clans. The Issaq and Darod clans in Sanaag are closely linked through marriage. The Habr Yunis in particular are intermarried with the Warsengeli and Dolbahunte.

Another motivation for the conference was economic, and had to do with trade, access to grazing lands, and access to water. In a sense the conference was a business meeting. The Issaq need to cooperate with the Dolbahunte and Warsengeli in order for business, trade, economic recovery, rehabilitation and development to happen and be sustained. The Habr Yunis also need the freedom to move southwards through Dolbahunte territory to their grazing lands in the Haud.

One of the effects of war is to undermine people's 'coping mechanisms' or 'survival strategies'. 'Low-intensity' warfare, which typifies much of the armed conflicts in the world today, in which 90 per cent of deaths are civilians, aims to destroy the social fabric of communities and cooperation — the first level of coping strategies. In the harsh post-war environment in Sanaag region, peaceful cooperation, which allows for the resumption of trade and sharing of resources, is in itself a survival strategy.

5.21 Local Government

The second item on the agenda of the conference was the establishment of a regional administration. What kind of administration will emerge was not clear and was up for debate. The most likely structure will be one that mirrors the one developed for central government, with a council of elders and an executive administrative body.

The challenge for NGOs working in Sanaag is going to be how to work with any new administration that is formed. The elders kept the 'politicians' out of the peace meetings, because making peace was not their 'job'. Now it will be the job of the politicians to run the administration, and the elders are likely to point the NGOs towards supporting the administration in order to build upon or strengthen the peace. As the situation in Somaliland changes, NGOs will have to adapt their practices from one in which there was no functional government, to one in which there is a representative government starting to function.

Sanaag may offer a way of dealing with this change. In addition to the regional administration, the innovative addition that was being considered in Erigavo was the formation of a 'Development Committee', or 'intellectuals committee'. The function of this committee would be to act as advisers to the elders and the administration, to gather data on the needs of the region, and seek funding for regional development. It was been proposed that each clan would pay the salary of one graduate for one year to represent them on this committee. The name being proposed by SDRA was the 'Peace, Planning and Economic Committee'.

5.22 Peace and Development

In Sanaag region a process is underway to rebuild a community damaged by war. The model suggested by the Sanaag Conference is that peace and stability can only grow by building peace from the grassroots. The model suggests that a locally initiated process is likely to be most sustainable. It also suggests that efforts by NGOs in Somaliland should be directed towards supporting these processes at the periphery.

For the purpose of this report, what is perhaps most striking when looking at the peace meeting in Sanaag is that processes used in peace-making, or peace-building are similar to those we look for in a sustainable development projects: a long-term process, community participation, community support, legitimate representation, traditional (indigenous) ways of doing things, common goals, and community ownership of the process. In this sense the NGO approach to self-reliant sustainable development is not so far removed from peace-making or peace-building. The goals of justice and development are surely common to both. Once this is understood, it does not require too great a leap of imagination to begin to look at ways in which NGOs can both support and learn from peace-making activities in Somaliland.

99

6 CONCLUSIONS AND RECOMMENDATIONS

The purpose of this report was to help to strengthen agencies' analysis of the situation in Somalia and Somaliland and to identify options for them to consider in supporting peace and reconciliation. With regard to the first task, I hope that the report will, if not strengthen, then at least widen their framework of analysis and understanding. The second task is more problematical.

From an anthropological perspective, Somali society works on a system of balanced oppositions between groups, orchestrated through, and institutionalised in, a segmentary kinship system and traditional laws and procedures laid down in a 'social contract' (xeer). This system is inherently unstable and therefore prone to conflict. If peace is thought to exist where there is an equitable balance, anything which upsets the balance will continue the conflict. The danger inherent in any 'intervention', be it foreign military or humanitarian aid, or externally initiated peace conferences, is that they can upset that balance. Agencies need to be conscious of this when supporting peace-making processes.[53]

A response to conflict depends on how one defines peace-making and peace. It is unlikely that 'peace', in the sense of a total absence of conflict, can exist in Somalia or Somaliland, or for that matter in other societies. How then does one define 'peace' and 'peace-making'?

6.1 What is Peace?

The following definitions of 'peace' were recorded by participants in Oxfam's workshop on Conflict and Peace in Hargeisa:

a) Types of Peace

badbaado	- safety
amaan	- security
degganaansho	- stability
samaan	- well-being
ladnaan	- well-being
xasi llooni	- stability
gallad	- blessing
salaamad	- peace
naruuro	- prosperity
nasteexo	- prosperity
badhaadho	- prosperity
barwaaqo	- prosperity
nabad-raadin	- peace-making
nabad-doon	- peace-maker
nabad-ilaalin	- peace-keeping
isafgarad	- understanding
heshiis	- agreement

b) The characteristics of peace and conflict

Nabad (Peace)	Colaad (Conflict)
Plentiful food	Famine
Milk	Drought
Rest	Poverty
Rain	War widows
Prosperity	Orphans
Helping	Displacement
Marriage	Divorce
High productivity	Refugees
Dances	Death
Harmony	Dispersal of family
Dialogue	Disability
Exports	Looting
Songs	Poor economy
Festivals	Hate
Conflict resolution	Lack of trust
Happiness	Destruction
Health	Lower birth rate
Imports	More weapons
Sound body and mind	No education
Tourists	No health
Schools	No accountability
Education	Disorder
Money	Chaos
Telephones	
No foreign troops	
Family reunions	
Free movement	
Ghee	
Lots of camels and sheep	
Livestock trading	
Less killing of livestock	

It was clear for those participants of the workshop that 'peace' involved more than an absence of conflict, as the Somali saying *nabad iyo caano* (peace and milk, i.e prosperity) implies.

6.2 What is Peace-Making?

If Somali society is said to be conflict-prone, then mechanisms also exist within Somali society to mitigate and resolve conflicts. Dialogue, the mediation of elders, religious sanctions, compensation, and indeed military strength are all traditional means for resolving conflicts. It is clear from the previous section that these means are currently in use in Somaliland. It would be wrong to think of these 'traditional' means of conflict-resolution as reactionary. They are dynamic, being updated and adapted to current needs. The people who understand this best are Somalis. Indeed, Somalis are as experienced at peace-making and conflict-resolution as they are at

101

making war. The models of Boroma and Sanaag suggest that reconciliation will be achieved only through a process which is 'bottom-up', that is one which is initiated and controlled by the participants. Again this was expressed clearly by the participants of the workshop in Hargeisa, when they contrasted the characteristics of a Somali peace meeting (*shir* Somali) with that of a UN peace meeting (*shir* UN):

Shir Somaali

- Involves legitimate representatives
- Uses traditional methods of problem-solving
- Uses experienced mediators (e.g. elders)
- Elders chosen by the community
- Involves the 'real actors'
- Community has confidence in representatives
- Elders have authority
- Held inside the country
- Common agenda/goal: peace
- Limited agenda
- Common rules, values (*xeer*)
- Ability of elders to enforce/ensure implementation of agreements
- Meetings structured to separate problems
- Consensus decision-making
- Equal representation by parties
- Community support, shared expenses
- Open time-table
- Traditional role of hosts and guests

Shir UN

- Lack of confidence in representatives
- Held outside the country
- Involves politicians, not elders
- Unequal representation
- Lack of understanding of the problem(s)
- External, rather than internal, support
- Lack of confidence in organisers/facilitators
- Lack of common *xeer*
- Short time-table

While the Addis Ababa meeting involved a broad range of representatives (religious leaders, elders, women, intellectuals), those who made decisions and signed the agreements were the politicians, or 'warlords'. Such people were consciously excluded from the peace meetings in Somaliland. On the other hand, the Addis Ababa conference did receive international recognition and therefore the possibility of international support, while the Boroma conference was not accorded international recognition, and therefore Somaliland is unlikely to receive the same level of international support for rehabilitation and recovery.

6.3 Options for Agencies Working in Somalia/Somaliland

The spectrum of peace-making is wide, and can range from physical to social rehabilitation. Relief work, if it helps to promote a return to a stable environment, can be considered part of a peace-making process. If relief becomes a source of conflict, then it is not contributing towards a peaceful and stable situation. It is a premise of this report that peace and stability, a return to constructive relationships, is a pre-requisite for long-term sustainable development. This also seems to be the understanding of the elders at Boroma and in Sanaag.

The question for relief and development agencies is to identify the level or levels at which they can support peace-making. The analysis in this report of efforts at peace-making in Somalia and Somaliland suggests that the most sustained and successful efforts at peace and reconciliation are those where people have been able to rebuild their relations of trust from the bottom upwards, as in Somaliland. It is a slow process. The aim should be to support, promote, or build upon local initiatives, working at the periphery to restore and empower the indigenous forms of peace-making and conflict-resolution.

In conclusion, the answer perhaps is to approach conflict-resolution and peace-making in the same way that one approaches development: in a style that is 'bottom-up' and 'participatory', allowing a relatively long time scale, and enabling participants themselves to control the process. In this sense agencies could usefully begin by assessing all their work in Somalia and Somaliland in terms of the extent to which they are helping to strengthen local institutions and promote a peaceful environment. Peace-building, rather than peace-making, is perhaps the level at which agencies should be working.

6.4 Recommendations

Demobilisation: As proposed above, the agencies present in Somaliland should make a substantial commitment to supporting the demobilisation process there.

Somaliland Programmes: The political, economic and military situation in Somaliland is different from that in Somalia. Somalia and Somaliland should be treated separately. Agencies should invest in strengthening their programmes in Somaliland and the capacity of their staff there to respond to the needs in Somaliland.

Advocacy: One advantage of UN peace-making efforts over indigenous ones is that they receive international support. Agencies should advocate international acceptance of the legitimacy of indigenous peace processes. They might consider commissioning further research, such as that initiated by ActionAid in Sanaag, on indigenous peace-making processes in Somalia, and feeding back the findings to UNOSOM and the international community.

Consultations: Agencies should consider supporting further 'peace workshops' in Somaliland, specifically for Somali staff of international NGOs and Somali NGOs as a means of strengthening the capacity of these NGOs and promoting dialogue and an exchange of ideas throughout Somaliland.

Agencies might also consider supporting a workshop for Somali women, from Somalia and Somaliland. This might best done as a workshop for Women of the Horn of Africa and might aim to identify broad issues affecting women throughout the Horn. Extending the scope to 'Women of the Horn' might help it to deflect some internal conflict.

Agencies might consider holding a Peace Workshop on Somalia, at which current research on and experiences of doing peace-work in Somalia and Somaliland could be presented. It might help to develop a framework and rationale for future NGO peace work in Somalia and Somaliland. It would also help to promote a more positive image of Somalia. As much work has been done, both practical and academic, by Somalis, the workshop should concentrate on their work. One could usefully consider bringing people in from other conflict situations, to share experiences.

The workshops might form part of the consultation process suggested for Somalia. Conversations with Somaliland elders suggested that they might be prepared to assist in consultations with groups in the south. This would depend, however, on the extent to which they felt they have solved their own problems.

Cultural Activities: Poetry and songs are extremely powerful media of communication in Somali society. Poetry in particular can greatly influence attitudes and situations. The peace conferences in Boroma and Sanaag both utilised poets. Agencies might consider sponsoring a Somali peace poetry competition, with the best entries broadcast over the radio, BBC Somali Service, and Addis Ababa Voice of Peace. This could be a high-profile media peace initiative. As with poetry at peace meetings, it could help to influence the situation psychologically. Ergada, the editors of *Hal Abuur* magazine, and Zeinab Jama have expressed an interest in such an exercise.

The agencies should consider promoting other Somali cultural activities, such as songs, music and theatre, both within Somalia and Somaliland and outside. Magazines such as *Hal-Abuur* should also be supported. Such activities can help to promote a more positive image of Somalia.

POSTSCRIPT

Several significant developments have taken place since Mark Bradbury submitted his report in October 1993.

1 On 3-4 October several US servicemen and numerous Somalis were killed in the Bakhara Market in Mogadishu, when US special forces attempted to capture the leaders of General Aideed's Somali National Alliance. As a result, the USA and UN took the decision to wind down their military operations in Somalia. In Mogadishu itself, UN and US forces have been largely confined to barracks, and only minimal protection has been offered to humanitarian agencies.

2 US policy is motivated by the attempt to withdraw completely from Somalia with some measure of honour. A temporary build-up of the use of military hardware was accompanied by an announcement that all US forces would be withdrawn by 31 March 1994. At the same time, greater diplomatic emphasis was put on scaling down the conflict with Aideed and the SNA. Much of this work was carried out by ex-Ambassador Oakley. It led ultimately to the withdrawal of the warrant for Aideed's arrest, and the release in January 1994 of all detainees held by the UN, among them several of Aideed's key aides.

3 The US decision to withdraw by the end of March 1994 was quickly followed by similar decisions by the Belgians, Germans, Swedes, and Italians — indeed, by all the European forces under the UN umbrella. As a result of these unilateral decisions, the UN has been forced to scale down its whole peace-enforcement operation in Somalia, with a target of approximately 18,000 troops on the ground after March 1994.

4 The impending withdrawal of the US and European contingents from UNOSOM created expectations of a drastic deterioration in security, and renewed clan fighting. However, while there has been an upsurge in random banditry, there has also been a quiet but noticeable increase in political 'peace-making' discussions between key clan groups and warlords — notably between Aideed's and Ali Mahdi's sub-clans. The combination of these renewed discussions, fuelled by a strong reaction against what is regarded as foreign interference in Somali affairs, plus a general public revulsion at the thought of renewed fighting, and the release of detainees by the UN, has engendered a more positive mood in Mogadishu and southern Somalia. It is interesting (and very much confirms the key thesis of this report) that *internal* processes now offer the best hope of improving the overall political and security situation. It is possible that the UN-sponsored humanitarian and peace meetings which took place in Addis Ababa between 30 November and 2 December 1993 contributed to this process, but there is little hard evidence for this, especially as some of the main Somali leaders did not attend, or attended only some short sessions.

5 Progress towards setting up District and Regional Councils (with a view to establishing a Transitional National Council by March 1995) continues, but at a slower pace. It is not yet clear how the various peace-making initiatives on the part of the clans will mesh in with the UN process of re-establishing civilian structures.

This will be one of the challenges for the future. Agency work in rehabilitation and development continues, as the security situation allows, and the challenge here will be to work out ways in which these activities can be taken on and taken over by genuine, popular Somali institutions.

Roger Naumann
Regional Manager for the Horn of Africa
Oxfam (UK and Ireland)
February 1994

NOTES

1 Unless otherwise stated, 'Somalia' refers to the territories of the Republic of Somalia, which include the (as yet) unrecognised 'Somaliland Republic'.

2 Some people have tried to apply a neo-Marxist analysis to explain the conflict, which makes a distinction between 'clanism' as ideological construct, and kinship, which represents 'basic values of society'. (Comment by A.I. Samatar at the European Somali Studies Association, September 1993.)

3 Oxfam Strategic Intent, 1993, statement of belief on poverty and avoidable suffering.

4 The precise make-up of these alliances has changed throughout the war.

5 Behind this move were Hassan Dhimbil Warsame (Habr Gedir/Ayr), Musse Nur Amin (Galjaal), and Mohamed Goodah Barre (Xawadle) (*Horn of Africa Bulletin*, April 1993.)

6 It is suggested that due to the preference shown to General Abshir by the UN, he has lost much credibility among the Somalis.

7 SWB = Survey of World Broadcasting.

8 Unconfirmed reports say that four American soldiers killed by a land mine on 8 August 1993, seven Nigerian troops killed on 5 September, and a helicopter crew killed in September were also mutilated.

9 *Horn of Africa Bulletin*, March-April 1993.

10 I did not meet anyone from the Justice Division, or anyone who was able to provide information on their work. This in itself indicates a lack of information-sharing in UNOSOM.

11 From UNOSOM Staffing Concept paper, June 1993.

12 It has been suggested that recent US policy in Somalia is to enable the Darod (primarily the Majeerteen) to regain power. If true, this may lie behind the dispute between UNOSOM and the Somaliland administration of Egal.

13 Reported by US lawyer Professor Tom Farer, *The Independent*, September 1993.

14 *Africa Confidential*, 30 July 1993.

15 Comment passed to me by Life and Peace Institute.

16 Comment by Dr Ahmed Yusuf Farah (see Part V).

17 Ecumenical Liaison Committee for Assistance to Somalia.

18 Jan Eliasson: Report to the UN ECOSOC, 21 July 1993.

19 This is a very rough division, especially as many groups practise both agriculture and transhumant pastoralism.

20 'Harti' is commonly used in the south to refer to the Warsengeli Dolbahunte and Majeerteen; in Kismayo it is the Majeerteen who are most significant.

21 I cannot confirm either of these historiographies, but it is interesting that people refer back to agreements of nearly 70 years ago, indicating the depth and protracted nature of the conflict.

22 The information in this section is largely based on interviews with the Zone Director.

23 Omar Moalim, an Ogadeni, was deputy PM in Ali Mahadi's administration of 1991. He was MP for Jamaama in the 1960s.

24 It is understood that the accord was signed between representatives of the following: SNF (Marehan), SPM (Awlihan, Bartiri, Jidwak), SSDF (Majeerteen), SNDU (Lelkasse, Awr Tabley), and Tuni and Banjuni, USC/SNA (Mohamed Zubeir, Sheikal, Galgaal, Habr Gedir), and SSNM (Biyamal).

25 General Abshir, a consistent critic of Barre, and moderate politician, has lost credibility among many Somalis for the preferential treatment shown to him by UNOSOM.

26 Alliances change quickly. Since the outbreak of fighting between UNOSOM and Aideed, Abdillahi Yusuf has sought to distance himself from Aideed, and play down their agreement. General Abshir has also commented that he and Abdillahi Yusuf have resolved their differences.

27 He is said to own UNICEF and ICRC offices in Kismayo, to have built Kismayo hospital and Afgoi hospital, and a number of mosques in Mogadishu.

28 The Zone Director also had fundamental doubts about the 'colonial' model of administration proposed by UNOSOM.

29 North-east Somalia, home to the Majeerteen, has also been largely free of conflict since 1990.

30 This idea is not supported by some historians and social scientists.

31 Comment by Garaad Abdulgani of the Dolbahunte.

32 It has been observed that these values have been destroyed in the south, where women, children, and prisoners have died in the carnage. While the rights of women, children, and prisoners were abused by the Somali army, the belief is that these standards of behaviour were adhered to by the northern clans.

33 A classic example of this happened in Jidalle, in Sanaag region, in 1992, when the Warsengeli and Habr Yunis (Issaq) held a peace meeting. The representatives of the Habr Yunis included a former SNM Commander and member of the SNM Central Committee, who attended the meeting as a representative of the SNM. The response of the Warsengeli was to argue that if they were to meet a political party (i.e. the SNM), then they would represent the 'Warsengeli Government'. The only way in which they were able to proceed with negotiation was to meet as two clans. As political parties they did not have the means to solve their problems.

34 Legends of warrior women, as in Islam, exist in Somali folklore.

35 Zeinab Jama has collected a number of war poems by women.

36 Interviews with SOMRA and Somaliland Women's Organisation.

37 Women are now more vulnerable to the religious movements than during Barre's regime. Under Scientific Socialism, women were given rights of inheritance, which goes against Islamic Law. Some eight Sheiks who opposed this law were executed by Barre when it was introduced. He revoked these laws in 1990. Therefore, while women's responsibilities have increased as a result of the war, they have also lost certain rights.

38 Reported by Zeinab Jama.

39 Article 10 of the National Charter.

40 Interestingly, the term Khussusi, from the Arabic *khas* ('special') was the name given by Sayid Mohamed Abdulla Hassan (the 'Mad Mullah') to his top council of advisers.

41 Musa Bihi is particularly unpopular with the Habr Yunis. As Minister for Interior, and head of the technical committee for disarmament, his personal dispute with the Habr Yunis could be a source of problems in the disarmament process.

42 Some serious questions need to be asked about why the UN is prepared to sanction the division of former eastern European countries, such as Yugoslavia, but not Somalia.

43 Interview with Hargeisa UNOSOM Zone Director, Keith Beavan.

44 Among the Majeerteen in the north-east, the bandits are known as *jiri*, the name of a bird. In the south they are known as the *morihan*, i.e. those who smoke

marijuana.

45 Reported by UNDP-OPS demobilisation consultants.

46 Reported by Omar Halim, UNOSOM Director of Policy Planning Group, July 1993.

47 The Somali anthropologist Dr Ahmed Musa Farah, working with I.M. Lewis, has undertaken a comprehensive study of the peace process in Sanaag and the role of the elders. The study, commissioned by ActionAid, will add extremely important information for our understanding of peace and peace-making in Somaliland and Somalia.

48 The study of Dr Ahmed Musa Farah has identified that it is in fact at the level of the *diya*-paying groups that the reconciliation process has been most effective. Reconciliation between the *diya*-paying groups has therefore provided the basic building blocks for a wider peace process.

49 The Garaad is said to have appointed his son to replace his brother.

50 The Manifesto Group were a group of politicians, elders, and businessmen, who petitioned Barre to step down peacefully in 1990.

51 See 1.3 above for characteristics of elders.

52 He was offered the post of Minister of Justice by Egal, but was asked by his clan to turn it down.

53 I was reminded of this when I learned that after my visit to the Sanaag peace conference, some questions were raised over the purpose of my visit there. There was some suspicion that I was 'spying' for the Hargeisa government. My mistake was not in visiting, asking questions, or showing an interest, but in not following the correct protocol in contacting people. Clearly there is a need to be sensitive.

REFERENCES

African Rights (May 1993), *Operation Restore Hope: A Preliminary Assessment*, London.

African Rights (July 1993), *Somalia: Human Rights Abuses by the United Nations Forces*, London.

Africa Watch (1990), *Somalia: A Government at War with its People*, The Africa Watch Committee, New York, Washington, London.

Africa Watch (1993), *Beyond the Warlords*, New York..

Agerbak, L. (1991), 'Oxfam's Work in Conflict: 1978/9-1988/90', unpublished paper, Oxfam (UK/I), Oxford.

Bradbury, M. (1993), 'Development in Conflict: Experiences of ActionAid in Somalia', a report to the Responding to Conflict Unit, Woodbrooke College, and ActionAid.

Boutros-Ghali, B. (1992), 'An Agenda for Peace', United Nations, New York.

Cassanelli, L.V. (1982), *The Shaping of Somali Society*, University of Pennsylvania Press, Philadelphia.

Compagnon, D. (1990), 'The Somali opposition fronts: some comments and questions', *Horn of Africa*, Vol XIII, Nos 1 and 2.

Drysdale, J. (1992), in Andrew Shepard (ed.): *Dream of Development, UNDP Project Plan 1983-1986*.

Duffield, M. (1990), *War and Famine in Africa*, Oxfam (UK/I), Oxford.

ELCAS (July 1993), Report of ELCAS Officer for Somalia, F. K. Pruller.

Fisher, S. (1993), 'Mediation and Training Agencies', unpublished paper, Oxfam (UK/I), Oxford.

Helander, B. (1992), 'The decline of clanship in Somalia', *Somalia News Update*, October 1992.

Human Rights Watch (1993), *Human Rights and UN Field Operations*, New York.

Lederach, J.P. (1989), 'NGOs and Peacemaking: A Prospect for the Horn', Horn of Africa Project, Institute of Peace and Conflict Studies, Conrad Grebel College, Ontario.

Lewis, I.M. (1961), *A Pastoral Democracy: A Study of Pastoralism and Politics among the Northern Somali of the Horn of Africa*, Oxford University Press, Oxford.

Médecins Sans Frontières France (1993), 'Communication on the Violations of Humanitarian Law in Somalia during UNOSOM operations', New York.

Menkhaus, K. (1993), 'Foreign Assistance in the Lower Jubba Valley: The Past Record', UNOSOM Lower Jubba Strategy Briefing Paper #3.

Omaar, R. (1993), 'The Best Chance for Peace', *Africa Report*.

Oxfam (UK/I) (1993), 'From Village Council to United Nations: Oxfam's Strategic Intent 1994-1999', Oxford.

Roseveare, N. (1993), 'Demobilisation: Post-Conflict Issues and Work', An Oxfam Review, unpublished, Oxfam (UK/I), Oxford.

Samatar, Said S. (1991), *Somalia: A Nation in Turmoil*, Minority Rights Group, London.

Third World Institute (1992), *Third World Guide (1991/92)*, Instituto del Tercer Mundo, Montevideo.

UN (March 1993), UN Security Council Resolution 813 (93).

Vizman, E. (July and August 1993), SITREPS of the International NGO Consortium, Mogadishu.

Watson, M. (1990), *Collapse of Somalia and the Science of Governance*, Management Resource Limited.

APPENDIX A

AGENCIES AND INDIVIDUALS INVOLVED IN PEACE WORK IN SOMALIA AND SOMALILAND

ActionAid
Hamlyn House
Archway
London N16 9HL
UK

Tel: 071-281-4101

African Rights
11 Marshalsea Road
London SE1 1EP
UK

Tel: 071-403-3383
Fax: 071-403-4023

Africa Watch
1522 K Street, NW #910
Washington
DC 20005
USA

Tel: (202) 371-6592A
Fax: (202) 371-0124

Amnesty International
International Secretariat
1 Easton Street
London WC1X 8DJ
UK

Tel: 071-413-5500
Fax: 071-956-1157

Bread for the World
802 Rhode Island Avenue, NE
Washington
DC 20018
USA

Tel: (010-1) 202 269-0200
Fax: (010-1) 202 529-8546

Coalition for Peace in the Horn of Africa
c/o Centre of Concern
3700 13th Street NE
Washington
DC 20017
USA

Tel: (202) 635-2757

Community Aid Abroad
156 George Street
Fitzroy
Victoria 3065
Australia

Tel: (010-61) 3-419-7111
Fax: (010-61) 3-419-5318

Christian Aid
Inter-Church House
35-41 Lower Marsh
Waterloo
London SE1 7RT
UK

Tel: 071-620-4444
Fax: 071-620-0719

Ecumenical Liaison Committee for Assistance to Somalia (ELCAS)
c/o Catholic Relief Services
11 Rue de Cornavin
1201 Geneva
Switzerland

Tel: 41-22-731-46-54
Fax: 41-22-738-48-14

(Includes CRS, Lutheran World Relief and Lutheran World Federation, Norwegian Church Aid, Trocaire, Caritas, Swedish Church Relief, and Christian Aid.)

**ERGADA: Somali Peace and
Consultation Committee**
c/o Mennonite Central Committee
Eastern Mennonite College
Harrisonberg
Virginia
USA

Tel: 703 432 4452
Fax: 703 432 4449

Hal Abuur
Journal of Somali Literature and
Culture
PO Box 3476
London SE15 5QP
UK

Tel: 071-277-1399
Fax: 071-372-6101

Horn of Africa Project
Institute of Peace and Conflict Studies
Conrad Grebel College
Waterloo
Ontario N2L 3G6
Canada

Tel: (010-1) 519-885-0220 (ext. 257)
Fax: (010-1) 519-885-0014

Professor I.M. Lewis
London School of Economics
Houghton Street
London WC2
UK

Tel: 071-405-7686
Fax: 071-242-0392

Life and Peace Institute
Horn of Africa Project
Box 297
S-751 05
Uppsala
Sweden

Tel: 18-169-542
Fax: 18-693-059

**Mennonite International
Conciliation Service**
Mennonite Central Committee
Eastern Mennonite College
Harrisonberg
Virginia
USA

Tel: 703 432 4452
Fax: 703 432 4449

MSF Spain
PO Box 11188
Nairobi
Kenya

Tel: 560345/564740
Fax: 568297

Nairobi Peace Initiative
PO Box 14894
Nairobi
Kenya

Tel: 254 2-441444/440098
Fax: 254 2-445177

**Ogaal Research and Publishing
Centre**
27 Laneside
Edgware
Middlesex HA8 9PL
UK

Peace Foundation (Africa)
Diakonia House
Naivasha Road
PO Box 60955
Nairobi
Kenya

Tel: 569493
Fax: 569485/569467

People for Peace
1st Floor
Waumani Building
Westlands
PO Box 14877
Nairobi
Kenya

Tel: 441372

Responding to Conflict
Woodbrooke
1046 Bristol Road
Birmingham B29 6LJ
UK

Tel: 021-415-4119
Fax: 021-472-5174

Scottish Action on Somalia
c/o Scottish Education and Action for
Development
23 Castle Street
Edinburgh EH2 3DN
Scotland

Tel: 031-667-5522/031-225-6550
Fax: 031-220-1290

Somalcare
Flat 5
2 Bedford Road
London N15 4HA
UK

Tel: 081-880-1343

Somali Counselling Project
5A-5 Westminster Bridge Road
London SE1 7XW
UK

Tel: 071-620-4589

**Somali Socio-Economic
Development Foundation
(SOMDEF)**
PO Box 73945
Nairobi
Kenya

Tel: 335002,338771
Fax: 331005

Somali Relief Association (SOMRA)
Oxford House
Derbyshire Street
London E2 6HG
UK

Tel: 071-729-3351
Fax: 071-729-0435

SORRA
Mohamed Barod
Hargeisa
Somaliland

Swedish Refugee Council
Torstenssonsgaton 6
5-11456
Stockholm
Sweden

Tel: (010-46) 86-67-68-99
Fax: (010-46) 86-61-65-98

US Committee for Refugees
1025 Vermont Ave., NW Suite 920
Washington
DC 20005
USA

Tel: (202) 347-3507
Fax: (202) 347-3418

Voice of Peace
Broadcasts every day between 2 and 3
pm on the 25 and 31 short-wave metre
bands from Addis Ababa.

APPENDIX B

SOMALILAND COMMUNITIES SECURITY AND PEACE CHARTER

Preamble

As we may all realise, security (of both life and property) and stability are indispensable pillars of the existence of mankind. Naturally, it is also central to the effective functioning of any central government as well as the attainment of sustainable progress. Moreover, history and experience have also shown us and attest to the fact that the security of the individual, both life and property, that of the community as well as that of the nation, are all inextricably linked together. However, as we may all recognise, historically the world has been subject to subsequent calamities and catastrophes comprising both natural and man-made disasters. These have caused wanton destruction of property and incalculable loss of life, as well as retrogression of both human progress and development.

Unfortunately, Somalia's experience in the recent years is something hitherto unknown to the world. The compounded effects of the disasters that have befallen Somalia have at last resulted in the destruction of the Somali state and the loss of its sovereignty. Furthermore, the Somali citizen has lost all his/her dignity, pride and honour, wherever s/he is in the wider world. This unenviable experience and circumstance that has been the lot of the Somalis for quite some time has resulted from the wilful disregard of justice, and the callous abandonment of all due processes of law, gross human rights violations as well as the criminal neglect of all the obligations of the government towards its citizens, including provision of basic social services.

It is after these events and agonising realities that the Somaliland Communities have declared an independent state. In addition to this, the other crucial issues that the communities also agreed upon include the promotion and strengthening of security and stability, maintenance of peace and the establishment as well as enhancement of peaceful co-existence among all of the communities of Somaliland. However, failure to realise these goals has perhaps dictated the collapse of the government that has been established. As the President of Somaliland has highlighted in his speech to the Grand Conference of the Elders in Boroma, lack of security was the single most important factor that dictated the failure of the government in its effective functioning and execution of its obligations, administration and governance. The President also further reiterated the impossibility of the establishment of any effective government while the security situation remains to be much improved.

As the President has emphasised, and we all concur with him as to its importance, the most relevant question that begs to be asked, therefore, remains to be if any possibility exists of confronting and tackling other daunting issues of national interest and the realisation of the desired cooperation of the Communities of Somaliland while these conditions of insecurity widely prevail? Perhaps the other crucial question we should ask ourselves and ponder on at this juncture is what are the factors that brought about this situation of insecurity in the first place?

To provide genuine answers to these vexed questions it requires us to reflect on the present circumstances that are prevalent in our country and the fundamental issues that brought about in the first place these conditions of instability and conflict as well as their perpetuation.

We all realise that arms and munitions are widely scattered among all the communities, and are mostly in the hands of immature and callous individuals. Among others, these facts have created the following difficulties and problems:

1. The use of these weapons for private interests and, perhaps more damagingly, their use against the Government in order to undermine its authority, not to mention their use in the destruction of the national assets and interests which the Somaliland Communities have wished to safeguard.

2. It has caused a large number of people and communities to become refugees and dislodged from their localities of residence and inhabitance, which in turn resulted in the undermining of security and threatened the peaceful co-existence of communities as well as the smooth movements of people and property.

3. It legalised killing, looting, banditry and a host of other illicit activities and attitudes that go against our cherished culture and sacred religion.

4. It has completely grounded and undermined the functioning of the administrative activities of the government and stopped all other commercial activities, as well as the free movement of people and trade.

5. It curtailed and resulted in the suspension of all the humanitarian, rehabilitation and developmental activities as well as all other assistance of the International Organisations. This has also had a negative and devastating effect on internal support and international recognition.

6. It drastically undermined the realisation of the peace accords that the communities have bilaterally and multilaterally agreed upon.

7. It has brought about for the individual citizen a perpetual fear and terror that bred mental instability and other numerous psychological problems for most of the population.

8. And other numerous problems.

All these critical issues and problems which we have mentioned above and which are all a threat to the security and instability of our nation have been previously given due attention and deliberated several times, as the attempts made towards their solution include:

1. The unification programme of the clan militias.

2. The latest of which was the WFP programme of demobilisation and corralling/kraaling of the militias.

115

3. The organisation of Peace Conferences between and among the communities and localities, including that of SHEEKH, of which the enactment of the resolutions passed remains yet to be seen.

Therefore, in order to realise the aims and objectives of the Somaliland State, and to redress and rectify our past mistakes, it is inevitable that all the issues that are currently outstanding and those potential tensions should be duly addressed and deliberated at this Grand Conference of Somaliland Communities, and all efforts should be directed to finding objective and lasting solutions to all the issues: this should also be witnessed by the international community in order to hasten recognition of our state(hood), increase humanitarian assistance and step up the rehabilitation and reconstruction of the infrastructure and social services institutions.

In view of this, the Grand Conference of Somaliland Communities (in **Boroma**):

After having seen: The recommendations of the Security (issues) Commission.

After hearing: The deliberations, views and recommendations of the Grand Conference.

*After appreciating:*The assessment of the general situation of the security in the country, the following articles of this charter have been hereby adopted:

Article I:
a. GUURTI: Council of Elders at the district, regional and National (Somaliland) levels.

b. BEEL: A community that shares common interest and neighbourhood (residence).

c. DEEGAAN: Locality.

d. DUULAAN: Ten or more persons who share common blood bond or kinship and who harbour interests that do not comply with this accord and the articles of this charter:

Article II:
The people of Somaliland should rely solely on its efforts and resources in maintaining and strengthening the peace and stability that is prevalent in the country.

Since the main threat to peace is at present the armed bandits (budhcad and day-day), the Grand Congress of the Communities of Somaliland hereby agrees that all armed bandits should be vigorously confronted, challenged and dealt with in order to prevent them undermining the prevailing peace and stability.

Article III:
This nation cannot dispense with outside help and assistance. Therefore, we should seek assistance from the International Community, be they governments or International Organisations.

Article IV:
Voluntary Organisations should be approached with the following requests:

1. Establishment of employment opportunities and vocational training projects in various skills and professions.

2. (Assistance in the) Maintenance of a clean environment.

3. Training and upkeep of the local security forces.

Article V:
In cooperation with the International Organisations, mines should be cleared from the roads and all other areas in Somaliland.

Article VI:
All weapons and munitions are a national (state) property. Therefore, their storage, use as well as other decisions relating to them are the sole province and responsibility of the Government (which calls for the following):

1. Firstly, the registration of all arms for the owners is required and called for, and then means and methods of exchanging arms for other useful projects should be given thought to as well as due consideration.

2. Secondly, arms should be forbidden to be carried in the towns and other places of assembly and congregation of people.

Article VII:
If a certain locality, district or a region for that matter is invaded from outside, it is incumbent upon the other Communities of Somaliland to come, in earnest, to its defence in unison and hurry to the rescue of the concerned entity, as such act is recognised as a blatant aggression against Somaliland as a whole.

Article VIII:
It is obligatory upon all the Somaliland Communities to give their utmost assistance and sincere support to any government that is established or chosen through the due process of law, in order to enable it to realise its administrative functions and governance obligations.

Article IX:
In order to realise the establishment of an effective government administration that can fully undertake the maintenance of peace and stability in the country, we propose the following:

1. It is required that each and every community should demobilise its militia and assemble or kraal the combatants in a certain barracks to be established in its locality, and should effectively restrain their movement. This should come into effect 15 days after this charter is ratified and endorsed.

2. It is incumbent upon every community to wage a relentless war against the armed bandits operating in its own locality and to secure and preserve its own security and stability.

117

3. In order to realise the satisfactory accomplishment of the above mentioned conditions, it is required that each community should establish its own local Police Force, which will serve as the basis for the establishment of a National Police Force in the (near) future.

4. Each and every region should start to hasten the operation of its judicial institutions in conjunction with the establishment of the Police Force.

5. The operation, inspection and monitoring of these issues is the responsibility of the committee of elders in each district.

6. An Inspection and Monitoring Committee with the responsibility to check and inspect the operation of the above mentioned obligations should be established (sooner rather than later).

Article X:
Each and every Community which resides in a certain area should establish a Standing Security Committee that will oversee the security matters in its own locality or area.

Article XI:
Each and every community should remove its own militia from the towns and their vicinities, main roads and other certain areas where people gather for social services.

Article XII:
It is obligatory upon each and every community to dismantle and demolish all the check-points established by the bandits and which are in operation in its own locality.

Article XIII:
It is obligatory upon each and every community to effectively safeguard the security in its own locality.

Article XIV:
The safeguarding and upkeep of any public property in a certain district, sub-district or locality, etc is the responsibility of the relevant committee in that area. It is also required that the Security Committee of that area take an inventory of all the public properties existing or found in their areas.

Article XV:
The Communities are hereby allowed to initiate their own by-contracts (xeer-hoosaad) and by-laws. Likewise neighbouring or adjacent communities can establish their own security by-laws that are compatible with this charter.

Article XVI:
Any assistance package (relief or otherwise) that is being assigned or provided for a certain community or locality, but requires to be transported through other areas or communities, should be given safe passage; it is incumbent upon each community to oversee its safe passage and security during the transit period in its locality and pass on this responsibility to its adjacent community, who are also required to do the same until the (assistance) package reaches its destination.

118

Article XVII:
The safeguarding of the security of the Foreign Nationals, and their properties, staying in a certain locality, is the responsibility of the Government and in particular that responsibility falls within the domain of the Security Committee of that area.

Article XVIII:
Each and every community is hereby required and should take a vow and a solemn oath not to attack any other community.

Article XIX:
a. If a conflict flares up between two communities, or if one community harbours a certain grudge against another, it is incumbent upon the Committees of Elders of the two communities to attend to, deliberate and strive to find a mutually acceptable settlement and just solution to the disagreement, whatever its magnitude, and in the shortest possible period of time.

b. If, however, they themselves find it difficult to find a mutually acceptable settlement, they should call upon the assistance of the Committee of Elders of other neighbouring communities.

c. If, again, a settlement is not found at this level, the matter should be referred to the executive committee of the Grand Committee of Elders of Somaliland.

d. The Committee of Elders who are assigned to mediate in the matter are required to address the case as soon as possible and in any case in a period of no longer than 14 days from the date of referral or registration of the case.

Article XX:
a. Every citizen of Somaliland has the right of ownership of his/her own fixed property existing in Somaliland, and no one has the right to misappropriate it or dislodge him/her from the property.

b. The Grand Conference of Peace in Boroma should appoint a committee that will engage itself in and oversee the mediation and settlement of the standing disputes and cases arising out of fixed properties that have been misappropriated (excluding those cases which have been settled already) considering the different circumstances of each locality.

c. Liquid or other movable properties which have been looted or misappropriated should be returned to the rightful owner/s in earnest (excluding those cases that have been already settled).

d. The safe transfer of the fixed and movable properties that have been misappropriated is the responsibility of the Security Committee of the locality in which the property exists or remains at present, with the cooperation of the Committee of Elders of the concerned communities.

Article XXI:
The meeting which the communities in SANAAG are planning to hold on 10-04-1993 should be given support and encouragement and assisted to fruition.

Article XXII:
The Grand Boroma Conference of the Communities in Somaliland should urgently nominate during its meeting a committee of elders that should find a solution and a settlement to the disputes currently outstanding in Awdal, and those of land disputes in Gebiley that are not yet settled, and should accomplish this feat within an assigned (preferably short) period of time.

Article XXIII:
a. A checkpoint and control post can only be established at the entrance and exit points of towns and should have a certain accountable administration.

b. A control post or checkpoint can only be established by someone authorised (by the relevant authority) to do so and must have a certain emblem that can be easily identified.

c. If a new and/or additional control post is needed to be established, it may be done so or established only by the discretion and authority of the Security Committee of the concerned locality.

Article XXIV:
Any damage (to life and property) caused by a certain bandit (budhcad ama day-day) should be accounted from his clan, but any damage against a bandit is non-accountable/accountable to no one (whatever the circumstances are).

Article XXV:
All other accords and charters that are not compatible with the articles of this charter are hereby repealed, rescinded and made null and void.

Article XXVI:
This charter will come into effect 15 days after its ratification and endorsement by the deputations and delegations representing the Communities of Somaliland in Boroma.

Article XXVII:
This charter is bound/bonded by the penal code, the shariah law and the articles of this charter.

(Translation by Mohamed Hamud Sheik)

APPENDIX C

JUBALAND PEACE AGREEMENT

Kismayo International Airport, 6 August 1993

We, the elders, religious leaders, intellectuals, politicians, business people and representatives of women's, youth, and various other interest groups and civic organisations of Jubaland:

Deploring the terrible loss of life and destruction of property resulting from the civil war which has raged throughout the country in general and in Jubaland in particular;

Recognising that continued armed conflict cannot bring about a lasting resolution of our problems;

Further recognising that we are one people having a common territory, religion, history and culture;

Mindful of the need to promote trust amongst one another and of the need for a freely negotiated and lasting peace as the only means to the rehabilitation of our normal daily lives including economic, social and political activities;

Appreciating the assistance provided by UNOSOM II in creating the environment and providing the logistical resources necessary for the peace conference which has culminated in this agreement;

Now, therefore, hereby declare peace throughout Jubaland and affix our signatures to this document signifying our unreserved, wholehearted and indivisible agreement to the provisions contained herein and by so doing pledge our commitment to their complete implementation for the benefit of our posterity and motherland.

1. This Agreement is the culmination of the Conference first begun at Mogadishu on 30 May 1993 to address the problems of Kismayo. A Declaration of Peace was issued on 3 June 1993, and a second phase, involving 152 delegates and approximately 50 observers, commenced at Kismayo International Airport on 23 June 1993.

2. The Delegates set up four Committees which worked on the principal areas of agreement herein, namely:

   a. Cease-fire and Disarmament;
   b. Reopening of Roads;
   c. Reunification of the People and Communities; and
   d. Return of Property.

3. We, the Delegates of the Conference, signatories hereunder, for ourselves and the people and communities of Jubaland whom we represent, hereby agree to the following provisions:

I. Cease-fire and Disarmament

4. All forms of physical and verbal hostility towards one another shall cease immediately and all communities and Districts shall be informed of such cessation within 30 days of the signing of this Agreement. Total disarmament shall be accomplished within 90 days.

5. Encampment sites for the two militia forces shall be established approximately 90 kilometres from Kismayo, that is to say, at Kamtirey to the north and Bulo Haji to the south.

6. There shall be provided rehabilitation of former combatants through reorientation towards civilian life, including vocational training, the fostering of good relations between one another, and the provision of jobs.

7. A regularly-sitting Committee comprising members of the various communities of Jubaland shall be set up to implement cease-fire and disarmament.

8. Violators of the cease-fire shall be prosecuted before a court of law and be liable for payment of blood money, return of property or compensation therefor.

II. Re-opening of Roads

9. All roads are to be free and open to movement of all persons for peaceful purposes and each community shall be held particularly responsible for the safety of the roads in the area it inhabits.

10. A suitably equipped and armed force shall be established to supervise free and peaceful movement on the roads. In this regard, the Delegates call upon the United Nations Operations in Somalia (UNOSOM) to give priority to assisting in the re-establishment of the police as soon as possible, to facilitate the apprehension of bandits.

11. Bandits and those aiding and abetting them shall be punished equally in accordance with Islamic law.

12. Any community or person who arrests an armed bandit shall be eligible for a reward of Somali Shillings 2,000,000. Any person who furnishes information on armed bandits which leads to their arrest shall be eligible for a reward of Somali Shillings 500,000 — 1,000,000. These rewards shall be subject to availability of funds.

13. Each community shall participate in the efficient distribution of humanitarian aid.

14. All dangers and obstacles to free movement such as mines, broken bridges, and impassable roads are to be removed and/or repaired in cooperation with UNOSOM.

III. Reunification of the People and Communities

15. The reunification of the people and communities shall take place within 30 days

of the signing of this Agreement.

16. Security shall be strengthened, and this shall be the responsibility of police and Chiefs of Districts.

17. A regular Committee for Reunification shall be appointed to work in cooperation with broadly-based District and Regional police as well as UNOSOM. This Committee shall determine when it is appropriate for a citizen who owns a house, farm or business in a District to return there, and shall be responsible for ensuring that this provision is fully implemented in cooperation with tribal elders, police and UNOSOM.

IV. Return of Property

18. Property belonging to the Somali State shall be returned to a broadly-based administration in Jubaland.

19. Private property shall be returned to its rightful owner, where ascertainable.

20. Where the rightful owner is not available, private property shall be returned to a person holding a court-authenticated power of attorney or to a minimum of three witnesses whose capacity to so act is certified by a court. Such property may be returned to a broadly-based administration in Jubaland by the order of a court.

21. A person or group found to have looted property shall be punished in accordance with the judgement of a court of law and shall either return such property or pay compensation to its rightful owner. In the case of livestock, it shall be returned to its rightful owner.

22. A Committee for the Return of Property shall be set up which, together with the courts and police, in cooperation with UNOSOM, shall be responsible for the implementation of the provisions of this section.

V. General Provisions

23. The message of peace shall be disseminated throughout Jubaland within 30 days of the signing of this Agreement. Dissemination of the provisions of this Agreement shall continue, using all available media resources including broadcasting facilities, newspapers and broadsheets, and through regular inspection visits to Districts, rural areas, villages, wells, and other locations. The public shall be repeatedly reminded that negative politics and propaganda that spread hostility are to be replaced by peace, brotherhood, trust and unity.

24. All Districts and villages shall form sub-committees comprising elders, businessmen, transporters, farmers, rural community leaders, religious leaders, women, youth and well-known personalities of Jubaland to foster and promote the message of peace.

25. The Delegates call for:

a. the reactivation of the trade that existed among the Districts of Jubaland;

b. the restoration of essential services such as water, health, electricity, education, agriculture, fisheries, resettlement of refugees, and the rebuilding of all institutions in cooperation with UNOSOM and non-governmental organisations;

c. assistance in assuring that humanitarian aid reaches all Districts;

d. the re-establishment of courts, police force, prisons and prison wards so as to bring stability to all the Districts forming part of Jubaland; and

e. the establishment of the presence of UNOSOM forces in each District and the assistance of UNOSOM in ensuring the execution of this Agreement.

26. Violators of the provisions of this Agreement shall be collectively challenged and dealt with according to law.

27. It shall be the responsibility of the tribal leaders and officers of the militias in cooperation with UNOSOM to ensure the execution of this Agreement.

28. Jubaland comprises the following Regions and their Districts:

Districts of Gedo Region

Garbaharey   Ceel Waaq
Bardhere   Doolow
Belet Hawa   Luuq

Districts of Middle Juba Region

Bu'aale
Jilib
Saakow

Districts of Lower Juba Region

Kismayo   Jamaame
Afmadu   Xagar
Badhaadhe

29. The Delegates declare their readiness to accord full collaboration with international and humanitarian agencies in the efficient performance of their activities benefiting the people and the land.

30. We appeal to the international community, governmental and private agencies to assist us in the fulfilment of the huge responsibilities we have undertaken in respect of the rebuilding of Jubaland.

LET US TRUST EACH OTHER IN THE NAME OF THE LORD

(Note: The above text is an unofficial translation prepared by UNOSOM from the original Somali.)

APPENDIX D

COLAAD IYO CAANO: HARGEISA WORKSHOP

Workshop on conflict and peace
Oxfam Somaliland

Hargeisa
5–6 September 1993

Introduction

After four years of war peace is returning to Somaliland. Oxfam's programme in Somaliland is also in a period of transition from short term emergency relief to longer term rehabilitation and development. A return to peace and a stable environment is the key to sustainable rehabilitation and development. The transition from conflict to peace is slow and Oxfam needs to ensure that its work in Somaliland supports the peace process. Oxfam should identify opportunities to support peace building in Somaliland.

The objectives of the workshop were to:

*   identify the role of NGOs in the post-conflict situation in and Somaliland

*   explore ways in which NGOs might support the transformation from conflict to peace.

The workshop was held in Hargeisa, over two days, 5th and 6th September 1993. There were 20 participants:

Name	Organisation	Profession/Training
1. Abdi Jama	OXFAM UK	Water Engineer
2. Mohamed Abdi Jibriil	Som/land Gov't	Management
3. Faduma Mohamed Aalin	-	Teacher
4. ZamZam Aden	SOMRA	Teacher
5. Rashid A. Arale	OXFAM UK	Accountant
6. Mohamed Sheik Abdillahi	SORRA	Chemic. Engineer
7. Yusuf Ainab	-	Engineer
8. Abdirahman Mohamed Ibrahim	OXFAM UK	Teacher
9. Sohrab Baghri	OXFAM UK	Water Engineer
10.Ali Ahmed Ali	ACTIONAID	Elec. Engineer
11.Zeinab Aideed Yusuf	SORRA	Women's Development
12.Zahra Aden	SOWDA	Office Management
13.Amina Haji Ibrahim	SOWDA	Teacher
14.Humphrey Pring	OXFAM UK	Business Management
15.Abdelkadir Sheik	UNOSOM	Diplomat/Economist
16.Dr Yusuf Hersi	-	Sociologist
17.Mohamoud Ali Sulub	OXFAM UK	Mechanic. Engineer
18.Abdulahi Abdelrahman Hersi	OXFAM UK	Business/Admin.
19.Qamar Ibrahim	OXFAM America	Teacher
20.Mark Bradbury	OXFAM (consult)	Anthropology

DAY I: CONFLICT

1.   Introductions

The group split into pairs and introduced themselves to each
other.

The 20 participants, representing 8 different organisations, came
from four countries and brought with them a range of professional
skills from engineering to sociology. Between them the
participants shared 193 years of experience of working in
development.

2.   Expectations, Roles and Goals

The participants were asked to consider the following questions.

1.   Why is your agency here in Somaliland?
2.   What do you think your agency's role should be here?
3.   What would you like to see your agency achieve in 12 months?
4.   What would you like to be doing in 12 months?
5.   What do you think Somaliland and Somalia will be like in 12
      months?
6.   What obstacles will prevent these things from happening?

The responses that followed were:

OXFAM (A)

1.   Original relief efforts were:
         - To assist in the development of the country.
         - Rehabilitation of the damaged infrastructure.
2.   To assist in rehabilitation and needs now.
3.   To finish the on-going projects and pending ones to be able
      to assess new projects.
4.   To put our full efforts into achieving the above goals.
5.   Think (hope) there will be stability in both.
6.   Suspicion and mistrust among the community and unwanted
      intervention from outside.

SOMALILAND GOVERNMENT UN/NGO OFFICE

1.   I am not an agency, I represent the government.
2.   To govern towards law and order and development.
3.   Maintain law and order.
4.   I would like to be doing proper coordination among various
      partners in rehabilitation programmes.
5.   I wish both will be peaceful and are moving towards progress
      in achieving self-reliance.
6.   Conflict and war are imminent threats to this.

ACTIONAID

1. It is here to work with and assist those who want to have a better way of life.
2. To support and enhance the ways of reaching a better way of life through the improvement of development programmes and empowering people.
3. Achieve it goals and implement all their plans of action successfully.
4. To put in practice all we wrote on paper, i.e. implement our objectives and achieve our goals and aims.
5. Somaliland/Somalia will be all right if the outside intervention turns towards support for what they (the people) want rather than the aims and objectives of the outsiders.
6. Unwanted outside intervention.

SORRA (Somali Relief and Rehabilitation Agency)

3. SORRA would like to realise its hopes in contributing to the rehabilitation and reconstruction of the country.
4. The same thing.
5. Only God knows!
6. Economic ruin, clan contentiousness. Lack of stabilising institutions and the trauma of recent violent conflict are the main obstacles.

SOMRA (Somali Relief Association)

1. Because it is our mandate to take part in relief and development initiatives in Somaliland.
2. My agencies role will be to gain experience and to contribute what we think will support our objectives, together.
3. I would like to see my agency achieving our plans in 12 months as we planned.
4. I would like to be someone who successfully achieves what was planned to be implemented, smoothly.
5. It is unpredictable.
6. Apart from natural obstacles, conflict will prevent these things happening.

SOWDA (Somaliland Women's Development Association)

1. To take an active part in the reconstruction of the country.
2. Our role is to mobilise women for the rehabilitation of the country.
3. In the next 12 months we would like to achieve:
    - income generating schemes for women
    - skills training institute
    - rehabilitation of the old Hargeisa tree nursery
    - focusing on primary education
4. As above (3)
5. Somaliland will prosper given the current environment of peace. As for Somalia we predict more conflicts, war!
6. If the security situation deteriorates, it will be an obstacle to achieving our aims.

OXFAM (B)

1. Oxfam is here in Somaliland to assist the people to improve
   their standard of living by:
     - providing clean and sufficient water supplies
     - improving public health
     - providing the inputs needed for agricultural development
     - education
2. Oxfam should be engaged in economic development activities.
3. Implement successful development projects.
4. Working in development projects in Somaliland.
5. Somaliland secure, politically stable and developing country.
   Somalia under UN Trusteeship.
6. Insecurity, political instability, lack of financial
   resources, inappropriate intervention.

UNOSOM

1. To consolidate and sustain the peace and support the
   administration in that respect.
2. Coordinate the international effort towards post-conflict
   peace building.
3. Demobilise the militia and integrate them into civilian life,
   rehabilitation of all sectors.
4. The continuum from relief to rehabilitation and development.
5. Peaceful and developing.
6. Donor fatigue.

These presentations were followed by an useful dialogue between
the representative from UNOSOM and the NGO representatives, on
the aims and objectives of UNOSOM in Somaliland.

The workshop then went on to explore whether there was common
ground among the agencies in terms of the role of the agency,
their future expectations for Somaliland and obstacles that will
prevent these. The following list was drawn up:

AGENCY ROLES	GOALS/EXPECTATIONS FOR SOMALILAND	OBSTACLES
* rehabilitation & development	* 6 groups were optimistic 3 were pessimistic	* unclear role of government
* economic development	* economic growth	* lack of resources
* listening	* positive change of attitude	* inequity
* encouraging community participation	* will reach common goals	* lack of accountability
* job creation	* develop government revenue	* conflicting interests
* maintaining peace	* continued role for traditional institutions	* lack of political will
* working with different interest groups		* insecurity

Overnight, Abdelkadir Sheik from UNOSOM re-worked this list and
came up with the following useful table:

AGENCY ROLES	GOALS/EXPECTATIONS FOR SOMALILAND	OBSTACLES
Rehab & Development	Create government revenue	Lack of economic/ resource base
Economic development	Increased economic activity	Lack of recognition Unresolved questions of governance
Job creation	Open roads	Accountability
Maintaining peace	Open roads	Equity & security
Working with various interest groups	Common values/goals	Equity/accountability

The question left for people to reflect upon, was the extent to which agencies are addressing those obstacles that stand in the way of achieving our expectations for Somaliland.

3. Understanding Conflict

The workshop went on to explore our cultural understanding of conflict, as expressed through language and proverbs. We started with the following examples:

> " Peace brings riches
> Riches bring greed
> Greed brings anger
> Anger brings war
> War brings poverty
> Poverty brings humanity
> Humanity brings peace
> Peace brings...."

"balaayo inta ay kaa maqan tahay qeyrkaa bey ku maqan tahay"

"Trouble is out there with others like you, when it is not with you."

a) Types of conflict

The participants went on to list as many words as they could to describe conflict:

Colaad	–	Hostility
Dagaal	–	War
Qaaquul	– }	
Khaakhuul	– }	Dispute
Ismaandahaaf	–	Misunderstanding
Shido	– }	
Shaqaaqo	– }	Calamity
Rabshad	–	Disturbance
Guluf	–	Strife
Xarbi	–	War
Iskahozimad	–	Confrontation
Iskudhac	–	Clash
Duulaan	– }	
Weerar	– }	Attack

In af-Somali there are many words for camel, but in English only one, and that comes from Arabic. However, in both af-Somali and English there are many words to describe conflict and different levels and stages of conflict. This suggests that conflict is a common experience in both societies.

b)   Maahmaaho Colaada: Somali Proverbs about conflict

Participants split into groups and produced a long list of Somali proverbs about conflict.

Colaad wiil baa ku dintee wiil kuma dhasho.
In conflict only life is lost but nothing is gained.

Colaad iyo nabaadi meel ma wada joogan.
Conflict and peace are bad bed follows.

Af-xumo nabadna waa kaa kaxeysaa colaadna wax kaagama tarto.
Offensive language only breeds trouble, but and does not help you in combat.

Geel doono geesao dhiigleey dhashaa.
Looking for loot (a camel) may end in destruction.

Nimaad fadhi kaga adag tahay looma sara joogsado.
Don't quarrel or fight with someone unless you have better weapons than him.

Colka ninka soo arkay iyo kan loogo warama si ugama wada cararaan.
The one who experiences conflict and the one who hears about it will have different fears.

Habar fadhida legdini wax uga fudud.
For idly sitting women things look easy. (i.e. for those watching everything looks simple)

Colaadi gurigaagana waa kaa kaxeysaa ku kalana kuma geyso.
Conflict only displaces from your home but does not provide you with another.

Dhagaal wiil baa ku dhintee, wiil kuma dhasho.
In war you lose a son may get killed but none is gained.

Belaayo baabkaaga ayaa laga soo xirta.
Close your door when trouble starts.

Belaayo buulkaaga laga galaa.
Hide from trouble in the inner chamber of your house.
(i.e. Keep away from trouble, do not seek it out.)

Haddaan af-xumaan gacani ma xumaato.
Any violence is sure to be proceeded by foul language.

Rag ciil cadaab ka doorey.
Resist oppression no matter the consequences

4. Some Conflict Theory

Another way we try and make sense of conflict is by studying it and creating theories about conflict.

In the west there are three dominant theories that have been developed to explain conflict.

Power Politics: This suggests human beings and groups naturally struggle for domination and power and that making war is part of human nature. It suggests that peace can only be maintained through a balance of power. This theory was used to explain Cold War politics and to justify strategic interests.

Structuralism: This looks at structures - structures of power, institutions, laws, economics, exploitation, environment - to understand the causes of conflict. It suggests that we are often not aware of those structures. When we become aware of them we struggle to overthrow them.

Liberal/pluralist: This suggests that many levels of human society are involved in conflict. It incorporates the idea of structures as a source of conflict. It also suggests that individual and group behaviour, attitudes and psychology, community needs and perceptions are important for understanding causes of conflict.

5. Human Needs

Another theory of why conflict happens is related to human needs. This proposes that conflict results from the denial or suppression of human needs.

The group brainstormed and came up with the following list of list human needs:

food	clean environment	transport
sleep	jobs/employment	family planning
water	recognition/approval	intellectual stimulation
peace/security	communication	faith
shelter	holidays	recreation/entertainment
clothing	respect	moral values
health	identity	privacy
education	achievement	government
human rights	sex	justice

The group then tried to prioritise these needs into those essential for "survival", those essential for a "good quality of life" and those that are a "luxury". There was considerable debate over whether the more "subjective" needs - human rights, identity, achievement, faith, justice - were essential for survival or a luxury.

It was recognised that people have different needs and the suppression of one person's or one group's needs by another could lead to conflict. The question was raised as to whether Somaliland could achieve peace and reconciliation if any of these needs were not met.

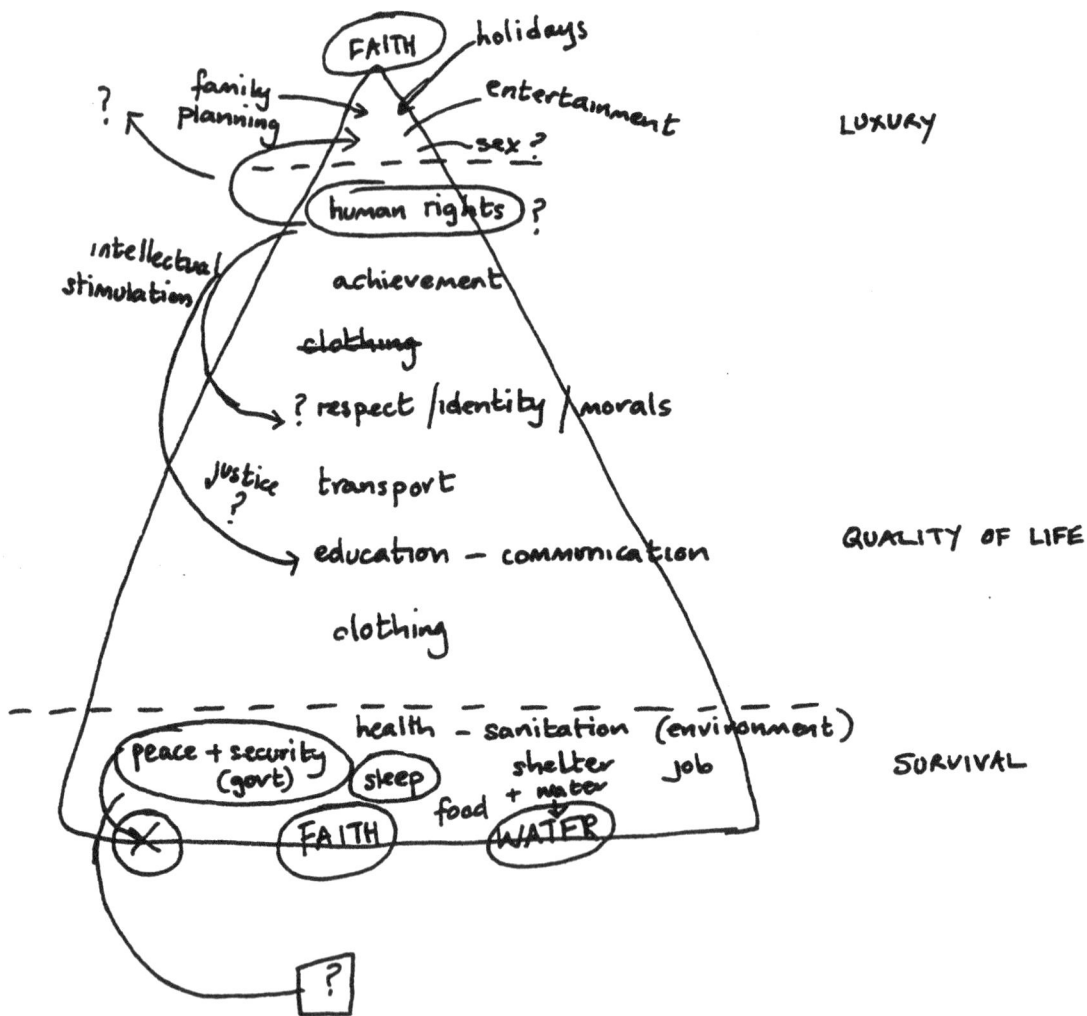

FAITH   holidays

family   entertainment
Planning   LUXURY
?   sex ?

human rights ?

intellectual   achievement
stimulation
                   clothing

                   ? respect / identity / morals

justice   transport
?   QUALITY OF LIFE
         education — communication

         clothing

         health — sanitation (environment)
peace + security   job   SURVIVAL
(govt)   sleep   shelter
                       + water
         FAITH food WATER

?

BASIC NEEDS

132

We reflected on how many of these needs NGOs were addressing in their programmes in Somaliland.

One thing missing from the list of needs was people. The workshop was offered a proverb from South Africa:

"umntu ngumntu ngabantu"

"you are a human being because of other people"

6.   Conflict Matrix

The workshop went on to consider (some of) the causes, impacts, responses to and solutions to the recent Somali conflict and produced the following matrix:

CAUSES	IMPACT
unequal distribution of power unequal distribution of resources injustice ethnic discrimination different political background & experiences different norms dis-enfranchisement of some groups in favour of others different ideology	destruction death alienation displacement refugees disunity hatred & hostility mistrust disease fear loss of confidence trauma loss of national pride poverty loss of faith

Conflict

confusion conflict high kat consumption disunity re-instatement of Somaliland UN intervention relief aid	reconciliation employment creation peace conferences economic improvement demobilisation international recongnition of Somaliland banning of kat positive involvement of UN sustainable development national peace commitment decentralisation of power

RESPONSES	SOLUTIONS

We then reflected on the extent to which the solutions suggested addressed the original causes of the conflict? Furthermore, to what extent are NGOs supporting these solutions to the conflict?

DAY 2   PEACE

1.   Introduction

The morning began with a review of themes discussed the previous day.

2.   Roots of Change

Development involves change. NGOs can be agents of change. Change can be both positive and negative.

The aim of the first main session of the day was to discuss roots of change. We did this by listing important events in the history of the Somali people this century.

* Darwiish (Sayid Mohamed Abdulla Hassan) war against the British and Italians 1900-1920.
* 1928 drought
* 1940-1945 Second World War
* 1943 SYL was founded, Somali nationalism started
* 1940-50's inter clan conflicts
* 1950 UN Trusteeship of Somalia
* 1950 "Habtii" famine
* 1954 Reserve area given to Ethiopia
* 1956 "siiga asse" drought
* 1960 independence
* 1961 attempted coup in Somaliland
* 1963 fighting in NFD
* 1964 war between Ethiopia and Somalia
* 1969 coup by Siad Barre
* 1974 "dabadheer" drought
* 1972 introduction of Somali script
* 1977 Ogaden War between Ethiopian & Somalia
* 1977 Djibouti independence
* 1988 SNM attacks on Burco & Hargeisa, outbreak of civil war
* 1991 Overthrow of the regime of Siad Barre

We noted that many of these events were related to or involved outright conflict. Since the beginning of this century, the Somali people have faced many long periods of conflict.

We then attempted to identify the five most significant events in Somali history and to rank them in terms of their positive or negative impact on Somalia's development, according to the following diagram:

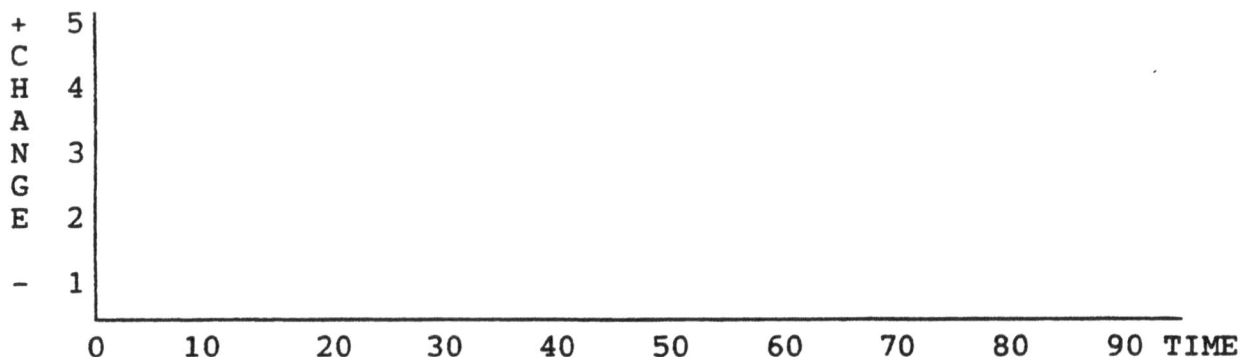

```
+  5 |
C    |
H  4 |                                                        .
A    |
N  3 |
G    |
E  2 |
     |
-  1 |
     |_____
     0   10   20   30   40   50   60   70   80   90 TIME
```

It proved extremely difficult to decide which events had a positive or negative impact on Somalia's development. It was felt that many of them contained both positive and negative aspects. This suggested to us that while conflict is often a source of change, it is not always perceived as negative, although this may be in hindsight.

We then went on to discuss what happened between these periods of conflict and ended up with the following diagram.

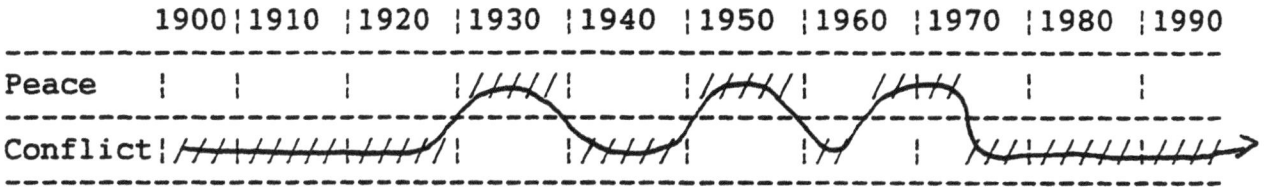

```
        1900|1910 |1920 |1930 |1940 |1950 |1960 |1970 |1980 |1990
--------------------------------------------------------------------
Peace   |    |    |    |  //// |   |//// |  ////  |    |    |
--------------------------------------------------------------------
Conflict|//////////// |    |   //// |    |/|    |  ///////////// →
--------------------------------------------------------------------
```

This exercise suggested that during this century the Somali people have experienced cycles of conflict and peace. This led us on to discuss whether it is feasible to aim for sustainable peace. To help us we used a model developed by John Paul Lederach.

Awareness of Conflict

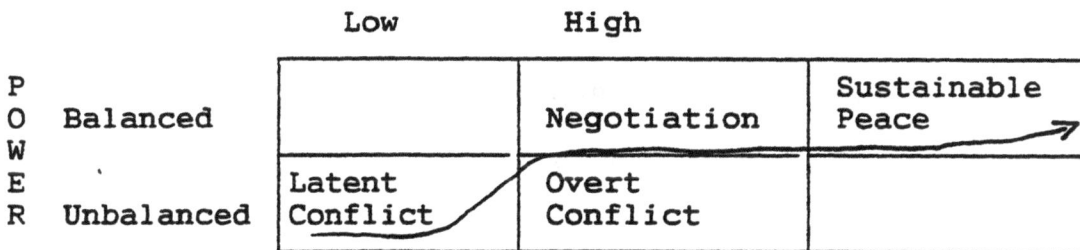

		Low	High	
P O W	Balanced		Negotiation	Sustainable Peace ↗
E R	Unbalanced	Latent Conflict	Overt Conflict	

3.   Power

On the first day, the "unequal distribution of power" was identified as one of the causes of the Somali conflict. The model by John Paul Lederach also suggests that conflict emerges from an imbalance in power relationships. On the first day someone had stated that the role of agency was to "empower people".

If conflict results from an imbalance of power it is necessary to reflect on what we mean by power, or how we define it. We went on to lists some definitions of power:

* Power is the authority to make decisions on behalf of the community.
* Power is the will to make change
* There are two types of power - legitimate and illegitimate:
   a) coercion - to make someone do something against their will
   b) authority - legitimate power delegated by others
* Power is domination over others
* Political power and economic power are balanced through legal power.

4. Defining Peace and Conflict

As we had done with conflict, the workshop went on to explore our cultural understanding of peace as expressed through language and proverbs. The group started by listing as many words as many words as they could to describe peace:

a) Types of Peace

badbaado	-	safety
amaan	-	security
degganaansho	-	stability
samaan	-	well-being
ladnaan	-	"
xasi llooni	-	stability
gallad	-	blessing
salaamad	-	peace
naruuro	-	prosperity
nasteexo	-	"
badhaadho	-	"
barwaaqo	-	"
nabad-raadin	-	peace-making
nabad-doon	-	peace maker
nabad-ilaalin	-	peace-keeping
isafgarad	-	understanding
heshiis	-	agreement

b) Maahmaaho Nabadeed: Somali Proverbs on Peace

The participants split into groups and produced a long list of Somali proverbs about peace.

Waxan nabad iyo caano aheynba waa la kala qaadaa.
People can steal anything but milk and peace.

Nabad baa caano macaan./Nabad baa caano lagu dhamaa.
At times of peace even milk tastes sweeter.

Dumarka kolba kii reeyey raacaan.
Those who women cheer for surely wins.

Adoo nabad u balawaadha balooy kaaley lama yidhaahdo
Do not call for trouble when peace is within reach.

Nabad iyo colaadi isku caano dhiqis maaha.
Milk tastes differently in times of peace and times of conflict.

Qonyar socde qodaxi ma muddo.
Thorns will not prick him who treads carefully.

Gal dad liqa ah ul baa la isaga dayaa.
Before doing anything, test with a stick the depth of the well.

Aan wada hadalno waa aan heshiinno.
An offer of talk is an offer of peace.

Nin gardarani ma guuleysto.
Victory is never with the aggressor.

Booraan hadimo ha qodin, ku dhici doontaana mooye.
Never dig too deep a hole for your enemy less you fall into it.

Rag walaal wuxuu ku dhaamo la waa.
Fairness may be the best you can offer to men.

Wax walaal loo diidey, wed baa leh.
Something you keep from your brother may end up lost.

Wax aad samaan ku weydo, xumaan laguma helo.
You will never gain through war what you cannot get in peace.

Ijiid aan ku jiidee waa gacmo daalis.
Tit for tat is a waste of effort!

Gar-diid waa Alla-diid.
He who refuses justice denies god.

Nabadi waa naruuro.
Peace itself is prosperity.

Guri nabadaa lagu nastaa.
The best home to rest in is one at peace.

Nabad la'aani waa nolol la'aani.
There is no life without peace.

Marka nabad la helaa nolol la helaa.
Life can be lived to the full only at times of peace.

Nabad baa nayaayir leh.
Peace has prosperity.

Nabadi maxay ku yeeshax?
Peace does not do any harm

5. Characteristics of Peace and Conflict

Referring to the previous day's work on conflict, the workshop went on to define and compare the characteristics of peace and conflict.

Nabad (Peace)	Colaad (Conflict)
Plentiful food	Famine
Milk	Drought
Rest	Poverty
Rain	War widows
Prosperity	Orphans
Helping	Displacement
Marriage	Divorce
High productivity	Refugees
Dances	Death
Harmony	Dispersal of family
Dialogue	Disability
Exports	Looting
Songs	Poor economy
Festivals	Hate
Conflict resolution	Lack of trust
Happiness	Destruction
Health	Lower birth rate
Imports	More weapons
Sound body and mind	No education
Tourists	No health
Schools	No accountability
Education	Disorder
Money	Chaos
Telephones	
No foreign troops	
Family reunions	
Free movement	
Ghee	
Lots of camels and sheep	
Livestock trading	
Less killing of livestock	

The conclusion was that peace does not just mean the absence of war.

6. Conflict Resolution: nabaad raadin, xaliin colaadeed

The workshop then went on to discuss means of resolving conflicts. This was done by looking at the characteristics of Somali peace meetings (shir nabadeedka or 'shir Somaali'), such as those that had taken place in Burco, Sheik, Boroma and Erigavo in Somaliland and contrasted them to a UN sponsored peace meeting ('shir UN'), such as the Addis Ababa meeting in March 1993. We considered why one type of peace meeting might be more successful than the other.

Shir Somaali	Shir UN
Involves legitimate representatives	Lack of confidence in representatives
Uses traditional methods of problem solving	Held outside the country
Uses experienced mediators (e.g. elders)	Involves politicians, not elders
Elders chosen by the community	Involves 'criminals'
Involves the 'real actors'	Unequal representation
Confidence of community in representatives	Lack of understanding of the problem(s)
Elders have authority	External, rather than internal support
Held inside the country	Lack of confidence in organisers/facilitators
Common agenda/goals - Peace	Lack of common xeer
Limited agenda	Short time table
Common rules, values (xeer)	
Ability of elders to enforce	
Power of elders to ensure implementation of agreements	
Meetings structured to separate problems	
Consensus decision making	
Equal representation by parties	
Community support, shared expenses	
Open time table	
Traditional role of hosts and guests	

In addition while the Addis meeting involved a broad range of representatives - religious, elders, women, intellectuals - those who made decisions, who signed the agreements were the politicians, or 'warlords'. These people have been excluded from the peace meetings in Somaliland. On the other hand, it was recognised that the Addis conference did receive international recognition and therefore the possibility of international support, while the Boroma conference did not get international recognition, and therefore Somaliland is not likely to receive the same level of support.

It was suggested that many of the characteristics that are important to make a Somali peace meeting successful, are similar to those we look for in a successful development project: long term process, community participation, community support, legitimate representation, traditional (indigenous) ways of doing things, common goals, community ownership of the process. Successful peace meetings are like good development projects. In this sense the NGO approach to development, is not far from peace-making or peace-building.

Conflict resolution has been described as a "balancing of goals".
In the west or north we would use a model, such as below, to
describe the process of conflict resolution.

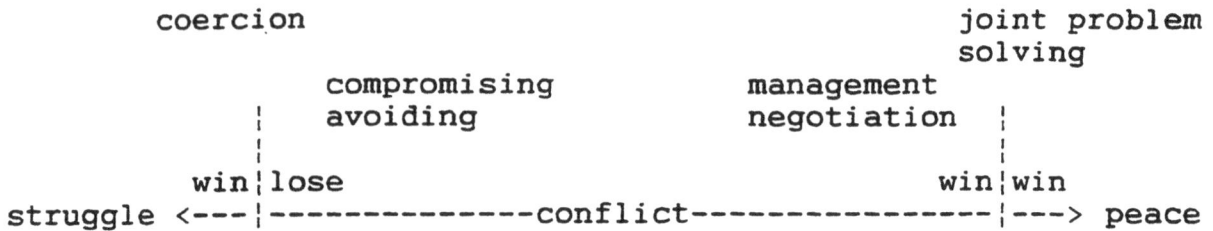

```
        coercion                                  joint problem
                                                  solving
                compromising        management
                avoiding            negotiation
                |                              |
                |                              |
        win|lose                       win|win
struggle <---|--------------conflict---------------|---> peace
```

In this process conflict resolution involves:

- a process of mediation, rather than facilitation
- getting people together
- joint exploration of problems
- respect of rights
- no preconditions
- maintenance of dignity
- cooperation
- expression of feelings

The Somali peace meeting will normally reach decisions through
consensus, rather than voting. They are therefore aiming for a
win-win situation.

It was concluded that the methods and techniques of problem
solving or conflict resolution used in the Somali shir nabadeedka
are very similar to those designed by theorists of conflict
resolution in the west or north. The west has a lot to learn from
Somali society in this respect.

7.   Learning by Doing

Having concluded that the Somali peace meeting shares many of the
characteristics that we look for in a good development project,
the workshop went on to compare and contrast the experiences of
ACTIONAID and OXFAM in rehabilitating urban water supplies in
Erigavo and Las Anod towns.

Participants from ACTIONAID and OXFAM described the background to
their projects, the problems involved, how they were overcome,
and the successes and unexpected successes of the project.

1. ACTIONAID: With their operational base in Erigavo, ACTIONAID
   was able to involve the community in the details of planning,
   implementation and long term management of the water supply
   system. The project faced some problems from local
   competition over jobs, inflation, the lead in time to recruit
   international engineers and delivery of materials. However
   their emphasis on working through local committees of elders,
   reaped some unexpected success in terms of contribution of
   some free labour, free storage of materials and transport.
   The project took seven months to complete from   initial
   designs to the commissioning. Now running, the system is
   self-financing. The main lessons learnt is that good training
   prepares the way for effective management.

2. OXFAM: The water supply system designed by OXFAM for Las Anod is larger than that in Erigavo. With no operational base in Las Anod, OXFAM initially commissioned a local contractor to undertake the first part of the project. Although the contractor completed his work, a dispute between the contractor and OXFAM delayed the project for 10 months. This persuaded OXFAM to implement the project itself, working with a community water committee. Working with the community, rather than through a contractor has been a better experience. The project is reaching a conclusion and OXFAM have begun to work with the community on developing a management system.

Considering the two experiences, there was general agreement on the importance of community involvement in any development project, not only for short term gains, but also the long term ownership and management of the project.

Taladaan la ruugin waa lagu rafaadaa.

An issue that is not well thought through at the beginning keeps returning.

8.   Sustaining Peace: The Role of NGOs

In the final session the workshop went on to discuss possible roles for NGOs in supporting, sustaining and building upon peace and reconciliation in Somaliland. The following proposals were made for NGO support.

Demobilisation - skills training for veterans
                 - peace workshops for fighters
Income generation programmes
Public works programmes
Keep out of politics
NGOs can act as liaison between government and communities
Influence the UN and the international into different approaches
Advocacy work for Somaliland
Presenting positive images of Somaliland
More peace workshops in the regions *
Protecting the rights of the private sector
Prioritising community needs
More coordination between NGOs

* It was suggested that Somali NGOs themselves might consider running workshops on conflict and peace.

The question was raised as to whether there was a role for NGOs in supporting local peace meetings (shir nabadeed). It was suggested that NGO's should be cautious. They should make the distinction between peace meetings and political meetings.

EVALUATION OF OXFAM WORKSHOP ON CONFLICT AND PEACE

In order to evaluate how useful the workshop has been we would be grateful if you could take time to answer the following questions. Please be open in your comments.

Name: Organisation:

1. How useful have you found the workshop?

a. a lot   b. a little   c. not at all

2. Please explain your answer:

Apart from the acquaintance participants achieved there, the topic was well selected, so the attitude was quite interesting and useful.

The workshop has addressed some issues which were overlooked before - such as why the Somali shir is more successful than the UN shir

It addressed all burning issues on the causes and consequences of the war and what went right or wrong in search for solutions too.

Logical assessment of events leading either to conflict or to peace.

Because of the problem of Somalia/Somaliland it is very important to make this kind of workshop.

I have gained a lot experience.

Being new to working in development projects, I found a lot of information which will be useful for any future work.

Because there are different people in the workshop, different experience so I found very serious workshop.

I have learnt a lot about Somali culture, especially settlements of disputes and reconciliation. Besides I now have an idea of what a majority believe to be the needs of the country i.e. development related rather than relief related projects. Successful projects seem to be those that collaborate with the residents and involve them in all stages. "listen a lot, talk less".

3. Which part(s) of the workshop did you find most useful or interesting?:

First, I found useful the participation of women and how they contributed, secondly, the experience and calibre of the participants was good, so the topic was well digested.

Those parts I found most useful were the parts on the nature of conflict and the history in Somaliland, the Somali shir verses UN shir.

All parts.

Causes of conflict; events happening in Somalia/land from 1900 till present, "the cycle of event" curve was interesting.

Both the peace and conflict discussion were very interesting, but peace is what I very much interested in.

All issues or the whole topic.

Community participation was very useful for me because there were some projects failed for this reason and every NGO agency will avoid that problem.

Somali history; causes, impact, responses and suggested solutions to the problems caused by various conflicts.

4. Which part(s) of the workshop did you <u>not</u> find useful or interesting?:

None at all!!
Every part was useful.

5. Would it be useful to have further workshops on the same or similar themes, or with other organisations?:

Yes, absolutely.

6. If yes, where?

NGO offices and their sites of work, if possible.

In a neutral venue (free from coercion).

In all five regions for the intellectuals and veterans.

Hargeisa, Burco, Berbera and other regions of Somaliland.

OXFAM, ACTIONAID, CARE.

Hargeisa and other towns.

Inside and outside the country.

Burco for instance.

7. If yes, are there things that were not discussed in this workshop that you would like to discuss in future workshops:

No, but I can say time will be better if it is a little more than one or two days, better to be 3 - 5 days.

To form a common approach by all NGOs to Somaliland provided they are acceptable to the local community.

To give sufficient time and space to the investigation of the roots of the conflict.

143

Invite the intellectuals for a workshop.

How to make peace and reconciliation between Somalis.

Identification of the sort of projects - in depth - that have the potential of having the most positive impact.

8. Any other comments:

I suggest the UN/NGOs should encourage the workshops/seminars etc. of this style because knowledge and experience can be passed on to one another. The development workers also learn from each other and cost-wise it is cheap.

Overall it was a positive sign.

Time was too short; not enough people invited; I appreciated the process; enjoyed the workshop.

I believe all the attendants have all profited greatly, in terms of ideas; all in all a very successful workshop.

INDEX

147

Saakow 55
Sab clan 9
Sahnoun, Ambassador Mohamed 15, 45
Samaale clan 9
Samaroon clan 9
SAMO (Somali African Mukti
  Organisation) 23, 26, 28
Sanaag 12, 66, 70, 76, 77, 81
Sanaag peace conference 62, 85-99, 102;
  peace and reconciliation process 88-
  89, 95-99; preparation 89-90; common
  objectives 90-91; representation 91;
  organisation 91-93, 95; problem-solv-
  ing 93-96; funding 96; security 97;
  property issues 97-98; and common
  interests 98-99; local government 99
SDA (Somali Democratic Alliance) 25,
  24, 26, 77
SDM (Somali Democratic Movement)
  13, 16, 23, 26, 28
SDM/SNA 23
SDRA (Somali Development and Relief
  Association) 93, 96, 99
Shahin, General 35
Shanbara group 50
Sharmarke, Abdirashid Ali 11, 30, 60
Sheikal clan 32, 50, 52
Sheikh 66, 72, 73, 76
Shimbiraale 88
Shinn, Ambassador David 33
Shire, Mohamed Ali 92
SLA (Somali Liberation Army) 55
SNA (Somali National Alliance) 27, 28,
  55
SNDU (Somali National Democratic
  Union) 23, 28
SNF (Somali National Front) 14, 15, 16,
  22, 23, 24, 26, 27, 28, 29, 30, 49, 54-56
SNM (Somali National Movement) 3, 9,
  10, 12, 13, 14, 16, 17, 19, 24, 62, 65,
  66-69, 70, 71, 75, 76, 77, 79, 87, 93
SNU (Somali National Union) 23
Somali African Mukti Organisation
  (SAMO) 23, 26, 28
Somali Development and Relief
  Association (SDRA) 93, 96, 99
Somali Democratic Alliance see SDA
Somali Democratic Movement see SDA
Somali Liberation Army (SLA) 55
Somali National Alliance (SNA) 27, 28,

55
Somali National Democratic Union
  (SNDU) 23, 28
Somali National Front see SNF
Somali National Movement see SNM
Somali National Union (SNU) 23
Somali Patriotic Movement see SPM
Somali Red Crescent 62, 64
Somali Revolutionary Socialist Party 9
Somali Salvation Democratic Front see
  SSDF
Somaliland 7, 16, 17, 20, 24, 40, 43, 65-
  104
Somaliland Government UN/NGO Office
  126
Somaliland Women's Development
  Organisation (SOWDA) 84, 125, 127
Somaliland Women's Organisation
  (SOWDA) 71, 72, 84,
SOMRA 71, 125, 127
Sool 12, 16, 66, 75, 77, 81
Sooyaal 82
SORRA 125, 127
Southern Somali National Movement
  see SSNM
SPM (Somali Patriotic Movement) 12,
  13, 14, 15, 16, 23, 24, 26, 28, 30, 49,
  53, 54-56, 57
SPM/SNF 11, 54
SSDF (Somali Salvation Democratic
  Front) 9, 11, 16, 23, 26, 28, 30, 31, 49,
  55, 56, 59-60
SSNM (Southern Somali National
  Movement) 16, 23, 26, 55
Summerfield, Dr Derek 85

Togdheer 12, 66, 81
Tuuni clan 50, 61
Tuur, Abdulrahman Ali, 65, 76, 77, 78,
  80
Twi, Dr 85

UNDP 36
UNDP-OPS 82
UNICEF 36, 53, 82
UNITAF (United Nations International
  Task Force) 1, 15-16, 22, 23, 25, 26,
  27, 31, 36, 44, 46, 55
United Somali Congress see USC
United Somali Front (USF) 23, 28

148

United Somali Party *see* USP
UNOSOM 4, 5, 15-16, 96, 103, 125, 127;
    conflict with Aideed 22, 28-30, 32-34,
    38-39, 61-63; and peace conferences
    26, 28-29, 30, 32; criticism of 33, 39,
    60; and inter-clan fighting 33-35; US
    domination 36; political factions 38;
    and District Councils 41-44; concern
    at military action 44-46, 83; staffing
    problem 47; and Kismayo peace con-
    ference 57, 58, 59, 61-63; rift with
    Egal 77-79; expulsion 77, 82; diplo-
    matic blunders 78; and demobilisation
    81-83, 84
UNOSOM II 16, 22; new mandate 25-26,
    78; politics of 34-38; structure of 35-
    36, 37
USAID 53, 82
USC (United Somali Congress) 13p 14,
    15, 16, 17, 23, 26, 28, 29, 49, 54, 55,
    65
USC/SNA 11, 23, 30, 55, 58
USF (United Somali Front) 23, 28
USP (United Somali Party) 23, 24, 26,
    28, 76, 78

Wagat, Abdillahi 54, 59
Walsh, Mark 56-57, 62
WAMO Women's Organisation 64
Waqoyi Galbeed 12, 66
Wardighigly, Mohamed 13
Warsame, Ali 92
Warsengeli clan 9, 11, 12, 26, 50, 65, 66,
    67, 75, 76, 78, 86, 87, 88, 89, 91, 93,
    94, 95, 98
Women's Family Life Institute 71
World Concern 53, 64
World Food Programme (WF?) 36, 82

Xawadle clan 26, 27, 31, 34, 50, 52
Yobe 88, 90
Yusuf, Colonel Abdillahi 11, 28, 31, 56,
    59-60

Zunguri 50

www.ingramcontent.com/pod-product-compliance
Lightning Source LLC
Chambersburg PA
CBHW080952050426
42334CB00057B/2605